The
naked
author

A guide to self-publishing

Alison Baverstock

BLOOMS

Bloomsbury Publishing Plc

1 3 5 7 9 10 8 6 4 2

First published in 2011

Bloomsbury Publishing Plc
50 Bedford Square
London WC1B 3DP
www.bloomsbury.com

A CIP catalogue record for this book is available from
the British Library

Print ISBN: 978 1 408 13982 0
E pub ISBN: 978 1 408 15709 1

Available in the USA from Bloomsbury Academic & Professional,
175 Fifth Avenue/3rd Floor, New York, NY 10010.
www.BloomsburyAcademicUSA.com

Typeset by Margaret Brain
Printed and bound in Great Britain by CPI Group (UK) Ltd, Croydon,
CR0 4YY

For Neil, Alasdair, Harriet, Jack and Hamish
To help with the story they will each have to tell

Contents

Foreword

Liberate your words, change the world

Your words are powerful. They long to be read. They hold the potential to inspire, educate and entertain. Your words might change the world. Self-publishing gives you the freedom and ability to reach readers with your words. Your success is not assured. Although self-publishing tools can make it quick and easy to publish a book, self-publishing doesn't make it easy to create a great book.

You've probably heard the stories of authors like Amanda Hocking, Brian S. Pratt and John Locke – all authors previously rejected by big publishers – who achieved enormous commercial success by self-publishing. While these stories are true and inspirational, they are also rare. The vast majority of self-published books do not sell in large numbers. This is true of many traditionally published titles as well. Few authors – traditionally published authors included – earn a living wage from writing. Most maintain day jobs.

Why do so many writers continue to write despite the fact that commercial success is so rare? The answer lies in this simple fact: writers write for reasons different to why publishers publish. Most writers write for the love of writing. The journey of self-expression is often more enriching than any promise of commercial success. Book publishers, however, are running a business. They're in the business of publishing books readers want to buy.

With the rise of commercial mass-market publishing, professional publishers controlled the printing press and access to retail distribution. Publishers sought to publish writers whose work had commercial potential. Therefore, publishers had the power to determine which writers became authors, and which books were published, marketed and most likely to be purchased. Before the advent of self-publishing, writers who wanted to reach readers with books had no choice but to work with a publisher.

While publishers have every right to judge books through this filter of perceived commercial merit, such a filter invariably denies many great writers the opportunity to publish, and denies readers the freedom to enjoy a wider range of writing.

The world's unpublished authors – possibly yourself included – possess a wealth of imagination and knowledge locked between their brains and fingertips. Self-publishing makes the writer's dream of publication more possible than ever.

Until recently, most self-published authors failed to reach large audiences, primarily because they lacked brick and mortar bookstore distribution where the majority of book sales took place. But this disadvantage is diminishing. Here in the United States and elsewhere across the world, physical bookstores are disappearing, sales of print books are declining, book sales are shifting to online retailers and sales of ebooks are rising. It's the addition of ebooks to the self-publisher's toolbox that has enabled self-published authors to finally reach readers in larger numbers.

The change is rapid. In the first two months of 2011, according to the Association of American Publishers (AAP), sales of ebooks rose 169% over the same period a year prior, while sales of printed books declined 25%. The AAP reports ebooks grew to account for 8.3% of the US book market in 2010, up from about 3% in 2010 and 1% in 2009. I predict unit sales of ebooks will surpass print books by the end of 2013.

Impressive as these numbers may appear, they dramatically understate what's actually happening around the world. As brick and mortar bookstores continue their decline, the playing-field will level between traditionally-published books and self-published books, both of which will occupy the same virtual shelves of online retailers. Books will compete based on their ability to satisfy readers. The author is the brand and the publisher on the spine matters less. Welcome to the new publishing renaissance.

But as the power of publishing shifts to you, the writer, so too does the responsibility. The best publishers honor their readers by publishing books worth reading. If you decide to self-publish you must honor your readers by assuming personal responsibility for the same professional publishing duties performed by the best publishers. You're responsible for hiring professionals (or bartering with fellow authors) to help you edit, revise and proof your manuscript. You're responsible for producing a professional-quality book cover. You're responsible for book production, marketing and distribution.

Most self-publishing authors discover effective publishing is much harder than it looks. Luckily, many of the tools for publishing and distribution are freely available to authors, and this book is one such. Alison Baverstock will help you learn how to self-publish like a professional.

Go forth, honor your readers and become the best self-publisher you can be!

Mark Coker
Founder
Smashwords
www.smashwords.com
August 2011

Mark Coker is the author of *The Smashwords Style Guide* (how to produce and publish an ebook), *The Smashwords Book Marketing Guide* (how to market any book), and *Seven Secrets to Ebook Publishing Success* (best practices of the most successful indie ebook authors).

IS PUBLISHING DEAD?

OR JUST THE PUBLISHER?

Introduction: why self-publishing is no longer a last resort

Publishing today is at a crossroads. The industry is obsessed by the drive towards digital content, formats and markets, and all stakeholders are nervous. Disintermediation and reintermediation – the outright removal or delivery of traditionally organised products and services through new mechanisms – is much discussed. The number of retail outlets willing to sell a range of books is declining at a worrying pace; there is no certainty over which ebook reader will predominate, or whether the public really can be persuaded to change their method of reading after over 500 years of close reliance on the printed codex. All involved are holding their breath to see whose position is preserved, and financial stake is secured, in the new order of things.

This atmosphere of uncertainty is particularly significant because the publishers up to now have had it pretty sweet. The industry has until comparatively recently remained a byway, largely ignored by bigger corporations. Publishers were the lucky beneficiaries of an ongoing buyers' market and competition to get published always exceeded opportunities for publication. Solidarity among authors was never strong, and new talent could usually be relied upon to undercut in pursuit of a possible book deal.

Of late, the odds on getting published have lengthened, as the amount of good material competing for an official contract has increased. Writing competitions attract huge numbers of high quality entrants,[1] and the widespread availability of creative writing courses has revealed the extent of publishable work that exists. There remains a glut: more good quality material available than there are publishing houses able to handle it.

---

[1] E.g. UK television Channel Four's The Richard & Judy Writing Competition of 2004, which attracted 47,000 entries. The standard was so high that the sponsoring publisher Macmillan awarded a book contract to the entire shortlist, and eventually built a new business model, Macmillan New Writers

What has however changed is the response of authors to this situation, and their increasing willingness to take their destiny into their own hands. Up in the outside lane has crept a new breed of informed and empowered author. Disintermediation benefits the position of those whose role cannot be replicated or replaced; and as the creators of content, authors can find themselves in a strong position.

At the other end of the scale, the emergence of the individual star author (and their commensurate demands) also threatens the old publishing business model. This has echoed developments in sport during the same period, where the international footballer became more important than the team they belong to. Sports journalist Paul Hayward commented: 'With good reason do today's top football managers emphasise 'the group' and the collective will. Mourinho, Wenger and the rest know they must resist the shift of power from the club to the individual. The modern sporting superstar is a floating corporation. Over the next ten years he might go freelance too.' A debate over the future of Wayne Rooney in October 2010 gave further insight into this situation. The club manager, Sir Alex Ferguson, has presented himself as a paternalistic figure for the team as a whole, but Rooney evidently derived this level of emotional support from his own agent, who was responsible to him alone, and his family, who had PR and marketing agents of their own promoting their various brands. In the process there was speculation over whether Rooney's individual ambitions were best served within the team, or could be better served elsewhere. An apology followed, Rooney to Ferguson, and a longer contract was signed, but in the process the issue of who is more important, individual or team, had been raised. The parallel between this situation and authors' relationships with their agents, rather than their publishing houses, is evident. Some authors (such as James Paterson and Daisy Meadows[2]) are setting up Italian Renaissance-style *scuola* to collaborate and hence satisfy the demand for new material; and from here it is but a short step to setting up their own publishing company.

[2] Most borrowed authors from UK public libraries in 2009. Daisy Meadows is not a person, rather the pen name for a group writing project run by Writing Partners, www.writingpartnersltd.co.uk

The new writer too has more options open to them. The widespread ownership of computers, with associated writing and project management software, has provided a new technical freedom; the ability to present material to a market and spread information on its availability is no longer reliant on the conventional gatekeepers of the publishing world. And the confidence to do this has often been promoted by a creeping disenchantment among authors for the practices of publishing.[3]

What the publishing industry did to promote the cause of self-publishing

Perhaps the most significant event for writers of the first decade of the 21st century was the public living out of a common dream. The huge sales of J.K. Rowling sustained lots of writing ambitions, as individual writers thought it might happen to them too. It showed what was possible.

But while substantial numbers were sold, the huge discounts available on these titles invited speculation in an area where traditionally writers had assumed publishers knew best. How was it sensible to discount bestsellers, when in every other industry you pay more for the new and the in-demand? At the same time, authors complained that the publishing industry had both contracted the number of titles it takes on, and become consistently more risk-averse. Having managed on gut feeling for so long about what was selling, the UK industry now has probably the best sales information service in any retail market.[4] And just as the widespread ownership of satnav systems for cars has meant that a generation of drivers has forgotten either how to plan a route or remember where they have been, the availability of such sophisticated sales information within the book trade has meant that statistics can be produced to support or discount the chances of any new writer/title being considered for

---

[3] This next section examines the industry from the writer's point of view. For consideration of the publisher's particular perspective on authors see A. Baverstock, *Marketing your book, an author's guide*, London: A&C Black (2007), pp 12–15

[4] Nielsen Bookscan, www.nielsen.co.uk

possible publication, followed shortly afterwards by actual sales figures that prove the point. Lionel Shriver's *We Need to Talk About Kevin* was taken on by small independent publishing house Serpent's Tail because the publisher, Pete Ayrton, liked the work; had his business been able to afford the annual £5,000 subscription to the Nielsen database he would have found the information that her previous novels had not been a success, and maybe not made the same decision. Repeatedly writers report that publishers are unwilling to build the demand for writing that they agree is first rate; to experiment with new types of work or to offer an apprenticeship by allowing a writer's reputation and following to grow over several books. It is significant that literacy initiatives to spread the habit of reading, from which publishers benefit, often come from outside the industry, within the charitable sector/funded by public money.

Given the sheer quantity of books being produced, there has been a tendency for publishers to use cover design as market research, *to try it and see*, with devastating long term consequences for the associated writer; poor sales of a particular title may be jauntily marked down to a 'poor cover design', over which the author had no consultation, let alone control, but whose reputation will substantially affect their chances of remaining in print in future. This often crystallises in the unhappy history of a writer whose varied output is given a uniform market presence, in order to impress a 'brand to return to' on the would-be consumer (who after all usually only buys a title once) but which at the same time repels large sectors of those who might also be attracted.

Expectations of author involvement in the marketing of their work have risen significantly over the period; today the author is part of the marketing package and unable to insist that the writing bit is all they do; publishers are in hot competition to secure the *promotable author* and new delivery mechanisms are heavily dependent on their contacts and connectedness. But makeover television programmes, transforming homes and gardens, have made amateur designers of us all. And for authors, being included in the marketing package, fostered a desire to be part of the decision making process too – about how both they and their work are being packaged and presented to the market. Watching celebrities being turned into bestselling authors, with the addition of a ghost writer and large marketing budget led many professional writers to question the basis on which publishers make decisions – and to take matters into their own hands. Others have felt that their age/sex/race or affiliation is against them, and instructed independent marketing support.

Author independence has also been fostered through a growing appreciation that they could invest in their writing development. The range of options is now dazzling. There are courses, short and long term, residential or 'low residency' (attendance not required very often; tuition and feedback mostly delivered by distance learning) and pricey writing holidays, particularly if the location is spectacular and the tuition residential, intense and star-dusted. There are fees and donations to facilitate entry to competitions, as well as a range of other forms of paid-for support for writing. Look in the back of any magazine on writing (and this too shows the spread of the writing habit) and you will find a wide range of literary consultancy and plot-doctors who have accustomed the nascent writer to understand that writing needs investment, in the same way that they would instruct an architect to help them realise the extension they had long anticipated but not been able to visualise. Even those already with contracts are not immune from the need to spend; published writers have appreciated that few publishing houses now have their own in-house editors, and that the freelance alternatives may be variable in quality – and they may decide to spend their own money on copy-editing and proofreading, just to ensure that their text is as correct as possible, and their reputation preserved.

Self-publishing acquires a new respectability

Self-publishing has had a dubious reputation in the past; it does seem ironic that in today's celebrity-obsessed world, the word 'vanity' is not in widespread use[5] – except with reference to writing. But there are many authors who have taken a financial stake in their publications, and doing so can be seen as a measure of your personal

---

[5] It's a word more commonly used in the 1950s; like 'dainty' and 'doily'. Its survival in the early 21st century is largely in the en suite bathrooms of upmarket hotels, where a 'vanity set' is commonly a complimentary selection of cotton wool and ear-buds

commitment. It can also be a stage on the path to getting a professional publisher to look at your material for the first time, or if you have been dropped by your publishing house, ensuring that your material remains accessible. The range of new products and services for writers means that *bespoke* or *independent publishing* (it's time we reconsidered the name) is returning as an option of choice, not the abandonment of hope.

These new services (e.g. consultancy, technical, marketing) create new options, not all of which necessarily result in widespread dissemination of an author's work. New services allow the author to park a project in a permanent format and then either enjoy the pleasure of sharing (a particularly good option for family memoirs or books of personal significance) or the opportunity to move on with whatever they want to do next, and return to it in six months time with a fresh objectivity. Sharpening a project for preservation, whether as a competition entry, blog or finished book, tends to deliver satisfaction – however it is eventually going to meet its market. Meanwhile competition for the delivery of these services means they generally represent good value for money.

Who is this book for?

This new book, significantly the first on the subject of self-publishing from a traditional publishing house, explores self-publishing as a concept, a mechanism and a future. It considers the philosophy of investing in yourself, and the associated mental adjustments required, before moving on to examine the mechanisms that will allow this to happen. My hope is that it will be engaging, motivating – and completely practical. Anyone seeking to write, or support the writing of others, would benefit from understanding the principles involved.

Finally, although this is just the introduction, I would like to suggest a few key principles to bear in mind as you continue (or to take away with you if you decide to go no further).

1 **Be honest about your expectations;** what you want out of self-publishing and what self-publishing can do for you. While it is very seldom a direct route to riches, it can be a route to self-fulfilment, and this may be just as important.

2 **Tailor your response accordingly.** While I firmly believe that all writing is worthwhile, as it permits reflection and clarity of thought, not all writing deserves to be more widely available. The beauty of self-publishing is that it allows you to preserve your ideas and thoughts in a format and a multiple that is commensurate with both appropriate and likely wider interest; even if that is limited to you, and a print-run of just two copies.

3 **It's not a race.** There are no prizes for finishing early, or pressing the 'send' button too soon – only resulting disappointment, when you see all the errors you might have spotted with a more careful reading.

4 **Get as much feedback as possible on your writing** before you allocate further resources or decide on the scale of your involvement.

5 **The most significant difference between conventional publishing and self-publishing is the need for marketing,** and if you want to sell your book you will need to devote considerable time, energy and resources to trying to make that happen. Be warned now that people can be surprisingly mean.

6 With self-publishing **the buck stops with you.** There is no one else to blame.

Case study: Siobhan Curham, The *Dear Dylan* story

'This time last year I made a momentous decision. I turned down a two-book deal to self-publish my first novel for young adults, *Dear Dylan*.

Dear Dylan tells the story of a fourteen-year-old girl who starts emailing her favourite actor. As things get increasingly difficult for her at home her emails go from being standard fan mails to an outlet for her feelings and frustrations. And then Dylan starts to reply. Or does he? The book is slightly unusual in that it is constructed entirely from emails (a structure that presented a certain amount of challenges as the story progressed, let me tell you!).

Once I had finished *Dear Dylan* I sent it to about ten literary agents. After the customary six week wait I started receiving rejections. Most of them were of the standard variety, but one gave a more detailed reason for turning it down – namely that they didn't feel the email structure worked. But the very same day I received that rejection a friend told me that a well known independent children's publisher were looking for writers for their new YA list. Deciding to go for broke I sent the first 30 pages off to the commissioning editor and later that same day got a reply asking me to send the rest of the manuscript immediately. Coming so swiftly on the heels of a round of rejections from agents you can imagine my excitement. And when, two days later, the editor told me that she loved the book, I was overjoyed. She also said that it had been really nice to receive a manuscript that was fresh and different, and how frustrated she was with all of the 'tired and unoriginal' books she was being sent by agents. I got the real sense that in today's uncertain market agents are playing it even safer than publishers. It was an important and interesting lesson.

Within a week I had been offered a one-book deal and pretty soon that was increased to a two-book deal and an advance was verbally agreed. It felt like a fairytale ending. Little did I know that it was actually a nightmare beginning.

At first it felt empowering to be acting without an agent, but that feeling didn't last for long. Having previously had books for adults published by Random House and Hodder & Stoughton I knew how long it took for a contract to come through, so when I had started writing my second book for the publisher and I still hadn't seen any paperwork for the first I started getting a little annoyed. But every time I chased it I was met with an excuse and the whole thing started getting very stressful. When I did eventually receive a contract I was shocked to see that the advance was considerably lower than had been verbally agreed. I then went through the entire contract comparing the terms on all of the various rights with my previous contracts and was once again shocked and disappointed at how low they were.

I'll admit that at this point I started feeling a bit out of my depth but thankfully I had previous contracts to use as a template, so I went back to the publishers asking for percentages in line with what I had previously received. The publisher improved their offer but it still fell short of what I had received before.

Now, I'm sure that if *Dear Dylan* had been my first book I would have accepted their revised offer and still felt grateful that they were publishing it but instead I felt angry. Especially when I spoke to a friend at a literary agency who told me that publishers will always try and take advantage of a writer acting on their own. And, to put things into a broader perspective, my partner had recently been diagnosed with a very aggressive form of cancer, so book deals didn't seem like the be-all and end-all any more.

When the publisher then started shifting the goalposts regarding publication dates and which book they would publish first it was the final straw. I refused to sign the contract and withdrew my book.

And then of course I felt awful. Any writer knows how hard it is to get a publishing deal – I couldn't help feeling I had completely blown my chances. I felt so disillusioned by the whole experience I decided to forget all about my writing and focus on my other career as an editor. But then, in spring 2010, I had a sudden flash of inspiration. I had felt let down by publishers and agents alike but I still really believed in my book. And I had written *Dear Dylan* to try and help teenagers going through difficult times in their lives so what use was it stuck away in a computer file? What if I self-published it and gave away the electronic version for free?

I wanted *Dear Dylan* to look just as good as any traditionally published book so I invested in the services of the designer Michael Hill and worked with him closely to get a cover that would both appeal to the target readership and stand out as a little different.

Then I contacted self-publishing company AuthorHouse and within a few weeks *Dear Dylan* was available both as a free download on my website and in book form from Amazon and AuthorHouse. Then I started investigating how I could use the internet to market my book. I discovered that there were a huge number of websites dedicated to reviewing YA books and that each of these websites had hundreds, sometimes thousands, of members. So to get reviewed by them would be a fantastic (and free!) way of reaching my target readership. I only approached one of the websites initially, unsure if the fact that *Dear Dylan* was self-published might make it exempt. But the woman running the site told me to send her a copy, and within a couple of weeks she had posted a hugely positive review. Encouraged by this, I set about sending copies of the book to as many of these websites as I could – on both sides of the Atlantic. Although some of them took longer than others, all of them posted reviews and thankfully all of them were favourable. After a while I saw that people had started posting comments about the book online and I realised that a word of mouth buzz was beginning. It was hugely exciting, especially as all of the other books being reviewed on these sites were from major publishers. It felt great to be on a level playing field with them.

Then, one day at work, I came across an article in *The Bookseller* magazine appealing to publishers to enter books for the 2010 YoungMinds Book Award. The organisers were looking for books for young adults that dealt with the issues that teenagers face growing up. *Dear Dylan* certainly fitted the bill but I felt sure that as it was self-published it wouldn't even be considered. However, realising I had nothing to lose but the cost of a stamp, I sent them a copy. I was overjoyed when a week or so later I received an acknowledgement email from the organisers saying that the book had been entered for the competition. I had cleared the first hurdle! About a month passed and then an email popped into my inbox from YoungMinds – my book had made it to the long list. I was so amazed and delighted it felt as if I had actually won. Especially when I saw the other writers on the list – highly respected authors such as Jean Ure and Bali Rai – it felt incredible to be in such company.

The next stage of the competition involved the long-listed books being sent out to schools and youth organisations across the country for young people to decide upon the shortlist of six books. This stage took a couple of months so I put the competition to the back of my mind. I was pretty certain I wouldn't get any further and anyway I felt delighted to have got as far as I had. Then, one day at the beginning of September, another email from YoungMinds popped into my inbox. I pressed open and did that desperate search for the key word that would tell me my fate, such as "disappointed" or "sorry". The first word I saw was "brilliant". I had been short-listed. I had to leave the office to do a quick celebratory dance in the ladies' toilet. It was unbelievable. How had a self-published book managed to get itself short-listed for a national award? And even more heart-warming was the fact that it had been chosen by young readers. I don't think I'd ever felt so honoured.

On the day of the award ceremony one of my work colleagues asked if I'd prepared an acceptance speech 'just in case'. I just looked at her and laughed. As far as I was concerned there was no way on earth *Dear Dylan* was going to win. But that night the unbelievable happened. When the magic envelope was opened, my name was called! It was the most incredible moment of my writing life. But I still wasn't quite at the fairytale ending.

A few days later, when the news of my win broke, I was immediately contacted by a flurry of literary agents all wondering if I was seeking representation. I seemed to have found myself in some kind of bizarre parallel universe where all of the tables had been turned. One of the agents who approached me, Erzsi Deak, had just set up her agency after years as a children's editor and literary scout. I really liked the idea of going with somebody new and we clicked immediately. Within a week of signing up with her she had sent *Dear Dylan* to all of the major children's publishers and at the end of December six of them had said that they would be interested in buying it. My book would be going for auction. It was a fantastic Christmas present!

In the end I signed a two-book deal with Egmont – a publisher I had previously dreamed of writing for. I also got my first ever French book deal and have had some interest from Disney regarding the film rights. Proof indeed that fairy-tale endings can be born from the most nightmarish of beginnings, and we writers should never give up on our dreams.'

1

Reasons for self-publishing.
A quiz

Why do you want to self-publish?

For the committed writer, who has been struggling for many years to get published, the 'helpful' suggestion that you consider self-publishing often produces a furious response. The thought can be seen as patronising, dismissive and, perhaps most crushingly, the final hint that you should give up on your ambition to get a professional publisher or agent to believe in your work. It is hoped that the information in this book will both teach you enough about the processes involved in publication, and make you aware of systems and services available to those who decide to proceed, to make an informed choice.

But embarking on self-publishing requires far more than just a technical facility, the time to manage the process or an available budget. For a satisfactory outcome it is vital for the author to be aware of the responsibility they are assuming. Even though in some cases the tasks involved may be spread between friends and wider family, still the responsibility for deciding to proceed will be that of the writer, and with this decision comes a whole range of associated considerations that in conventional publishing are looked after by someone else (Is it good enough to be published? Would anyone want to read it? Does it need reorganising or rewriting? What is the best format?).

Assuming responsibility is easier if you have both thought about how much is involved and considered your associated motivation. So before we go further, and to avoid you wasting your time, I am offering a short quiz. How many of the following statements do you agree with?

Good reasons for self-publishing

I have not been able to find a commercial publisher to invest in my writing.

> 'Self-publishing should be seen as a last resort. It is better to get your book published and distributed at someone else's risk and expense, and to have the process handled by experienced people with adequate staff and equipment, than to struggle with it yourself. Even if your book turns out to be a big success, it is highly unlikely that you will do better with it in terms either of sales or of profit by publishing it yourself than you would have done with an established publisher.
>
> There are three rules for those considering self-publishing. The first is only do it as a last resort. The second, don't risk more money than you can afford to lose. The third, take all the advice you can get from anyone who knows what they're talking about.'[6]

To this excellent advice, from two people who have been through the process several times, I would add one further point: don't give up on finding an external investor too soon.

I want to set this project to one side, in a finished format, and move on to the creation of other things.

Contacting publishers and agents takes time and energy; each submission needs to be accompanied by a specific pitch explaining why this is a project that should interest them, and goes off with an accompanying investment of adrenalin and hope. While you should not underestimate the amount of time required to turn a manuscript that you have finished into a finished product, self-publishing does offer you the prospect 'passing Go' and progressing towards completion; of parking a project in a finished state, and moving on to whatever you want to do next.

[6] Jill Paton Walsh and John Rowe Townsend, 1995. They were already experienced publishers of niche material when they published Jill's 3rd novel, *Knowledge of Angels* in the UK, a title that was nominated for the Booker Prize, and had found a professional publisher in the US, but had been turned down by her previous publisher in the UK. It was subsequently picked up by another UK publisher. They have since self-published other titles together

I have a specific market in mind for my work, in this case my family and close circle of friends (or it could be your community or school). I have no desire to make it more widely available.

Self-publishing will allow you to put a copy of your book in the hands of everyone you intend (or in their inbox for an ebook), and say 'see what an interesting family we come from' or 'now you know more about where you grew up'. Putting a set of thoughts and experiences to bed in one convenient format that can be shared with others can bring immense satisfaction, at whatever stage in life you do it.

I have no ideas for follow up books or material that could be developed. As far as I am able to say at the moment, this is a one-off book.

Publishers and agents are on the lookout for authors who can repay their initial investment (it takes time and money to get an author noticed) by producing replicable, reliable material at regular intervals. If you have just one book in you, unless you are particularly famous or the story you tell absolutely compelling, self-publishing may be a good route.

I have a very particular idea for how I want my book to look.

Publishers will of course have their own ideas for how a project should be structured and presented, and this will be shaped by their experience, what the potential reader might expect and an appreciation of how the associated costs impact on their return on investment. So if you are dead set on a particular format, then self-publishing is a good option – you can choose the typeface and insist the picture your sister painted goes on the front. As an example of this, Ben Schott's *Miscellany* was produced to a very exacting specification, as a Christmas gift for his friends – he wanted it 'to look like something his grandfather might have owned'. But even after the project was taken on by Bloomsbury he still does all the typesetting – because he really cares how the final product looks.

I can sell the book myself.

Some authors can sell their book themselves, maybe in conjunction with training or after-dinner speaking, or via an effective website through which they can market the title. Or you may want to hand out a copy of your book as a calling card for a business that offers consultancy. If you have a specific expertise and the contacts that back this up, then self-publishing means you can communicate directly with that market, without sharing the profits with anyone else.

As an example of this, a friend is an expert in fireplaces. Such is his reputation, through his business he holds the names of all the relevant dealers and installation experts. His first book on fireplaces was published by a conventional publisher, but for his second he is considering managing the process himself making full use of his contacts and expertise.

I want to write something different from my usual output.

Publishers tend to pigeonhole writers; not out of a desire to entrap but because it takes time to get a reading public established for a particular writer, and it helps get their name known if they are producing a particular type of book. One of the reasons it took Hilary Mantel so long to achieve the reputation she so richly deserves is that it was impossible for her publishers to do this; each book was completely different. While this arguably makes her a more significant and estimable writer, the unifying strand to her work was that each title was the new Hilary Mantel, rather than belonging to a specific, and identifiable genre. So if you have established a name as a particular type of writer, and you want to try something different, and are not sufficiently established with your publishing house that you think they will back you, whatever you produce, or can risk selling fewer copies of a title and so having your profile reduced in house, self-publishing might be a useful way to proceed.

My last book did not do well.

Sales are under constant scrutiny and the author whose sales pattern is in a downward direction will find it hard to maintain their previous position, no matter how well reviewed/highly respected/ fast selling their work has been in the past. No author today who 'has a publisher' can consider it an ongoing arrangement. To counteract the accompanying feelings of insecurity, it may be pragmatic to investigate the mechanisms of publishing work yourself; the investment of time and money that would be required were you to be forced to go it alone.

4

My work is about to go out of print.

Once a title is nearing the end of its print life (i.e. there are few copies left), or sales have slowed down, the publisher has to decide whether or not to keep it in print. If they decide not to, the stock may be sold off at a substantial discount to a remainder merchant, or pulped. Alternatively, the author will be offered the option of buying up the remaining stock, which they are free to sell at speaking engagements or give away. Once a title is declared out of print, and the rights have reverted to the author, they may decide to have more printed at their own expense; through self-publishing, or perhaps to change format and disseminate as an ebook. At a time when you inevitably feel vulnerable, learning more about the processes involved in self-publication may help you feel empowered.

My ego feels bruised by constant rejections from agents and publishers.

If you decide to self-publish, you become the customer – and so rather than facing endless rejections you will find that firms offering you their services tend to be pleasant to deal with. They are helping you develop your dream. It's a bit like buying a house you have wanted to own for a long time, the various legal and practical processes confirm you on the path towards ownership – but happily with no one else competing for the property.

Decision making in publishing takes so long; I want to get on with it.

> 'I am afraid as you do not write – that the 3rd volume has occasioned some disappointment. It is better, however, to speak plainly about it, if it be so. I would rather at once know the worst than be kept longer in suspense.'
>
> Charlotte Brontë to her publisher, George Smith, 1 December 1852[7]

Publishers are careful people. They take their time to think about whether the market needs the product offered, whether what is suggested is right for the market (or needs adaptation), and then

[7] The Brontë House Museum, Haworth

whether the writing is appropriate for the product (they may like your idea but decide you are not the best person to produce it for them). They are also committee-based, so work tends to get discussed between colleagues not all of whom see literary excellence as the chief criterion for making a decision (would we be better off commissioning someone better known?).

It's possible for decisions to be stalled, or revisited, after commissioning. And the irony is the larger the publishing company, the longer the process may take (more committees to consult). If you decide to self-publish you can almost certainly get a product to market more quickly, although whether you can replicate the quality product of a professional publisher is less certain.

Time is not on my side.

The other reason for speed is perhaps the age or physical state of the writer. The publishing world is not particularly ageist (there are examples of people who get published later in life, consider Raymond Chandler, Laura Ingalls Wilder, M.M. Kaye, Diana Athill and Mary Wesley) but a commercial publisher or agent who decides to invest in you will want to build your reputation as a writer over years to come. You may also feel that trying to get published is eating up too much of your time – that could be spent doing other things.

There may also of course be an additional personal agenda here: you are aging or seriously ill and suspect your writing time may be limited; you want to capture the memories of a key member of the family before they are no longer with you. Ensuring the survival of information they alone have, and recording it as a self-published book, will ensure permanence.

I have got £10k to spare/available to access and a project I have always wanted to see in print.

The very wise father of a friend of mine commented recently that when he looked back on his life, the thing he regretted was not the money he had spent, but the money he had not spent; when life circumstances made expenditure difficult and as a result they had all missed out on something they would have enjoyed at the time or appreciated later. My husband and I still regret a picture we passed up in 1985 – by the time we came back to the artist he had become much more collectable and the prices had gone up accordingly – but the experience did influence our future buying habits. Having sufficient resources (or an ability to cut your overheads) to complete a project that has been a long-term fantasy is a good reason for deciding to go for it, particularly if the funds are now accompanied by sufficient time for you to nurse it into life. Roddy Doyle:

> 'I had no family. I lived in a bedsit so I didn't need to save. Not a bother in the world. I went into the bank and I did a bit of homework with my agent. We figured out the printing wasn't all that expensive, same as buying a second-hand car. I lived by the train station so I didn't need a car so did this instead. It was a great adventure.'[8]

I want to learn more about how the publishing industry works.
Receiving just a couple of rejection letters from publishing houses can make the industry look very joined up, and exclusive. While invariably polite, publishers tend to use the same phrases in their rejection letters ('I did not fall in love with it'; 'does not fit our list as currently developing'), leading aspiring writers to feel this is a club of which they are not members. While dispiriting, authors often do not appreciate just how much material they have to choose between, and hence the difference that an attractive package or effective introductory letter can make.

Self-publishing is an excellent way of learning more about the industry, and the amount of effort that goes into the creation of a book. As broadcaster Libby Purves said after self-publishing her son's writing: 'We did get a sense of what they do all day.'[9]

I have a lot of energy to put into this project.
Self-publishing will require this, and the generally accepted starting point includes a combination of determination, grit, assertiveness and some experience of negotiation. There is also considerable power in energies that may be just as forceful, but less willingly acknowledged. A self-publishing project may be fuelled by anger,

---

[8] From 'An interview with writer Roddy Doyle', Platform, Open University Community online http://www8.open.ac.uk/platform/news-and-features/interview-writer-roddy-doyle
[9] See chapter 17

frustration, loathing, a burning sense of injustice, isolation, neglect, jealousy and a determination to set the record straight.

Several years ago I heard a blind marathon runner interviewed on the radio. The interviewer began by concentrating on the difficulties of running such long distances when you cannot see, and the kind of special support needed. So far, so predictable. But he concluded by asking the runner about his motivation in taking on something so difficult. The response was obviously a surprise – 'Bitterness'. Asked to amplify, it was clear the interviewer felt increasingly uncomfortable as the runner talked of his determination to prove that he could do something that others had been confident he could not; after years of feeling patronised. Negative content was not appreciated and the interview ended with the host trying, unsuccessfully, to extract a positive message from the overall discussion. The 'b' word lingered in everyone's memory.

Writers need to think about the emotions and personal attributes that they will bring to the task of self-publishing. These will necessarily include determination and forcefulness, but maybe also a dash of bitterness to keep you going. And who's to say that it is positive emotions that progress a project more than negative ones?

Bad reasons for self-publishing

I want to make money.
Please accept now that it is seldom that the amount of effort that goes into writing a book is compensated for by its subsequent sales.

If you decide to self-publish, and to try to make money out of the venture, you will have to try to sell the work: to friends, colleagues and even family. You will find that most people seem to expect a free copy ('I bought you dinner two years ago'; 'we have known each other for thirty years'; 'you are my brother-in-law') and the logic of being willing to pay more for a round of drinks than you are asking for your book is not widely accepted. You may well feel frustrated that they are so mean and end up either losing friends – or just liking them less.

I am furious with the publishing industry.

'Certainly anybody whose experience has been gained in the literary field cannot believe that merit alone decides the success or failure of a writer.'
Rebecca West, 1960

Publishing is a business. And to remain in business, risk gets spread – across different markets through the commissioning of different types of product. In the process, it is true that good manuscripts do get overlooked; books commissioned from those who cannot write, and remain stubbornly un-bought by the general public because their role as 'author' stretches credulity; bad decisions made. But this happens because judging the taste of the book buying public is tricky and is notable precisely because it is unusual – there are far more good decisions from professional publishers than bad ones.

If you are going to manage the process of publication yourself it is better to begin by being really objective about your work (is this really worth investing in; will others want to read it?) rather than as part of a one-person vendetta against an industry that will always be bigger than you.

I want a real publisher to snap me up.
This may happen, but is more likely not to. The internet abounds with stories of self-published books that become bestsellers, but they stand out as stories because in general they are rare.

I want my family and friends to read what I have written.
Again, this may happen, but it may not. You can't force people to read. Of course they may do later on, once you are no longer around – one of the marks of maturity seems to me to be that you suddenly wish you had asked your parents more about their life. But whether or not you get asked in your lifetime, if you have written it down, it is there for all to consult – whenever they decide they are grown up enough to want to know.

I can do it myself. As someone with a sharp eye for detail, I can do the bits the publisher would and how hard can the rest be?
A tempting thought, but every book hides a wealth of specific decisions and experience – and the process is not as easy as you

may think. Bear in mind that it's notoriously difficult to edit yourself – we tend to see what we thought we wrote, not what is actually there. If you do decide to self-publish there will be a huge number of things you will have to learn about; from dealing with bookshops to organising storage, postage and packing – and most of them have nothing to do with writing.

How did your responses shape up?

There is no right answer to this quiz, or easy way of totting up the scores. If you have answered yes to all the good reasons for self-publishing, and no to all the bad ones I feel you may not have been entirely honest with yourself. The process will however hopefully have sharpened your understanding.

You do not have to have a final response to the question of whether you should self-publish right now. You may consider self-publishing for one project and pursuing publishing deals for others. And nor should you think that embarking on self-publishing for a project will stop you getting a 'proper' publishing deal for it in the long term. It won't – indeed there are several case histories included within this book that prove this is not the case.

And meanwhile, while you are just embarking on an under-standing of the processes of publishing, which includes self-publishing, if someone tells you they have self-published, find out how the process went, ask what they wish they had known at the outset that they now realise – and then buy a copy from them!

Case study: Paul Hurst

Paul Hurst left school after 'A' levels, and having been unable to decide what to do at university, entered the world of work instead. He became skilled in bookkeeping and accounting and eventually started working in the Civil Service. Here he found he was surrounded by people who were ironically trapped by their (excellent) pension prospects; unable to retire or move jobs, with their personal development and creativity stunted. It was not a happy environment and he decided to get out, opting for a combination of life as a band leader and provider of freelance accounting/bookkeeping to small businesses. But his consultancy services continued to introduce him to a range of people facing similar difficulties, and his desire to help them led to the creation of *Business Survival and Prosperity Guaranteed*, a compendium of financial and management advice for those seeking to nourish a small business.

He did begin by trying to publish through conventional means, and found an agent, but she was unable to find a publisher who was interested, so he thought he would sell it himself via Amazon and directly from his website.

As regards the production of the book, it was laid out by an editor friend and then printed by professional printers, although looking back he wonders if he could have managed the layout himself. He chose a primarily typographic cover design and strong colour scheme (blue and yellow) based on what other business books looked like, arranged for an ISBN and sent copies off to the UK copyright libraries.[10] And he got a real kick from the thought that, when playing at a gig near Oxford recently, his book was somewhere on the shelves in the nearby Bodleian Library. The first edition revealed typographical errors he had not spotted while writing, and a second has just been delivered. It sells well via the website and with Paypal handling the money side of the business, purchases come in from all over the world – the most distant so far being Africa. The small print run of the first edition allowed him to trial his ideas – and then announce its sell out with the publication of a second (for which he also shuffled the chapters around and added a couple of new ones).

He had established a relationship with the marketing guru Paul F Gorman, firstly as a paid mentor, and later as a friend after Gorman retired, and they remain involved. Together they have worked on the website that promotes Hurst's book. The copy follows the conventional advertising formula of attract

---

[10] A copy of any new book with an ISBN should be sent to the following libraries: The British Library, London; Bodleian Library, Oxford; Cambridge University Library; National Library of Scotland, Edinburgh; National Library of Wales, Aberystwyth; Trinity College Library, Dublin. US authors send to the Library of Congress in Washington

(good headline), interest (long introduction to the product), desire (effective description of benefits; samples for the reader to inspect the kind of advice on offer), conviction (through quoting third party endorsement), and action (persuading the individual to order).[11]

His life today is a happy juggling of both accounting and music, deliberately kept at a sufficient level to fulfil his priority of operating from home. The music side of his activities has been helped considerably by the licensing in the UK of venues other than churches and registry offices in which to host weddings and civil partnerships; considerably widening the range of venues available. This has created a much bigger market for the services of musicians and other part time entertainers. Bands for a school or church barn dance often tend to be informal groupings, happy to play in return for beer money, but weddings/civil partnerships attract a more considered and considerable expenditure. This income funds his writing time.

In the long run he sees writing and offering business advice as a more sustainable career, for when – as happens to all musicians – his fingers become less flexible. Having a book in his name also benefits his business consultancy service; people are inclined to rate the advice of those who have written about what they do, and it can be given away to those who are considering his services. He is actively developing an ebook version of his work as a way to increase market awareness of both title and services and enable its swifter updating, and is thinking of expanding his information service for those planning weddings into a bigger website or ebook.

'My book helped me scratch a particular itch – I had wanted to write one for some time. The biggest jolt was seeing it properly laid out; looking like a 'real' book rather than a Word document. It also gave me confidence – the learning curve was steep but I now have a lot more confidence about future projects.'

[11] Or AIDCA. AIDA (attract, interest, desire, action) was first advocated by advertising agencies in Madison Avenue, NY in the 1950s. The 'C' was later added by direct marketing copywriter Roger Millington, from Kingston-upon-Thames

2

The stages of self-publishing; the competencies and assets needed

There are firms which offer a complete service, and, for a fee, will help guide you through all the following stages (see chapter 15). On the other hand, it's a good idea to know what needs to be done, and in what sequence, in order to turn a writing project into a book that can be read by others. You will need:

An appreciation of what it means 'to publish'

Professional publishers get irritated by authors who dismiss the part they play in book creation as 'pressing a few buttons'. So for self-publishing authors who must manage the processes themselves, it's worth bearing in mind that the verb 'to publish' is multi-layered. For example, it will involve deciding what kind of audience you are seeking to reach, and managing the implications this has for language, font size, format, binding and level of durability – and at what anticipated selling price. And then there are much subtler considerations, like the impact the typeface you choose will have on the text, and the way your cover blurb and design will resonate with the prospective reader. Publishing is a complex endeavour and the self-publishing author does well to begin by appreciating this.

A manuscript or an idea
In the beginning was the word. In whatever format you decide to share your ideas – traditional book, ebook, picture book or zine (home-made magazine) – the words, or a visualisation of words, are the starting point. This idea may be at the back of your mind

and still be formulating or it may be partly developed, with some chapters written and an outline available. But until you have a product that can be assessed by others for wider dissemination, it is difficult to proceed.

Within traditional publishing, work may be commissioned on the submission of a 'partial' (part of a completed manuscript; usually a detailed outline/synopsis and the first three chapters). But for the author who is planning to self-publish, for the project to be effectively costed, your potential suppliers will need material on which to base a realistic quotation (ideally an overall word count, typesize and an anticipated number of typographic characters per page). This is easier (and likely to be more accurate) if the work is finished and you are ready to proceed.

This principle is not inviolate. Self-publishing can proceed for years as a bit-by-bit process: accessing memories with the help of a close friend or ghost writer who can organise them for you; gaining feedback on your manuscript; commissioning an illustrator to give life to what is in your head. However, once you start proceeding towards a finished format, your costs will rise significantly if at that stage you start changing your mind about the text and/or illustrations. Digital formats can be amended much more easily, but the metamorphosing into the final openable and readable object will still need to be redone.

To use an analogy from everyday life, the manuscript preparation is the assembling of the basic ingredients for cooking. The various stages of text preparation are the method; the production processes are the application of heat, which fundamentally changes things. See chapters 10 and 11.

Material that is worth preservation

I took an old watch to a jeweller in Northern Ireland and asked if it was worth repairing. His response intrigued me:

> 'I cannot say because I do not know what it is worth to you. Are you going to tell me it belongs to your father and is therefore very precious? What I can say is that it would be very expensive to repair, and is probably not worth it, unless the value to you is more than that.'

It's a good analogy for the preservation of writing. The value of the writing you are seeking to preserve or share depends on a series of criteria, from your life-stage to your relationships with others. Are you seeking to hang on to last testament of a close relative or to preserve your own manuscript? Value has no single measure, but the product you create in the process must have some value for someone. See chapter 9.

How much assistance does the manuscript need?

Does it need a structural edit; moving the substance around to ensure the material is complete and everything is in the right place? Would the opening of the book be achieved best through flashback rather than chronology? Is it too long or too short? Does the ending need strengthening? It's hard to be objective about your own work; further assistance may be found in chapter 9.

Does it need illustrating?

A children's picture book will need images, and you need to consider where to source them. Ideally, you need to see an artist's work in isolation (on a website or in a portfolio) before you meet the artist. You need to separate the individual from their work: do you like the artist's style; does it represent how you want your ideas to be conveyed; do you need to get used to it before making a decision? You also need to think about the time and effort involved in creating appropriate illustrations, and the likely associated cost. For more ideas see chapter 11.

Copy-editing

Copy-editing is not the same as the structural editing mentioned above. Copy-editing requires the establishment of editorial standards and then their rigorous application to the manuscript, for example looking for consistency in spelling; effective grammar; management of detail (the heroine's eyes are blue in chapter 1 and green in chapter 7) and chronology (when was the character born and what are their key dates?); the resolution of gaps, irrelevancies and unnecessary repetition. Professional copy-editors are meticulous individuals who are trained to look out for lots of different things at the same time. Their time will be costed on how much intervention is required. Many copy-editors can provide a structural edit, while people who describe themselves as structural editors generally do not copy-edit. See chapters 9 and 10.

A decision on format

You will have to decide how you want your material to reach its market; physical (with what kind of binding?) or e-resource? Chapters 14 and 16, on production and preparing for publication in e-format book will give you more ideas.

Typographic design

You can type your manuscript, but you will probably need the services of a trained typographic designer to indicate what the final product should look like. Effectively managed, the details of typographic design are not evident to the general reader, who merely gains easy access to the content; it is the careful handling of design that often creates a distinction between the professionally and amateurishly presented text.

Typographic design is the composition of the pages by using the attributes and styles of typefaces and space to create the desired overall effect; to ensure an appropriate reading experience for the user. This involves deciding not only which typefaces to use and in what sizes, but also how many columns on the page, how many lines on the page, how long the line of text should be, how much space between the lines (leading), whether the text should be aligned on both edges (justified) or on one side only (unjustified), whether any headings should be centred or aligned with the left margin, and how wide the margins either side and on top and bottom should be.

The decision of which typeface(s) to use will depend on the nature of the text and the intended reader. Although typefaces can be used in various sizes, seldom is a book typeset in one typeface only. It is more common for 'families' of related typeface to be used; perhaps one for the main body of the text, another for headings and page numbers, maybe a third for footnotes. See chapter 12.

Typesetting

After all these careful decisions about how to treat the text have been made, and the text has been copy-edited, it is typeset. Many people confuse typing with typesetting, but typesetting is the implementation of the decisions made by the typographical designer. The designer's decisions are implemented using typesetting software that is more refined and detailed than any word-processing programme.

Cover design

Unhappiness with the cover is one of the most frequent gripes between authors and their publishers. Authors frequently report feeling misrepresented by the image chosen and that their book, and they themselves, are being packaged in a way that is more relevant to what other people are publishing than their particular writing. This is often true; given the sheer amount of material available, all manufacturers try to offer potential buyers 'category clues' from packaging – hence most bleach products are 'cold' colours (blue green or yellow), whereas products for car maintenance tend to be 'technical looking' (black and red). Books are targeted in similar ways so that a customer can quickly spot and hopefully choose the kind of books they like; 'commercial women's fiction' may be presented in candy colours; crime is usually in black, white and red.

Commissioning your own jacket or cover offers you the potential to present yourself as you want, but getting it right is vastly harder than it may appear – and a friend with a passing acquaintance with Photoshop is not enough. The market is highly competitive, people make very quick decisions on whether a book needs a second look, and the cover is crucial in prompting appropriate attention. If you want your product to sell, the market's perception of what they expect it to look like, given its content, is more important than your own personal preference – or sense of obligation to that very talented nephew. See chapter 11.

Promotional/jacket copy

Again, this is crucial. Many studies within the publishing industry have shown that whereas it is the cover that draws attention, it is the cover copy that persuades the viewer to purchase. Even if you are not planning to sell your work, the text here will be read as a summation of the product, and it offers the clearest possible indication of whether or not the content is worth reading. Brief author information usually appears here too. See chapter 19.

Proofreading

Once the manuscript has been typeset and laid out, it will need to be proofread against what was originally provided. If it has been typeset from an electronic file then there should be no *fresh* mistakes, but it will still need to be read for odd word-breaks, in particular at the end of a page, stranded text (often called 'widows') such as the first line of a new paragraph that gets separated from the balance with a page turn, and correct styling of headings, captions or other text features. A proofreader may check against the text supplied, and also on occasion blind proofread (reading without the original text). Both are very valuable and are best done by someone other than the writer, who will see what they thought they wrote, often filling in missing words in their head. Last-minute corrections are always possible, but the closer you get to the finished product, the more expensive they become. With professional proofreading, only minor errors are likely to get into print, and you just have to live with them unless they are dangerous or libellous, and they can be corrected if and when there is a reprint. See chapter 13.

Choosing a supplier and deciding to print/preparing for digital dissemination

The decision on who is going to manage the production of your title is a difficult one, options now being spread worldwide, and you will need to juggle the issues of cost, value, ease of communication and delivery. There are traditional printing firms where your book will come off the same presses that handled the work of writers you admire, and other firms who can offer digital printing that means a print run of just two copies is economically viable. See chapter 14.

An ebook publishing service can help you upload a document in any form and turn it into an ebook very quickly, but it still pays to have it professionally edited, typeset and proofread first. See chapter 16.

Arranging for delivery and storage

Deciding that you are ready to print (dubbed 'passing for press') brings a temporary relief, and if you are using print on demand (see page 216) no associated large parcels. But if you are having a longer run, the problem then arises of what to do with the stock. Books damage easily and the purchaser wants a perfect copy.

Where can you store the stock? Both damp and heat adversely affect paper and weaken the glue on the spine, making it soggy (for damp) or brittle and hence liable to crack (for excess heat). Think of all the titles on your own shelves that, in theory, have probably had optimum storage conditions, but now probably have both yellowed pages (because they were not printed on acid-free paper) and broken spines. Storage space in outhouses and garages is liable to variations in temperature, flooding, rodents and other temporary or ongoing hazards. See chapter 17.

Marketing

This has come low down the list but is the single factor that puts most people off self-publishing – or prevents them from trying it again. It is labour intensive, demands time and determination, skill and energy – and can feel demeaning. However great the self-published author's lack of enthusiasm for marketing, if you want your work to sell, you have to engage. Of course additional promotional support can always be paid for, but bear in mind that you will be paying for the service provider's time rather than a guarantee of column inches or airtime – and you may retain a nagging suspicion that they will never do it as well as you. See chapters 18, 19 and 20.

Other useful competencies for the self-publishing author

An ability to timetable

Working back from the date you want your material delivered, in order to meet key buying seasons or a specific anniversary, you need to establish when each stage needs to be finalised, to allow enough time for checking, processing and contingencies. See chapter 5.

Coordination skills

One of the particular challenges of self-publishing is coordinating simultaneous stages, to ensure a product comes out in a timely fashion. This is much harder than it looks, particularly when there is only one individual managing each function, which within a publishing house would be spread between several different departments. Thus your jacket visual needs to be prepared at the same time as your jacket copy; space will need to be left in the manuscript for cross-references but you will not be able to fill in the page numbers until after the page design, typesetting and proofreading have been done. If you are proposing to sell the title, marketing will need to be considered as soon as you start planning, and those on whom you depend for retail sales will need to see a 'cover rough' long before the book is ready. Editing will need to be done while keeping an eye on production planning, as time on the printing press will need to be booked ahead.

These various stages require different skills. An eagle eye for detail is not necessarily the same as a marketing brain that can spot likely opportunities. It can be useful to bring in friends with different aptitudes to help you with your project; small writing support groups consisting of several people producing different kinds of material can work particularly well, both face-to-face and online.

Self-belief
The conviction that this project is an appropriate beneficiary of your time and resources will be needed to maintain you when the going gets tough. At some point you will almost invariably wonder why you started.

Funding self-publishing

'Book writing is not booming. In plain terms, it doesn't pay enough. It doesn't pay as much as it *ought* to, in a country with a growing appetite for books. The British public wants, increasingly, to read: it does not, on the whole, want to pay for reading... A golden nucleus of book authors, not necessarily the best, build up small fortunes in ways denied to the pop novelists of the past. But hundreds more – and these by no means flops or failures – squeeze only a miserable dole from their work. Britain is getting its books at the expense of its authors and on the cheap...'

Richard Findlater, *Observer* journalist and editor of *The Author*

The extract comes from a pamphlet called *The Book Writers: who are they?* Although it dates from over 40 years ago (1966), the problems are still entirely familiar. The writers of books are those on whom it is easiest to place financial pressure when things get tight; they are 'the least entrenched party in the business of book production'[12] and so tend to be the easiest to budge.

Reading back through the archives of The Society of Authors, the scenario is depressingly consistent – from the reduced royalty suggested as a convenient step towards moving the industry towards profit, when price rises in the raw materials after the second world war made publishing temporarily uneconomic, to the drastic cuts regularly proposed to Public Lending Right whenever public spending is under pressure.

Yet publishing costs money, and the list offered in this chapter of component parts to your self-publishing project, will all need to be funded – or otherwise secured.

Writers must also fund their own development time. Some individuals may be able to set up paid writing time, perhaps as a sabbatical from their place of work, or by taking unpaid leave. If you are trying to negotiate here, bear in mind that creative projects which bring credit on the organisation as a whole, or provide a means of staff bonding, may be positively viewed – and provide useful fodder for reporting through official organisational channels such as the staff newsletter or the PR department.

* If you are managing the process of publishing yourself, then you can set your own price and try to recoup your costs, but bear in mind that unless your product is for a specified and targetable niche, this may be very difficult. And to establish your overall profit from the project the surplus you generate has to be divided by the number you print, not the number you sell.

* If you are using a publishing solutions company (see chapter 15) be very clear about how the process will be paid for and the associated financial commitments you are accumulating. You will pay up front for the finalisation and then preparation of

[12] Victor Bonham-Carter, *Authors by Profession*, Volume 2, London: The Society of Authors (1984)

your book but may find yourself locked into much longer term arrangements. Some companies charge high fees for servicing orders and/or lock the author in for a period after publication (perhaps one or two years). Others count the stock produced as the author's and act as a distribution or sales agent, retaining a small commission for the sales they make. Check the contract.

- If you are selling online through etailers (e.g. Amazon), you will be charged a percentage of the selling price as commission each time a sale is made; and the percentages may vary according to the price level (in general, low prices attract higher levels of commission). If you use an online payment service (e.g. Paypal) they will take another percentage.

- Booksellers and other retailers agreeing to stock will need a discount to cover the associated costs of displaying, listing and selling your title. They may also only pay you once the titles have been sold, and retain the right to return them to you if they do not sell at all (see chapter 17 on distribution).

- Individual sales through bookshops may be at one rate, but outlets taking 'bulk sales' such as supermarkets demand much higher discounts. Similarly, promotional schemes (e.g. the use of a book as a giveaway with a magazine or subscription) may attract little profit at all; usually on the grounds of associated publicity. Think whether this is worth it from your point of view: unless you have other things to sell your market in the near future, getting your name better known may not fully offset the cost of production.

Case study: financial arguments against – and then for – self-publishing: Lucy Raby,[13] writer for television

'Having been published[14] I was keen to maintain my profile as a writer and about five years ago I wrote a science fiction novel. This has been doing the rounds of publishers, but to date has not

---

[13] www.lucydanielraby.co.uk

[14] *Nickolai of the North* (2006) and *Nickolai's Quest* (2007), London: Hodder & Stoughton Children's Books

been picked up. The option remained to self-publish, but what put me off was the initial cost and the fact that the whole thing looked extremely unviable economically. Having spoken to many self-published authors, and questioned them closely about costs, it looked like a great way of throwing away time and money in return for seeing your name in print. Even traditionally published authors have to do a lot of work self-publicising, as I have done, but self-published authors were funding their writing time too. It seemed to take two or three years of hard slog, hand-selling in branches of Waterstone's every Saturday, to even pay off the initial outlay; and discounting made it even harder to make a profit. The resulting hourly rate of pay was hardly making a living.

Which is what I am used to being able to do with my writing; I have always earned my living in this way. Working in television, you can earn £2,000 – £3,000 for a month or so, plus royalties. With self-publishing, if you "don't do it for the money", it seemed you could not expect to make any real return out of it. And if you can't make a viable living at it – surely that is just vanity publishing by another name?

What changed my mind however was the option to self-publish through digital publishing or ebooks. It does not have the same cost implications as print, and is a good way to test material on the market and get noticed by publishers and the market alike. It does however require a similar amount of marketing and promotion. If you just dump an ebook on Amazon or a similar ebook site, it would be the same as putting a book in a warehouse. You have to get it out there in the digital shop and drive visitors to both the ebook site and your own home website. You also have to provide a certain amount of free content and marketing initiatives to build up a following and hook readers in. But all this can be done online, rather than trudging round UK bookshops hand-selling. This is the way forward. My new book, *Goddess in Pyjamas*, a science fiction fantasy for 9–12 year olds, is out now on Smashwords, priced at $2.99; available as a download on all platforms including Kindle, and free from Amazon. The first book in a trilogy, I will be marketing it with short story giveaways and competitions.'[15]

[15] http://www.smashwords.com/books/view/59203

Public Lending Right (PLR)

Many governments now include some form or compensation for authors for 'lost sales' arising from loans made through public libraries; a book stocked in a library may generate just one sale (and resulting royalty as associated income), but in fact be read by hundreds of people. It is important to register your titles with PLR so that loans can be counted, and particularly important if a book has been issued in a new edition and the ISBN changed.[16]

Rather than count every single loan, in every single library in the country, PLR is based on a sampling strategy of certain libraries within certain library authorities (which change at regular intervals) and whose loans are then averaged out over the whole country. So if you should happen to find out that your own local library is part of the sample, a donated copy might be pragmatic. The maximum receipts of an individual author are capped, and the number of beneficiaries is wide. Even for an author whose works are out of print, PLR receipts can still form a useful income.

Legal understanding

Just because you are self-publishing, does not free you from observing the law, and there are a range of legal issues to which you should pay careful attention.[17] In a traditional publishing scenario, within the contract between author and publisher there will be a clause that requires the author to confirm that their material is not legally actionable now and that they indemnify their publisher from legal action in future. In practice, those who were offended

---

[16] 28 countries have a PLR programme, and others are considering adopting one. The first was Denmark in 1941 and others include Canada, UK, all Scandinavinan countries, Germany, Austria, Belgium, Israel, Australia and NZ. There is ongoing debate in France about implementing one. There is also a move towards having a Europe-wide PLR program administered by the EU. In the UK this is managed through www.plr.uk.com

[17] I am indebted to Nicola Solomon, General Secretary of The Society of Authors, and Dan Townend of Kingston University, for help with this section

by an author's work would be more likely to pursue a case against the publisher than an individual author (hence Penguin's difficulties as the publishers of Salman Rushdie in the 1980s). A firm offering self-publishing will require similar confirmation from authors whose work they publish, but will not provide a similar umbrella of legal protection, because the choice to publish is the author's rather than the publisher's.

Self-publishing may involve producing material in digital formats, rather than in print, and spreading information about your work through social media. Blogging and Tweeting feel informal, because they are so quickly executed and disseminated, but be aware that the internet is not a law-free zone. You should be as careful as if your work was going to be traditionally printed.

The following are the rights to be aware of:

Copyright

Copyright is a branch of intellectual property law – it protects the products of people's skill, creativity, labour or time. 'What is worth copying is prima facie worth protection'.[18] The key legislation in this area in the UK is the Copyright, Designs and Patents Act of 1988, which came into effect on 31st July 1989

The first owner of copyright is the author, or the employer if the work is done in the course of employment (unless there is agreement to the contrary). There are moral rights to protect photographs which individuals commission but for which they do not own the legal copyright (e.g. wedding photographs), and it may be an actionable breach of confidence if a person who has obtained information in confidence takes unfair advantage of it. Injunctions can be granted by the courts to help prevent its further spread.

There is no copyright in facts, news, ideas or information, but copyright does exist in the form in which information is expressed and the selection and arrangement of the material by others, all of which involve skill and labour. So taking the ideas from someone's argument may not be copyright theft, particularly if done in order to extend the debate, but using their wording, selection of facts or arrangement will be.

---

[18] N.J. Peterson in University of London Press Ltd versus University Tutorial Press Ltd (1916) 2CH 601

A defence of 'fair dealing' for the purposes of reporting current events for the use of other people's copyright work requires sufficient recognition of the original work and its author, and it must be 'fair' i.e. the new material must not compete commercially with the copyright owner, and the amount of reused material must be reasonable. Significantly, photographs are not subject to a defence of 'fair dealing for the purposes of reporting current events.' Also, be aware that if someone commissioned a portrait photograph, such as a family member, they may have moral rights of privacy which allow them to object to a picture being published.

Thinking digitally; be clear that your blog does not include anyone else's work. Ensure that you have copyright clearance for use of any photos or illustrations. It is easy to cut and paste images from Google Images but even if there are no copyright notices on them, re-use will normally be an infringement of copyright for which you could be sued. Be careful when using photographs of others. Photographs taken in a public place can still offend privacy laws.

While considering copyright, think too about your own. Think about what use others can make of your work. Would you be distressed if they re-used it? If so, include appropriate copyright notices and terms of use. If you don't know how to draft these consider using a creative commons license http://creativecommons.org/worldwide/uk with which you can keep your copyright but allow people to copy and distribute your work on conditions which you can choose from a simple checklist given on the website. For example, you could allow your work to be used only non-commercially and amended so long as you are given a credit.

Accuracy

Make sure your work is accurate; if following your advice could be risky include an appropriate disclaimer: you don't want to be sued if a recipe for your favourite dish causes an outbreak of food poisoning.

Privacy

An individual's right to privacy is often linked to a potentially actionable **breach of confidence** and the courts need to achieve a balance between Article 8 of the 1988 Act (the right of respect for private and family life) and article 10 (the right to freedom of expression).

Everyone is entitled to respect for their private and family life, home, health and correspondence (including digital correspondence) and it is unacceptable to harass, intimidate or persistently pursue individuals once asked to desist or leave. The law is sharpened with particular effect for children under 16, who must not be interviewed or photographed unless a parent, or adult with similar authority, consents. Considerations of privacy have also been affected by Max Mosley's case against the *News of the World* in July 2008, for invasion of privacy. This may cause difficulties for the increasingly popular genre of 'life writing', and some publishers now adopt a process of 'good practice' whereby they check that living individuals referred to (in such a way that they can be recognised) in such titles are approached for approval; usually this means giving them a copy of the paragraphs in which they are mentioned.[19] There may however be a defence of public interest, which includes detecting or exposing serious crime or impropriety, preventing the public being misled by an action or statement, an individual or organisation.[20]

Sex offences and associated privacy

The Sexual Offences Act 2003 effectively gives anonymity during their lifetime to alleged victims (male and female) of most sexual offences from the point that they make the allegation. This applies even if there is no physical contact involved (e.g. indecent exposure, trafficking for prostitution). This anonymity remains, even if the allegation is later withdrawn or the accused is later cleared, and not identifying the alleged victim, but detailing specifics which enable the individual to be identified, may also break the law. This protection ends with death. Anonymity can be waived, if the case is deemed to be in the public interest, but would need written consent, without interference, and only be in the case of victims over 16. In such circumstances, reporting restrictions might be lifted.

The Criminal Justice Act of 1925 prohibits the taking of any photographs (or portrait or sketch) in the court or its precincts, of any juror, witness, party or judge and it is also an offence to publish the same.

---

[19] See the Press Complaints Commission Guidelines www.pcc.org.uk
[20] Article 10

Defamation, libel and slander

Defamation is based on the principle that 'everyone has the right to have the estimation in which he stands in the opinion of others unaffected by false and defamatory statements and imputations' (McNae's 2009).[21] Judges tell juries that a defamatory statement will expose the complainant to hatred, ridicule or contempt; cause them to be shunned or avoided; lower them in the estimation of right thinking members of society or disparage them in business or professional matters. To win a libel case a complainant has to prove that the statement is defamatory, that it may reasonably understood to refer to them and that it has been published by a third party. They do not have to prove that the statement is false (the court will assume that), or that they have been damaged, only that the information tends to discredit them. Defences may include justification (proof that the allegations are true); fair comment (e.g. the comments are commonly and honestly held beliefs that are without malice); the information was obtained through privilege (e.g. court reporting, but the Defamation Act of 1996 requires that reports must be fair, accurate and contemporaneously made or a statement from an authority such as the police, the council or a government); accord and satisfaction (settlement of a claim by an appropriate and agreed means); offer of amends (the publication of an apology or the payment of suitable damages). Given that English law depends on precedent, new cases arise that extend the courts' understanding all the time, and there are current debates about the relative importance of the urgency of the story, whether comment was sought from those involved (in order to gain a variety other sides of the argument), and the prevailing tone of the writing.

Defamation can take place in a digital environment (e.g. a blog, website or Tweet) as well as a printed one. Slander cannot as it relates to unrecorded spoken words only. You have freedom as to what to write in a blog but not if it is defamatory of another living person. Therefore ensure what you say is true, accurate and can be backed up by facts.

Libel is written (the origin of the word is liber; Latin for 'book') and it applies to digital writing as well as print. Emails and website

---

[21] T. Welsh, W. Greenwood & D. Banks, *McNae's Essential Law for Journalists*, Oxford: OUP (2005)

copy are legally binding and can be actionable. **Slander** is spoken or transient defamation, unless it is broadcast as part of a public performance, and to make it actionable it must be published to a third person (although making a public performance available on your website for downloading would probably count as libel). Unlike libel, where damage will be assumed, to fight a case of slander the claimant must prove damage, unless it falls into one of four categories (suggestion that someone has committed a punishable crime; that they have a contagious or objectionable disease; that the chastity of a woman is questioned; the suggestion is calculated to damage an individual's prospects in their profession or business).[22]

An action for **malicious falsehood** can be brought following the publication of a false statement that the claimant can prove is untrue, was published maliciously, and tends to/is calculated to cause financial damage.

The Rehabilitation of Offenders Act of 1974 is designed to allow people to live down relatively minor convictions, which become spent after the specified period of time. Writing about such convictions can be done on the grounds of justification, but this will not succeed if it can be proved that the writer was acting with malice. Rehabilitation periods are ten years for a prison sentence of six months to two and a half years, seven years for a prison sentence of six months or less and five years for a fine or other sentence. A sentence of more than two and a half years cannot be spent.

An accusation of **contempt of court** can arise if extraneous information is published during a trial which jurors or potential jurors might read, and hence the likelihood that this (or similar) material would be ruled inadmissible as evidence. The main concern of the law is to preserve the integrity of the legal process rather than to safeguard the dignity of any individual court or case. This is obviously more likely for a journalist than a writer of books, but if a writer were tweeting or blogging information related to their work, perhaps as a promotional technique, and this could be prejudicial to a trial, then the same charge could arise. The risk of an accusation arises from the moment proceedings are active (say

---

[22] At the time of writing, the UK parliament is considering reforms to the libel laws

29

an arrest is made or a warrant issued) until the end of the proceedings (a verdict, the case is discontinued or no arrest is made). Other possible contempts could include seeking to find out what happened in a jury room or making recordings in court.

Case study: Barbara Horn, Editorial Consultant

'I have self-published one book (*Editorial Project Management, with exercises and model answers*, *EPM* for short) and produced a second book (*Copy-editing, with exercises and model answers*, or *CE*) that is a co-publication. The only difference in the procedure is that I market and sell *EPM*, and the co-publisher markets and sells *CE*. As the titles indicate, both books are instruction manuals for people working in, or hoping to work in, publishing. Therefore, they have a clearly defined market, which influences the content, design, price and marketing.

Because I have considerable experience in publishing and have project managed and copy-edited an enormous number of books, I knew exactly what I had to do and, for the most part, how to do it. I produced the books a few years apart but the process was the same in both cases.

I began by considering when the best time to publish would be. September was the logical choice because I hoped both books would be recommended reading for students on academic publishing courses and because that is the month when the Society for Editors and Proofreaders (SfEP), of which I am a member, has its annual conference. I worked backward from the conference date to schedule each stage in the process, from preparing the text to delivery of the printed books, including my own time as author and project manager. I made sure that the schedule took account of all my other time commitments and allowed 'contingency time' for unforeseeable problems.

When you work backwards from the final date to the day you can start work, you see how much time is available for producing the text. My texts are adaptations of distance-learning courses I had written. While adapting the text would not take as long as the original writing, it was important not to underestimate the time needed to make the changes required for a different market and format; for example, I had to re-do most of the diagrams and all of the model answers to fit a much smaller page.

Then I drew up a budget. Again, experience was invaluable. I knew what services I would need and the range of costs for the editorial jobs. I obtained quotes for typographic design and typesetting, cover artwork, and printing different quantities, and for the supply of ISBNs – essential if you plan to sell your book through any retail outlet. For *EPM*, I also got quotes for producing and mailing a leaflet, and for envelopes and postage for mailing the book itself. I used these figures to calculate the cost of producing a single book – the unit price. I researched the market to see what price would be reasonable and estimated how many I might sell directly and how many at discount through other outlets. I used these figures and the unit cost to calculate how many copies I would have to sell before I made a profit – the breakeven point. I did some research too, to determine how many copies I would be likely to sell through different outlets. You have to know how much money you will need to spend and how long it will be before you get it back before you can decide whether or not you can afford to proceed.

My schedule told me when I would need the services of different professionals. Again, experience was a major advantage. I knew how to access the appropriate people and – essential – how to negotiate with and brief them. It's vital for any self-publishing author, even a professional editor like me, to employ a good copy-editor, proofreader, indexer (for non-fiction only, of course) and book designer, and to be able to explain to them the purpose of the content, who the intended reader is, what specific elements you want them to deal with, and when you need them to begin and to finish. I took advice from a friend and colleague in dealing with the printer, where I have more limited experience. My first contact with these service providers was on the telephone. In every case I confirmed our agreement, in every detail, in writing.

It's nice to report that all of this went according to plan up to and including delivery of the printed copies. I was less successful at marketing and sales, which refers only to *EPM*. I sold copies at the SfEP conference and paid for leaflets to be included in the mailing of their regular newsletter. The number of copies I had been advised to bring greatly exceeded the number I sold. I sold a good number quite quickly through the return of the leaflets and advertising on my website, and I sold (and continue to sell) a number through the Publishing Training Centre (PTC), where at the time I taught a relevant course. I sold a fair number at other institutions where I taught similar courses, and I reached breakeven point in good time. However, after I stopped teaching, sales slowed down. I had e-mailed every academic institution in the UK and some abroad that offered publishing courses, but I was unable to see which, if any, sales resulted. I tried to interest a limited number of bookshops in the title, but failed. Eventually, being nicely in profit, I joined the Amazon Advantage programme, and continue to sell this book through it and directly: contacthorn-editorial@btinternet.com. I am currently planning a second edition.

The production of *CE* was equally satisfactory: on time, to budget, and of the required quality. The marketing and sales were not my responsibility. It is available from PTC: www.train4publishing.co.uk.

Self-publishing is a lot of work, and I cannot imagine how I would have coped on my own without my experience and connections; I would certainly have wanted to find a firm or individual to do all this for me.'

THE HISTORY OF PUBLISHING

AN EVOLUTION

3

Climbing over the fence: a history of self-publishing

with Judith Watts and Lindsay Brodin

The digital revolution is taking out the middleman. From my laptop direct to your smartphone, from her Mac to his PC, the artist's search for an audience no longer depends upon securing the interest of the professional gatekeeper. In photography and film, in music and the written word, the creative entrepreneur is on the rise.

The publishing industry has experienced many revolutions in its long history. Today, mainstream publishing remains a risky business. To deliver a book into the reader's hands, significant investment is needed in production and distribution technology and in the involvement of skilled staff at every stage of the process. Publishing houses can't afford to take on manuscripts that won't sell. The gatekeepers make pragmatic decisions based on what has sold before.

But what about writing that is not fashionable, or that is breaking new ground, or that is aimed at a limited audience? From Jane Austen and Marcel Proust to Roddy Doyle and James Patterson, in every generation, writers encountering indifference or interference from publishing middlemen have found ways of bearing at least some of the financial risk involved in getting their work into circulation. Their methods are aspects of self-publishing.

In this chapter, we'll consider the story so far. We'll look at the development of the publishing industry, at the difference between self-publishing and so-called vanity publishing, and at some of the creative entrepreneurs of the past – writers who stopped knocking on the closed gate and simply climbed over the fence.

A glance at the history of publishing

The relationships between writers, illustrators, printers, booksellers, publishers, agents and readers have evolved over hundreds of years. They have been affected by technological revolutions, by social changes such as the rise (and some might say fall) of literacy, and by economic fluctuations affecting levels of disposable income. And given that a recognition of an author's copyright and swift mechanisms for mutiple dissemination arrived relatively late in the day, you could argue that the history of self-publishing is the early history of publishing.

The first literary revolution took humanity from an oral to a written culture. Stories and records no longer relied upon memory and face-to-face transmission. Ancient cultures used a variety of materials for storing their words; texts were engraved in and painted onto stone and metals, carved into and written on wood, and pressed into wax and clay tablets.

The spread of papyrus from Egypt and the development of parchment (made from animal hide) led to the ubiquity of the scroll. This recording system – a single, long sheet of material wound around two wooden axes – was easily manufactured, inscribed, edited, transported and stored.

Technological innovation undermined the scroll's pre-eminence. In Pompeii, a wall painting shows a woman holding a stylus and four bound wooden tablets. Each wooden leaf had a recess filled with wax, creating a surface that could be inscribed and repeatedly reused. When Romans replaced the wax-filled wooden leaves with parchment, and bound the parchment sheets within a separate cover, the codex was created. More portable than the scroll and, importantly, allowing sections of text to be accessed out of sequence, the codex was a significant innovation in production. The format survived from Roman times until today; this was the birth of the book.

Trade in manuscripts – texts copied by hand – was known to the Ancient Greeks and Romans, but this early commerce faltered at the end of the Roman Empire. For 700 years, the reproduction of manuscripts in the West was largely confined to the monasteries of the Christian church. In the Middle Ages, the market for manuscripts re-emerged. Books were sold at fairs throughout Europe. Stationers supplied vellum (calfskin, an improved parchment) and co-ordinated the work of scribes, illuminators and book binders. Scribes reproduced texts; they were not authors in the creative sense. Until the role of the author was legally recognised hundreds of years later, texts could be freely copied, distributed, and even altered as the scribe, or later the printer, saw fit.

Demand for texts in Latin and in European languages grew. The European papermaking industry developed in the 14th and 15th centuries, providing a material cheaper than parchment and more readily available than papyrus. With Gutenberg's invention of the printing press in the 15th century, the role of the publisher began to take shape. In England, William Caxton was a merchant, printer, and bookseller. He served the limited domestic market, offering wealthy individuals his personal selection of romances, poetry and histories. Caxton was, in essence, a publisher and an early literary gatekeeper.

The Industrial Revolution in the 18th century brought significant economic change and the rise of literacy. Fundamental aspects of book production, such as papermaking, the manufacture of moveable type, printing and binding, had been small-scale and handcrafted, largely unchanged since before Caxton's time. These were gradually mechanised, leading to an increasingly specialised printing industry that concentrated on the physical production of books. This allowed the emergence of publishing as an industry in its own right. Focussed on the selection and development of texts for the market, this is the publishing business model we would recognise today. Industrialisation, urbanisation and education stimulated demand for printed material. Technical innovations made production faster, easier and cheaper.

The role of the author had become increasingly recognised over the years. If writers were paid at all in the early days of printing, it was often by a single copy of their book. In the 18th century, Alexander Pope's business acumen allowed him to become one of the first writers to live by his pen. The idea of the professional author took root. In the Copyright Act of 1814, first legislative reference was made to the author. Previously, copyright for texts had been held by stationers, booksellers, printers or publishers. The 1814 Act recognised that the book's author was its originator, and authors looked to copyright law to strengthen their financial position. The subsequent 1842 Act finally granted authorial ownership, lasting for the writer's lifetime and for a defined period after their death. In 1884, the Society of Authors was established, giving authors a professional voice, influencing trade issues such as developing international copyright law, and arguing for the payment of royalties as the fairest form of recompense for authors' intellectual property.

The age of the novel dawned in the 19th century. Publishing became big business, working on a modern scale. Text was the primary form of entertainment, and publishers created new products, such as serials and penny-a-part novels in the 1840s, and new concepts, such as children's books designed to amuse rather than to educate. At the end of the 18th century, a typical print run had sold out at 500 copies. By the end of the 19th century, Victorian novelists were selling copies in hundreds of thousands. This was the genesis of mass-market publication. As more and more books were published, increasingly specific readerships coalesced around the emerging literary genres.

With a growing volume of written work to process, changes had to be made in the way that publishing houses selected texts. They employed professional readers to assess the literary and commercial value of submitted manuscripts. On the author's side, the end of the 19th century saw the arrival of literary agents,[23] responsible for ensuring that manuscripts were submitted to the most appropriate publishing houses and for securing the best possible financial settlement in an expanding international market. The bookselling business also found its modern form, with retail and wholesale supply chains growing to service the growing readership.

Further far-reaching changes in society and in technology emerged in the 20th century. Radio, film and television challenged the book's pre-eminence in entertainment and, to a certain extent, in education. Publishers responded to these challenges by taking advantage of new opportunities. Penguin was founded by Allen Lane in 1935. Lane recognised the public appetite for good stories that were well told, and reasoned that the right text could be sold in large quantities to a those who simply could not afford to buy the standard hardback book. He developed the paperback format and placed it in non-

---

[23] One of the first was Curtis Brown in 1899

traditional outlets, such as Woolworths, establishing the Penguin brand. The cheap paperback introduced book ownership to a new sector of society.

In the first half of the 20th century, books regarded as unsuitable for public consumption could not be freely published in the United Kingdom. To maintain public decency, literature deemed unacceptable had to be altered or sold privately, often at a premium price. But the first half of the century had seen two world wars and significant societal change, and a new generation of publishers and authors challenged old assumptions. With the Obscene Publications Act of 1959 and the acquittal of *Lady Chatterley*,[24] it was no longer possible to suppress books on moral grounds. This led to an expansion of subject matter and genres.

Developments in technology impacted upon all areas of 20th century life. The advent of word processors and computers allowed writers to create, edit and submit text without laborious hand-copying or typewriting. In publishing, computer systems were developed to handle typesetting and layout. As computers became more powerful, sophisticated software packages were written, until desk-top publishing in the 1980s let everyone try their hand at book design. The previous introduction of the International Standard Book Number (ISBN)[25] allowed computerised systems to underpin the supply chain, refining stock and distribution systems.

The arrival of the internet and the World Wide Web has generated a seismic shift in the publishing industry. From the solitary blogger to the biggest publishing house, there are unprecedented opportunities for content creation, for reproduction, marketing, promotion, distribution and sales, and more ways than ever to connect with the reading public.

The digital revolution continues. Creative entrepreneurs may find that the self-publishing successes of the past can show us how to take advantage of today's possibilities.

---

[24] In 1960, 30 years after D.H. Lawrence's death, Penguin moved to publish his most provocative novel, *Lady Chatterley's Lover*. What followed was the most significant obscenity trial of the century as Penguin defended the book's literary merit against the government's Act

[25] W.H. Smith implemented the SBN in 1967 as they moved to a computerised warehouse. It was adopted internationally in 1970, becoming the ISBN

So how does self-publishing fit in?

Literary fashions change. Millions of pages of text are released, read and forgotten. Publishers continually create new products, battling for the reader's attention in their drive to turn a profit. But, as famously illustrated by Harry Potter's search for a publisher, the industry does not always spot a good thing. Thanks to authors who refused to accept mainstream publishing's indifference and who shouldered at least some of the publishing risk themselves, the wider public has been able to enjoy books as diverse as Marcel Proust's *In Search of Lost Time* and Roddy Doyle's *The Commitments*. Those risk-taking authors are self-publishers.

There is no one simple marker of self-publishing; different tactics can be employed at the different stages of publication. In thinking about tactics, it is helpful to break down the publishing process into three phases.

1 **Development** – concerned with getting the right words in the right order, this phase includes writing, commissioning and editing, and results in a finished text.

2 **Production** – putting those words on to the page, steps include design and reproduction. They take us from the bare text to the finished artefact, traditionally the book but increasingly the screen.

3 **Delivery** – ensuring that the page reaches the public, the third phase involves marketing, distribution and retail, and ends with the reader accessing the written words.

Sometimes these phases overlap. For example, marketing and sales may begin before a book is printed, never mind released. Many of the writers that we will mention have taken action in more than one phase, and some have taken control of the entire process, bearing all of the financial risk by setting up their own publishing houses and even establishing retail outlets. Not all self-publishing writers need to go that far. The following examples are not intended to be a comprehensive list of the self-published made good. They have been chosen to illustrate the variety of aspects of self-publishing.

Phase 1 – Development

In Caxton's days, the printer might develop, produce and deliver his own texts, from writing the words to selling the pages, and everything in between. They were effectively all self-publishers with the highest degree of control, and bearing the highest possible risk.

By the 18th century, it was common for unknown writers to supply at least some of the financial backing to launch their work. This was called private or subsidy publishing. In 1797, a manuscript was submitted to a London publisher by the proud father of an unknown author. *First Impressions*, a three-volume novel, was offered for private publication; the writer's family would pay to see the work in print and on sale to the public – and in the process mitigate the publisher's financial risk. The publishing house turned it down. Revised and renamed, it was finally published fourteen years later to good reviews. Today, with a proven sales record, as popular as ever with the reading (and viewing) public, and now a cornerstone of English literature, Jane Austen's *Pride and Prejudice* drives a whole author-centred business. Private publishing continues today. A Christian allegory, *Shadowmancer*[26] ran counter to the fashions in children's fantasy fiction. It was privately published in 2002 by author and former Anglican vicar, G.P. Taylor. After the self-published edition sold well by word of mouth, the book was picked up by mainstream publishers Faber & Faber.

Charles Dickens received considerable publisher interest. Already a successful author, a dispute with the publishers of his previous periodical led him to create a weekly literary magazine called *All the Year Round* as a new vehicle for his writing. He retained control of the entire publishing process, through all of its phases. In relation to the development of the text, his practice of writing in instalments is of interest. Rather than have the whole novel written in advance, Dickens developed individual characters' story lines according to feedback from his readers. This interest in and responsiveness to public opinion shares characteristics with the focus group in today's film and television industries, and with the interactivity inherent in blogging.

Even if publishers recognise the value of a piece of writing, censorship can prevent its publication. Writers may retain creative

[26] Graham Taylor. http://www.shadowmancer.com

control by self-publishing rather than revising their text. James Joyce's novel *Ulysses* could not be freely published in Britain due to its perceived immorality. Less tolerant administrations may ban critical writing altogether. 'Samizdat' is a Russian term which was coined during Stalin's regime, meaning 'self-published.' It is an ironic name for the underground copying and distribution of banned texts, including practices such as hand-writing, carbon-copying, and secret printing. Circulation takes place below the official radar with copies being passed from friend to trusted friend, often in spite of considerable personal risk. Mikhail Bulgakov's novel *The Master and Margarita* was a samizdat text that was posthumously published in the mainstream a decade after Stalin's death.

Phase 2 – Production

Industrialisation defined the Victorian Age. The rapid development of technology opened up new markets, but mass-produced goods were often poorly designed and made. William Morris reacted against this. A designer, artist and writer, he led the Arts and Crafts movement, championing the artisan. He set up his own press and hand-printed more than fifty books including his own work. Morris controlled all aspects of book design. Heavily influenced by medieval illuminated manuscripts and the printing of Caxton's era, he even created his own typefaces to ensure that all design details added up to a beautiful and harmonious whole. This revived interest in the artistry of book design and influenced many other small presses in turn.

At the end of the Victorian era, a writer and illustrator couldn't find a publisher willing to take on her first book. Her black and white drawings were out of step with the fashion for colour pictures. Beatrix Potter stood by her original design for the story of Peter Rabbit and Mr McGregor, and self-published. The initial run of 250 books sold out quickly and snagged the interest of one of the publishing houses that had previously turned her down. Potter went on to become one of the first writers to realise the potential of merchandising.

Julia Cameron's non-fiction bestseller *The Artist's Way*[27] began life in modest production, as copied and mailed out classroom

---

[27] Julia Cameron, *The Artist's Way*. New York: Tarcher/Putnam (2002)

notes. Similarly, in the 1970s, student teacher John Cassidy wrote down step-by-step instructions on the art of juggling. After success in the classroom, Cassidy and two university friends self-published the instructions in book form and sold their books with a set of beanbags attached. Extending production in this way, including the items needed to turn instructions on the page into an experience, was a successful innovation. The friends went on to set up Klutz Press, creating product lines stocked in toy shops as well as traditional book outlets.

Phase 3 – Delivery

From manuscript, to industrialised printing, to print on demand, technological changes have reduced production costs until they are no longer a significant barrier to self-publishing. Until recently, the third phase of the publishing process, involving marketing, distribution and sales, has been the most difficult for writers to undertake independently.

Creating interest in a book has always been key to its success. Sam Clemens created his own writing persona. He incorporated the name 'Mark Twain' as an enterprise and trademark, developed a strong personal image, and supported his books through energetic promotion and public performance. Unhappy with his publishers, he established his own company. Webster & Co. sold titles such as *The Adventures of Huckleberry Finn* on subscription, with book agents delivering a pre-scripted marketing spiel on the doorsteps of prospective customers. Production began when sufficient orders had been placed to make a healthy profit. Mark Twain became a household name.

Today, all authors must be involved in promoting and marketing their books, regardless of how they are published. Some writers bring particular skills to the table. Before the release of *Along Came a Spider* in 1993, James Patterson's publisher refused his request to run a television commercial to promote the book. An experienced advertising executive, Patterson used his skills and his own money to create and air the ad. Today he is one of the world's bestselling authors.

A key function of the publisher is to sell and distribute their selected titles to book retailers. In the past, if authors did not have access to the established distribution networks, they had to find alternatives. Sylvia Beach of Shakespeare and Company, a book-shop in Paris, helped James Joyce to sell the banned *Ulysses*. She contacted potential customers and took payment for the edition before it was printed. In 2009, Christopher Herz[28] took to the streets of New York City to sell copies of his first novel, *The Last Block in Harlem*, to passers-by. This earned him money, attracted publicity and proved the saleability of this book.

Now, limited access to distribution networks is no longer the barrier to reaching the public that it once was. Books can be printed on demand and shipped directly to the individual reader, and epublishing bypasses the need for physical distribution altogether. Writers use the online community and social media to promote their work and to build their fan base. In 2000, established mainstream author Stephen King experimented with digital self-publishing, releasing installments of his novel, *The Plant*, to readers who subscribed via his website. By early 2011, Amanda Hocking, [29] indie author of paranormal romances, had sold 185,000 copies of her novels in nine months, mostly through ebook sales, and in the month of January 2011 alone, she sold 450,000, making her now the world's bestselling ebook author. The electronic market place gives authors direct access to the distribution and sales network, an aspect of the industry that was previously the preserve of the mainstream publisher.

Many self-published writers, like Dickens, Morris and Twain, went on to publish other authors' work. Virginia Woolf founded the Hogarth Press. Its list included Woolf's own titles and the writing of others in the Bloomsbury Group. Lawrence Ferlinghetti established the City Lights Bookstore[30] and Publishers in San Francisco, producing his own poetry and that of his fellow Beat poets. More recently, Dave Eggers set up a publishing house, McSweeney's,[31] with a quarterly literary journal and a progressive book list. These independent publishers often took risks in helping other writers over the fence. Although not all self-publishing writers need to go this far, they must share the passion for getting quality writing to the public.

---

[28] http://www.publishersweekly.com/pw/by-topic/industry-news/publisher-news/article/17731-author-publisher-gives-new-meaning-to-handselling--.html

[29] Amanda Hocking. http://amandahocking.net/

[30] Lawrence Ferlinghetti. http://www.citylights.com/publishing/

[31] McSweeney's. www.mcsweeneys.net

Self-publishing and 'vanity publishing'

In the eighteenth century, self-publishing was a common and perfectly respectable route to public readership. In the twentieth century, its reputation was sullied by association with vanity press.

Generally, when we pick up a book in a shop, the text has already passed through many guarded gates. In development, the book has been crafted by the author until an agent is willing to represent it and a commissioning editor in a publishing house is happy to take a gamble on its commercial appeal. The text has undergone various stages of editing and refinement. In production, the pages have been designed to be easy to read, and the cover created to signal the book's genre, helping us with our selection. In delivery, the retailer has actively chosen to stock this book on their limited shelf space in place of another title because this book is likely to sell. A great review may have prompted our final decision to buy. For any mainstream published book, the reader can be reassured that several competent professionals have approved this product. Inside the fence, the reader's money is relatively safe.

The danger of self-publishing is that, in dodging the gatekeeper, the writer loses the benefit of quality control. It can be difficult for a writer to assess the quality and marketability of their own work, yet the drive to publish is strong. Vanity presses prey on this desire to see work in print.

Vanity presses will publish anything. They are not concerned with quality or commercial prospects because they make their money from the writer, who pays handsomely for all production costs. We've already seen that author controlled and funded publication isn't necessarily a bad thing. However, vanity presses misrepresent the status of the publication to the writer, implying that the work has passed assessment, that it has the approval of the mainstream, that it will appeal to the reading public and will be made available for purchase. These presses rely on writers' lack of knowledge about the complex publishing industry. This is not active and informed self-publishing.

Diminishing printing costs means that just about anyone who wants to self-publish can afford do so. However, not everyone has the range of skills needed to make a good job of it. The self-publishing writer can play to their strengths, but they must also address their weaknesses and seek professional help as required. When a writer refuses to acknowledge or mend the flaws in their work, vanity publishing is a sure fire way of displaying those flaws to a limited public.

Conclusion

Self-publishing has a long and dignified history. By actively engaging in aspects of self-publishing, authors have retained control of their work and of its presentation to readers. Some of them have made a profit. But, even in the mainstream, few people get rich from their writing; much self-publishing is done without profit in mind. It can help an individual to pass their life story down to future generations, or help a charity to get their raison d'etre into the public domain. It can help unknown writers make names for themselves; Margaret Atwood self-published a run of 200 copies of her first poetry collection, *Double Persephone*, after college. It was her calling card to the literary world.

In recent decades, self-publishing has suffered from links with vanity publishing. The denigration of artists who are self-funding and working outside the mainstream doesn't happen in music or in film-making; our culture celebrates indie musicians and directors. With the digital revolution opening up new technical possibilities and the rise of the creative entrepreneur, this cultural bias against those writers who self-publish is being challenged, at long last.

The relationships between writer, publisher and reader have always been subject to change. A new phase in the history of publishing has begun. Writers who are ready to take control of aspects of publication can take heart from those who have already climbed the fence.

4

What to write about? Developing content for self-publishing

'I think it is important to be clear on one's motives. One often hears of books that begin with the market – you know, writers who begin with the idea of "what will sell". There is a certain intelligence here, for all the obvious reasons. There is an understanding of who the readers might be, a convergence of interests, a recognition of what appeals, and so on. This is not by any means a bad place to begin, but it is not the only place.

Another place is with what Philip Lopate[32] calls "the supposition that there is a unity to human experience". This is not about some cultural phenomenon or interest that has been confirmed by the market. Rather, it has to do with the opportunity to pursue that alliance between experience, thought, and language with the belief that it is, can be, will be shared. Honestly, I know this sounds terribly sentimental, but I do stand by it, the possibilities in saying something true about a chair or a river or a person, or anything else. And after that, the form could probably be a tweet or an essay or an entire book.'

Akiko Bush[33]

What to write about

It is common for professional writers to talk about a writing life as an inevitable choice:

[32] US film critic, essayist, poet and teacher
[33] Akiko Bush, essayist and author of *Geography of Home*, writings on where we live, Princeton Architectural Press (1 January 2004)

When did you know that you were going to be a writer?

'About the age of eight the need to write became vital to me. I had neither the knowledge nor the desire to become a novelist but I knew I had been drawn into storytelling.'

What does it mean to be a writer?

'I never ask myself why I write. It's so inevitable for me. You wouldn't ask yourself, "Why do I eat, why do I breathe?" It's my way of connecting to the universe.'[34]

But whereas a desire to write is widespread within society,[35] for some the frustration comes at a very early stage – not knowing what to write about. Potential authors dream about the physical entity that is a book but can't see what is written on its front; like stories of patients undergoing psychoanalysis who find a room but don't know to whom it belongs. Indeed the very strength of the desire to have something finished can block its development. Others can feel frustrated about writing that occupies them but is not what they really want to write, either through the demanding requirements of their job or the misdirected attentions of professionals,[36] meanwhile there is a book shaped hole inside them, which draws frustration but insufficient energy to get started, the way depression (a tendency which is a frequent trait in writers) gets written about:

'Usually I feel a sense of emptiness in the middle-distance, approaching. You can try all you want, but there's nothing you can do to stop it.'   Alastair Campbell, 2011[37]

[34] Elif Shafak, 'Small Talk', *Financial Times*, 19/20 February 2011
[35] A YouGov poll in 2007 found that almost 10% of Britons aspired to being an author, followed by sports personality, pilot, astronaut and event organiser on the list of most coveted jobs
[36] Poet Gwyneth Lewis has linked her depression to not directing her creative energies where she really wanted to be involved – in her case by working in broadcasting rather than on her own writing. In *Sunbathing in the Rain: a cheerful book about depression* (London: Harper Perennial, 2002) she talks about her return to writing poetry
[37] 'Up Front', *Observer Magazine*, 13 March 2011

For some the decision of what to write about will be made for them – they desire to write a memoir or to put their point of view in a complicated situation; others will have poems that they want to develop and then record. The difficulty is spotting a subject to sustain you through the project – it's relatively easy to start a book, the difficult point tends to come later when you run out of steam, usually about half way through:

'Twice I've started novels and got stuck; three I've had published. Now I can see why the unfinished ones failed: I didn't know where they were headed. Having enough wind in your sails is vital; although they started well, they drooped at about 40,000 words, and I just couldn't get the momentum going again.

For a novel to work, I think you have to know where you are going, and to have an ending in mind from the outset. I like the idea of allowing a narrative to flow and a story to tell itself – over-tight planning can mean you end up writing as if you're ticking off a list – but I've learnt from experience it's important to have enough impetus – and passion for your subject – to keep your book going.

To use another metaphor, a narrative is like an arrow flying from a bow. You need the strength in your elbow to pull back the arrow so it flies up high into the air, reaching its zenith around two-thirds of the way through and then falling slightly to hit its target. If you don't know what you're aiming for, you're – literally – shooting in the dark. This doesn't mean you can't change your ending as your narrative evolves, but it's important to know what you're trying to say, and have passion for it as you'll need that to drive you onwards.

What is true for novels is true for other kinds of writing. I spent 20 years working as an advertising copywriter, and trying to write about a product where you don't know what it is you are trying to say (i.e. sell) is just as impossible. That's why agencies develop slogans and strap lines: they summarise the unique selling points of a brand in a few words. So you could say the most successful brands know where they are "headed", too.'[38]

[38] Sarah Rayner is the author of *One Moment, One Morning*, London: Picador (2010). Her fourth novel, *The Two Week Wait*, is due out in 2012. www.thecreativepumpkin.com

Is it worth writing about – and hence worth reading?

For the writing to be worth preserving, and certainly worth reading by others, arguably there has to be some central truth or believability to it, something that holds it together; even if the subject matter is fantasy or science fiction it has to be a world that others can believe in. Or as Kevin Rudd, former diplomat and Prime Minister of Australia said in a recent interview:[39]

> 'I believe in politics for the two questions it asks of us. One is, "What do you stand for and why?" And the second is, "Do you know what you are talking about?"'

If you replace the word 'politics' with 'writing', or any other creative activity, the questions work well as a philosophy for justifying work worth sharing.

Another useful set of benchmarks for what to write about is the advice we give to our MA Publishing students at Kingston University when planning a dissertation; to help us all identify whether or not there is sufficient mileage in the subject they want to explore. We advise them to choose a topic that offers the prospect of:

1 Sustaining their interest – because they spend a lot of time on it, and it is worth a large section of marks out of their degree as a whole. I usually ask students to prepare for the first meeting by thinking of three possible subjects; and then watch their facial expressions as they deliver. They invariably start with the two that are less interesting – and then their eyes light up as the third is outlined.

2 The availability of both expertise and information – the Rudd quotation works particularly well here.

3 A tight focus. Broad subjects are difficult to cover in any depth; you can find it easier to keep going, and hence have more impact, exploring a relatively small area of operation than a large one.

---

[39] 'Life and Arts', *Financial Times*, 19/20 February 2011

4 Creating a wider value for both themselves and their ideas; perhaps to an area of work they want to join or to their planned future career. We advise them to find a subject that others will be interested in too, and through which they can both contribute to the debate and progress their subject.[40]

Once we have established a subject area, I advise them to write the central thesis, or question they are seeking to explore, and to henceforth carry it with them (if they are itinerant) or stick it in a prominent location close to their main place of work. This then serves as a beacon to signify the pathway throughout the research and writing. This is good advice for any writer: choose something that has enough meat on the bones to sustain you, and a subject that fascinates you; and if you start dreaming about it, that's a good sign.

It must also be something that matters to you. It's relatively common for writers to get blocked by trying to write the book they think they ought to write, whereas there is another inside them that they long to write.

> 'You can persuade yourself that you should be writing such and such a book, because it will sell or because it is topical, but I think usually there is a book or story that is restless and yearning to get out of a writer, the one that almost aches in your body and which you long to get onto paper. I'm sure these are the books and stories that ultimately have soul and pertinence.' Hattie Gordon[41]

The speed at which your ideas flow out of you may be a sign of where you should direct your attention. The precious time when ideas flow easily has been described by psychologists as 'subliminal uprush'; to me it has always seemed close to projectile vomiting.

---

[40] Although bear in mind that what you write is not necessarily what other people experience when reading your work, they will have their own reveries and thoughts. Being a writer 'means you have the challenge of providing the sheet music for the reader, who always sings the song.' Joseph O'Connor, interview in the *Financial Times*, 26/27 February 2011

[41] Author of *The Café After the Pub After the Funeral*, London: Continuum (2004)

Using your unconscious

Playwright and lecturer Matt Cunningham comments:

'An "automatic" thought is one that comes to us unbidden and fully-formed. It seems uncanny. You'll be washing your hair, sorting the laundry, sitting through purgatory on call-waiting to the bank, something totally unrelated to your project – when suddenly it comes to you: the solution to that problem in the plot, a killer curtain-line, even an entire, muscled concept for a story or play. Famously, J.K. Rowling claims she was looking out the window of a train when a boy named Harry Potter, replete with back-story, jagged scar across his head and acceptance note from Hogwarts, strolled nonchalantly into mind. I can well believe it. The truth is, even when we're not actively working on our projects, our unconscious minds are toiling away at them, turning them over, squinting at them from different angles, making brilliant, unlikely connections. Rowling had already been putting Harry Potter together; it just took her conscious mind a while to catch up.

This is why I actually encourage my students to take time off. I tell them to daydream, stare out of the window, take a long bath, a walk, an afternoon nap, sleep on it – because it's at these times, I believe, that we commune with our unconscious. Of course, that encouragement comes with a stern disclaimer. If you don't enthuse your unconscious, pose questions to it – if, in other words, you're not also clocking up hours at the desk – then it's not going to respond. But when we really get excited about a subject, something clicks, the call goes through, and we engage our in-house writing partner. The great thing about her is she's prepared to put in overtime.

As a writer, I find the lessons of Freud and psychoanalysis, and the affirmation now given them by modern neuroscience, hugely comforting. They say our conscious self – our inner-monologue, that voice in the head we call "I" – suffers under a peculiar delusion. It believes that it's running the show, when in fact it's only a very puny part of our mental make-up. One way to read this is quite depressing. You can view it as an affront to your sense of self. Who are you if you're not that voice? But another way, the way I prefer, is to see it as a wonderful liberation. There is so much more to you than you're usually aware of. You're sitting on treasure.'

Nor do you have to come up with a completely new subject. You can write about the same area as other people but from your own point of view, and in your own voice. For example, the histories of 9/11 have been written but there will always be room for the personal tale of someone with a particular and so far unexplored viewpoint. My husband's cousin is a teacher and has often commented that the teacher's experience has yet to be heard. At her school in New Jersey, which had enrolled many pupils whose parents worked in Manhatten, they spent the day keeping the children busy; unclear at what point parents would turn up, and wondering if any would not collect at all. They passed each other notes to inform about what was happening, and did their job well. The next day one of the parents reported that her child had said 'the teachers knew nothing about this'. There may be real long-term value in personal memories of this kind, and recording them now ensures they survive for the future. At the request of my cousin, my uncle recorded his experiences during the Second World War. Four copies were produced, one each for his wife and two children, and a fourth for his regiment; the last is now with the associated museum, and is being used by historians of the period.

The other benefit of writing about familiar areas is that those to whom you may end up trying to sell your material will know how to categorise it ('Have I heard of this subject before?', 'Am I interested in learning more?'), and in the case of a retailer, where to stock it within store. And both readers and potential stockists may be positively influenced by the judgement of professional publishers, who have already invested in this subject area.

Possible themes

Writing about what you know – or don't know but would be interested in finding out about

The advice that writers should 'write about what they know' is regularly proffered, but if what you know about feels over familiar, or bores you, there may be more energy available through putting yourself in a situation where you are finding out at the same time as your characters.

Author Wendy Perriam does a lot of research for her books, and always enjoys exploring something with which she is not familiar. Research not only enables her to authenticate the experience, but also to find the right words:

> 'For my novel, *Breaking and Entering*, there's a key scene in the finale of the book, which involves a father and daughter walking into a remote Welsh lake and submerging themselves, fully-clothed, in the middle of the night. In order to make the writing more powerful and the scene more realistic, I knew I must experience it myself. And my personal immersion did, indeed, provide the details and the sense of danger I needed for this crucial scene: the padlock-grip of the icy water creeping up my body, inch by inch; the sensation of my waterlogged clothes, leaden, bloated and dragging down my limbs; the oozy mud beneath my feet and steeply shelving ground; the matt blackness of the sky contrasting with the darkly glimmering water; and then the sudden disorienting blindness as I plunged below the surface and plummeted deep down.
>
> OK, I wasn't in the wilds of Wales, but in my local park, and it wasn't midnight but only latish evening, and I even had a friend in tow, to ensure I didn't drown. None the less, it gave me that "truth" I needed to write with real conviction.'

Previous writings

If there is a most common type of 'bottom drawer manuscript', it will probably be a novel, drafted at a particular point in your life and then cherished ever since. There can be a strangeness in reviewing old material; it is evidently by you, but you no longer feel like the person recorded – a bit like listening to an old tape recording or watching a cine-film of your childhood self. But time is a great sifter. After re-reading, you may decide it offers merit, wider interest, or just deserves to be held in a more permanent format to ensure it survives.

Bundles of letters

Along similar lines, bundles of letters that have been stranded by time can be an excellent resource for any writer. Transcribing and recording, and in the process trying to establish a chronology and the historical background against which events are set, can reveal a story – or illustrate a particular event or period through the eyes of a significant bystander. What they do not know of contemporary events can be as revealing as what they understand, and history since can add a particular poignancy.

Poetry

Poetry can work well as self-published content. Poetry is notoriously difficult to sell and the number of publishing houses that specialise in this area is increasingly limited. A vast proportion of poetry sales are of the work of a limited number of poets, and the major selling opportunities are through poetry readings, literary festivals and similar specialist events, at which the author who is reading sells their work. Even if a major poetry publisher has offered you a publishing contract, if the book is to sell you will need to take part in its promotion. So the self-published poet is not at much of a disadvantage.

A decision to self-publish poetry creates an opportunity for a particularly careful attention to format, the space around the poem and the typeface used. Most poems are extracted and read aloud, and it is worth taking trouble over their isolation in a harmonious physical space on the page.[42]

A book for children

Many famous children's books began as tales told to the author's own. Some were written down at the time, others remained in oral forms (there will probably be several) in the collective family memory. These can make excellent self-publishing projects; drawing together threads of what everyone remembers and capturing the material before it is lost forever. Some family members will have stronger memories than others, and involving widely may spread the appreciation and eventual value of what is created in the process.

The individual/family memoir

Family history is a good starting point, and can create a book of strong interest to a defined circle of people, as well as material that interests others who lived through the same thing. Publishers are often approached about such works, but if they cannot see a

[42] See story of June Davies, pages 188–189

wider applicability – and hence market – such material can be well managed through self-publishing, particularly if you have no time to lose (you want a book finalised before the main protagonists are no longer around).

Similarly, your path through a significant time in history can make a good subject. A word of warning here. All writing offers you the chance to explain yourself, and in self-publishing, without an in house editor looking over your shoulder, it can be tempting to make it *just* your point of view. Consider the following letter, written by Ernesto Che Guevara:[43]

> 'Pablo,
>
> I read your article. I must thank you for how well you portray me; too well, I think. Furthermore, it seems to me you portray yourself pretty well, too.
>
> The first thing a revolutionary who writes history has to do is stick to the truth like a finger inside a glove. You did that, but it was a boxing glove, and that's not fair.
>
> My advice to you: reread the article, eliminate everything you know is not true and be careful with everything you don't know for certain is the truth.
>
> A revolutionary greeting, Commander Ernesto Che Guevara'

Personalised histories

To mark a particular anniversary or birthday, or a key event that others share, a personalised history, often in the form of a collection of photographs, can be a very special project. This is an area of growing popularity, formalising material that would otherwise be lost, either through the main memory holder no longer being there to recognise who is who in the pictures, or a failure in technology (usually insufficient backing up/poor storage systems).

Niche market

> 'The best prospects for self-publishing are books of local or minority interest for which you can identify the potential audience. With these, you might begin by asking around to find a small local publisher or a

---

[43] To Pablo Diaz Gonzalez, 28 October 1963 quoted in *Che Guevara Reader: writings on politics and revolution*, Melbourne: Ocean Press (2003)

local printer who would take your project on and even take or share the risk. The toughest to sell are fiction, poetry and general interest books for which the audience may be sufficient but is spread out at large among the whole population, so that you have no way of getting at it.'[44]

A niche market may be defined as 'one most people don't want but is ideally suited to those who do – products such as dating websites.'[45] Niche is topical right now.

As an example of this in practice, *Matterhorn Vision*[46] tells the story of local banker Brian Bonner's lifelong ambition to climb the Matterhorn; his 15 years of preparation and then the 1980 achievement of his dream at the age of 57, comparatively elderly for climbers. Published shortly afterwards, the book has been through five editions, has a supplementary DVD, and is still selling. It is hard to pin down why this has proved so popular. Perhaps because of the very practical nature of the advice given (choose boots with rings rather than holes for lace insertion – they are easier to tighten quickly) and the book's direct appeal to the clearly vast number of others with the same ambition.

A local project

Writing for a local audience can make a particularly effective project, and if tied in with local publicity and marketing, can offer a strong prospect of local sales.

Case study: Robert Mayfield of Horsham

'I have found self-publishing to be a very happy experience.

Having taught English and History for a number of years I tried to dramatise events and experimented with this through a novel in which a wizard and his friend fly through time visiting different historical periods. I had no luck in interesting publishers in this.

[44] Jill Paton Walsh and John Rowe Townsend, Green Bay Books (1995) http://www.greenbay.co.uk/advice.html

[45] *Review of Niche: why the market no longer favours the mainstream*, James Harkin, London: Little Brown (2011), reviewed by John Kay, *Financial Times*, 26/27 March 2011

[46] Brian Bonner, *Matterhorn Vision*, Woodgate Press (1990) www.brianbonner.com

'By 2005, however, I had discovered the romance of a small castle-like building; the old town hall in my home town of Horsham in Sussex. Realising that the building was most likely to be lost to the community I wrote *Dan Roberts's Dream and Space Visitors*. Dan Roberts had come to my attention when I read that he was the only benevolent ghost in Britain. He had been the custodian of the town hall in the 18th century for the Duke of Norfolk, and he haunts the hall in the hope that one day it will be returned to its former glory. This burst of writing lead to the writing of a collection of stories called *The Flying Castle Stories*, which will be published as two books. In these stories the town hall flies off, filled with characters inspired by features around the hall. And the characters I first invented in my stories about the time-travelling wizard have made a re-appearance.

All these stories were finished but as no one had shown any interest I went into self-publishing, which introduced me to other authors in the area. It is very satisfying to see these books slowly coming out and being made available to the local reading public, through our local library and through the Flying Castle Stories website.[47] The stories are illustrated with the help of a local artist, and again this has been a very pleasing collaboration. By the end of 2012 all five books will have been published; made possible because of computer technology and the ability to order short print runs. I don't know whether there will be wider demand in future, but at least the dream to write the stories and see them in print has been fulfilled.'

Personal trauma and the opportunity for catharsis through writing

The 'misery memoir' has been a strong genre in recent years, and the supermarket book aisles offer ongoing access to tales of other people's wretched upbringings; so much so that one writer speculated that a happy childhood was a terrible legacy to a writer.[48] Such books are usually presented through combining a grainy

[47] www.flyingcastlepublications.co.uk
[48] Andrew Collins, *Where Did It All Go Right?*, London: Ebury Press (2003)

image of a child at a pleasing age of innocence with a title packed with irony; the reader is quickly informed that all is not as it seems.

It can be appealing to think of loading all your hurt and unheard point of view into a single document; putting the record straight and in the process bringing to the surface issues that have been at the back of your mind for years. But be aware that deciding to investigate in more detail may not bring the peace and sense of closure that you seek. Catharsis may not follow; your trauma is still your trauma.

Rather you may be left with a nagging sensation; wishing that you had dealt more effectively with the issues at the time, or that you still had the option to confront the chief protagonists. Your family may be particularly resistant to raking-over issues until now apparently forgotten or suppressed. And if you plan on wider circulation of the material, journalists who get involved will be looking for a story that has a wider message; not just the opportunity to make an exposition from your side of the fence. Rather than restating a summary of the hurts done to you, they may find there is more value for their readers in the story of how you could not move on.

That said, putting all your memories in one place, and recording the situation from your point of view, can bring a sense of completion, and there is no need to circulate private material more widely.

Individual expertise

Areas of specific understanding work well for self-publishing, particularly if you have an expertise that others would pay for or find useful to access. If you are a subject specialist, and can see a market for your work, you may be well placed both to know when you have finished, and to whom your work should be disseminated. Such titles can be promoted through relevant internet forums (associations and interest groups) as well as after-dinner or general speaking engagements (see chapter on marketing) and function as an incentive for training and consultancy jobs.

Summary

My sweetshop approach, which itemises various writing options available, may feel artificial. Rather than consciously choosing a subject, maybe the writer should allow a subject to choose them. Wendy Perriam again:

'Write from passion! Whatever fires you up, or makes you furious will endow your writing with energy and power. Perhaps you crave the wildest extremes of love, or you thirst for freedom, or itch to murder a rival in cold blood. Pour all that onto paper and your prose will reflect the sheer strength of your emotions. Whereas if you write to please the market, or opt for "fashionable" subjects, in the hope of attracting readers, your book will lack exuberance, enthusiasm and any real sense of personal involvement.

In my view, fiction-writing offers a number of enticing possibilities to the writer. As a novelist, you can explore:

- Your own shameful or appalling thoughts; or even the immoral or senseless actions you may have contemplated but never had the boldness (or opportunity) to carry out. By putting such thoughts into someone else's head, or making your fictional characters take action in your stead, you can think through the "what if" consequences, and vicariously experience heightened levels of emotion. For example, David Vann's recent novel, *Caribou Island*,[49] presents a picture of a doomed and destructive marriage in a particularly fearless and original way, far from the usual pieties and clichés of a so-called "bad" relationship. I suspect many will find it cathartic.

- How it would feel to be the person you were born to be? Many of us fail to follow our natural talents or inbuilt inclinations, bowing instead to society's norms or to the wishes of parents or teachers; taking a conventional route, instead of being true to our true selves. I explored this concept in my novel, *Second Skin*, first asking a whole variety of people if *they* felt they were living a life that honoured their intrinsic gifts and their God-given

[49] London: Penguin (2011)

temperament. A remarkable number of friends and business acquaintances said no, they weren't; they had ignored their gut-feelings and settled for compromise. A solicitor I know admitted he'd always wanted to be an actor, but lacked the courage to follow his dream, while an office-worker, tied to a dreary daily round, said she really wanted to travel the world: cross the Gobi desert on a camel; catch narwhal in the Arctic. Fiction is an ideal way to try out the possibilities. Your characters can renounce the values they have so far lived by; ditch their commitments and strike out in a new direction.

- Secrets – everyone has them, yet they're often a source of shame and embarrassment. As a novelist however, you can explore and yet disguise your own intimate personal secrets by putting them into the lives and heads of your characters. This affords the chance to work out how what might happen were all to be revealed – possibly devastating consequences for the character's family and friends. Of course, memoirs can deal with exactly the same material and issues, but are often just too traceable, or may even result in a libel case!'

Extracting the content

A thought can exist without words, move from poetry into prose, or remain something just out of reach, with no words at all. Desire to have formulated words can exist in your mind, in intangible form.

Just start writing. What you produce does not have to resemble a book from the outset. There are various writing books that recommend exercises to get you scribbling. Julia Cameron's *The Artist's Way*[50] suggests morning pages, which open the writer to both their ideas and their environment, and help important themes rise to the surface. Nigel Slater's autobiography *Toast*[51] shows that life remembered through something as basic as the food eaten can be very powerful. And chapter six of this book will offer further thoughts.

[50] New York: Tarcher/Putnam (2002)
[51] London: Harper Perennial (2004)

Find a time of day (early morning, late at night), a location (garden shed, spare bedroom, kitchen table) and a means of recording (computer, laptop, beautiful paper and a particular weight of pencil) that appeals to you, and make a promise to yourself that you can keep: getting up half an hour earlier; working during your lunchtime; an hour once you have eaten or put your children to bed. Deferring the starting point ('Once I have a job', 'Once my children are at school', 'Once I have retired') has a message to your writing self: that other things matter more.

Case study: niche publishing
Sarah Nock, *Ponderings on Parkinson's*, Ferry House Books

Sarah Nock has had Parkinson's for more than twenty years. Her eloquent testimony, revealed in two books and an audio tape, is not directed so much to the Parkinson's community, but to those that support them: carers; family; friends. Life can go on, despite this illness, given the understanding of these all-important people. Her approach is pragmatic and insightful, and in taking her principled stand she uses a range of soothers to the spirit: poetry, laughter and the love of friends.

'My book was suggested by Professor Lees, who treated me, and wrote a wonderful foreword. *Ponderings on Parkinson's* is intended particularly for carers and family, and hopefully casts, with the help of metaphors and humour, some illumination on this funny job-lot of an illness. Actually it seems to work out that the afflicted one mostly pushes it under the nose of their "civilian" with directions to read it (no one with Parkinson's Disease likes to be labelled as "suffering" or "a sufferer" and in the US "civilian" is what they call the non-afflicted).

I haven't had any dealings with publishers myself, not having written a book before, but I have many friends who are authors and it seems to me that the publishers behave rather like the carers in Romanian orphanages; they quite forget who are the ones that count in their operation. It's routine to hear of them not sending an acknowledgement after receiving a manuscript, churlish in these days of the simplest forms of communication;

hanging on to it for perhaps six months before returning it with an inadequate rejection, after having stipulated no one else should see it till they have made a decision. I am left wondering how does anybody ever write anything topical?

Although I felt there was a demand for information about my condition, I was pretty sure they would not want my book, and so decided to go it alone – with the support of friends and family. One son controlled all the printing, another managed the finances, a daughter did the proof-reading and so on. Friends who had been/were authors or publishers took us through some of the intricacies and the best order of things. One splendid chum organised a launch party at a local bookshop, a wonderful location in one of the most interesting old buildings in town. Articles in the local papers followed – I do believe journalists have a soft spot for the word "grandmother"; if a "grandmother" does something it is worth paying heed!

The publishing part has been enormous fun, and we have managed to have good reviews and to be pretty successful – the book is now in its second printing. I do realise that the tricky bit of being publisher-less is publicity, you just have to get some, but by sending the book out for review and to known sufferers, we have received some strong endorsements in return:

> "She describes with wit and verve the many consequences of her illness as it has affected her over the past 20 years... the resilience of the human spirit is revealed."
>
> Dr James LeFanu, *The Daily Telegraph*

> "I've endured it (PD) with help from many sources, but few more useful than Sarah Nock's little book in which she modestly, and from personal experience, provides a touching footnote to the battle...this is a moving and useful guide."
>
> Leo Cooper, *The Daily Mail*

It was important to make access to the book easy, given that many potential readers are elderly and the internet is a big black hole to them. A bookshop is where they want to go – and even that may be difficult for them, as they will find a wheelchair involved eventually. Early orders were all solicited and fulfilled by mail. My son took a picture of this and captioned it "My 75 year old mother earning 3p an hour". My complete lack of knowledge about internet selling didn't help, but we now have a new website www.ferryhousebooks.co.uk which makes it easy for potential customers to see what we have to offer, and what other people think of it. And we also found an excellent manual on the subject.[52]

And we have now published a book on the disease, an audio version of the same (read by me) and *Sarah's Midnight Anthology*, a book of poetry to sustain people living through this malady (or others) – whether as carer or patient. I just love this second volume, which is already out. *Sarah's Midnight Anthology* contains 180 of my favourite poems by over 80 poets. I never tire of it, and as long as I can find someone to read to me (thereby making another convert) my worst times of pain and discomfort are mollified and diminished. And we have other ideas for books. Next comes a remembrance by my mother of her Edwardian childhood. Not an amazing book but a charming one and printed particularly to trumpet the cause of "Get your elderly relations to remember, write and re-tell". It's good for us; social history takes on a new life when it's family – and it bewitches and bewilders them, the old aunts and uncles as well as the parents, that they can remember so much more than they would ever have believed. And we have a couple of other ideas in the pipeline, on a variety of subjects.

Looking back, perhaps we had it easy with *Ponderings on Parksinson's*. It was our first book, on an emotive subject, and no doors were rudely slammed in our faces – even if they were never really opened. Self-publishing is a tricky and demanding business but there is a lot to learn and it is you who are in the driving seat. You even choose the cover picture.

In fact you make all the decisions. When it came to a question of re-printing I wrote to Professor Lees. "I do think you should reprint," he replied. "It has brought great solace to many of my patients." Who could ask for more than that? Thank goodness I didn't wait for those inevitable rejections that would have consigned it to the back of a drawer forever.'

[52] Alison Baverstock, *Marketing Your Book: an author's guide*, London: A&C Black (2007)

5

Checklist: defining the scope of your project: setting parameters and targets

Here is a short, check-in section, offering you the chance to become more specific about your proposed self-publishing project; to begin to define your goals. There will be an opportunity to explore all these issues in further chapters, but it is a good idea to sharpen your thinking early on.

1 What kind of book are we talking about (novel; 'how to' book of practical advice; personal memoir; family history; children's story etc)?

2 What is the purpose of writing it down (to ensure it is not lost while you can still remember it all; to share with your family; for commercial sale)?

3 Who is the intended reader? Try to be specific about the person you imagine reading it once it is finished (you; your descendents; people who like autobiographical tales; those unknown to you who are trying to write an after-dinner speech; children).

4 Any thoughts so far on the format? Hardback, paperback, spiral bound book, ebook?

5 What about illustrations? Even if you decide you do not need any, try to factor in the cost of professional design input on your cover, as this will make a crucial difference to how your book is perceived. See chapter 11 on any form of design or illustrative support.

6 Cost. What resources do you have available to fund this project? Is there a definite and prescribed limit or do you want to make this an ongoing source of involvement, expenditure and pleasure – as most hobbies are funded?

7 What is the book called? A working title helps you visualise the product you are trying to create and the effect you want it to have. (See chapter 19 to start the thinking process).

8 What is the name of the author? (See chapter 19).

9 If you are self-publishing a printed book, and planning to manage the production yourself, start thinking about the imprint (the logo/company name on base of the spine) under which you will publish. You can just use your surname, but giving your self-publishing firm a name can look less self-interested.

10 Establish the time frame. Is there a date by when you need to have finished copies? In general, this will take 6–12 months from the time you finish writing, to allow time for all the associated processes such as copy-editing, typesetting, proofreading and production. If you are managing these processes yourself, you need to allow for their effective management (doing things too quickly will result in errors). If you are employing others, you will need to allocate time to finding appropriate services, explaining what you seek, and then instructing them. The period of time you allocate to them to do the work will have to take account of their schedule (they may not be able to start straightaway), and for you to absorb feedback and make corrections. You also need to factor in weekends, and holidays – as an author you may work through them; suppliers may be less inclined.

A rough schedule

Publication date:	1st April
Despatch of reading copies to key accounts/reviewers:	18th February
Delivery of stock to author:	15th February
Pass for printing:	1st February

Marketing information to potential stockists:	1st September
Proofreading:	2 weeks
Typesetting, formatting and uploading the manuscript:	1–2 weeks
Instructing a cover designer and reviewing proofs:	3–4 weeks
Copyediting:	1–2 months
Manuscript review, structural edit:	2–4 months
Finalisation of manuscript by author:	1st May

6

The author's calling

This chapter is intended as a warning before you start writing – or thinking about presenting your writing. It is not designed to put you off, simply to encourage you to see writing a book in its true context: something that is difficult to do – but worth striving for.

> 'Writing a book is easy! If you can voice an opinion and think logically, you can write a book. If you can say it you can write it.... The prestige enjoyed by the published author is unparalleled in our society. A book can bring wealth and an acceleration in one's career.'
>
> Dan Poynter[53]

I am an admirer of Poynter's upbeat determinism, and feel sure his brand of encouragement may prompt some people to do just as he says. After all, if you project positive vibes about a project, others are likely to take you at your own estimation. But it seems to me that there is vastly more involved in writing a book than being able to talk, and that the prestige he implies will immediately follow is much more uncertain. There will be times on any publishing journey, self-imposed or otherwise, when you wonder if it really is all worth it. Thinking about your motivation before you start will help sustain you – or perhaps decide to postpone this particular trajectory until a later moment in your life.

---

[53] Dan Poynter's *Self-publishing Manual: how to write, print and sell your own book*, Santa Barbara: Para Publishing (2006), www.parapublishing.com. Dan is widely regarded as the father of self-publishing and foresaw the opportunities well ahead of others. His book remains available in print and ebook version

What are the attractions of writing a book?

1 Validation

Writing a book feels utterly validating; you feel as if you exist. Holding a volume with your name on the cover offers a very special sensation – I have yet to meet a writer, published or self-published, who does not feel the same. The sheer weight of the volume in your hands is uplifting; time stands still and you just think 'I did all that'. In this fast-moving world, life can feel reduced to a series of physical actions that confirm your existence: filling up the deep freeze; taking out the rubbish. A book confirms that you are there.

2 Permanence

The publication of a book offers a bit of solidity in this temporary world. Even if you subsequently use all your books as loft-insulation, or give them away to family and friends who never read them, what you created still has substance. What is more, if you have applied for ISBNs and sent copies to the requisite copyright libraries,[54] your book will remain part of their body of published work forever. The book will outlive us all.

3 You enter the catalogue – and perhaps the vocabulary

Assuming you have applied for an ISBN, if you ask for your book in a library or bookstore, it will appear on a database of titles available, referred to by your authorial name. You move from the frail individual – outward appearance concealing a wealth of insecurities – to a line entry in a database of similar products, many of which were created by the vastly more famous. If your book is used in universities and colleges, you can find yourself quoted and referenced.

4 Your voice can be heard

Even if you are not going to be a mass seller, writing it down and getting it into a shareable format means you have recorded material for the future: for your family; for the wider community; for fellow professionals. If this is material or a viewpoint that only you have access to, you ensure your point of view survives for when you are no longer around to represent it.

[54] See page 11

But there is also a negative side to the experience of authorship.

1 It's no longer special

The amount of high quality writing being produced today has led to an assumption that its creation has been easy.

> '...we assume that, because there are still plenty of writers practising in all the media, almost anybody can write a book, a script or a play. Sheer abundance depreciates the currency, and familiarity breeds contempt for both the act of creation and the creator.'
>
> Victor Bonham-Carter[55]

Bonham-Carter was writing in 1984. Since then Creative Writing classes have burgeoned, at all kinds of institutions (universities, local authorities, informal groupings); a similar swelling of therapy and counselling has encouraged many more people to write; the internet has created new ways to share words (email, texts, social net-working); writing competitions attract huge numbers of entrants.

Wider participation in writing, and improved access to published writers (through literary festivals and in the media), has made inroads into the respectful distance that used to exist between author and reader, impacting on the writer's role as isolated seer. Readers can now access writers, decide whether or not they like them, and vote with their purse. And the self-publishing author will have to work doubly hard to get noticed and make their book sell.

2 Lack of public acknowledgement

There is a difficulty here because writers are essentially individuals, and not good at joined up thinking; although universities have sought to fill the gap, there is still no fully acknowledged training qualification for authorship:

> 'Writing is an empirical art, which can only be learned by doing it, there is no formal way of graduating in authorship and no way of enumerating its practitioners. For them independence is of the

[55] Victor Bonham-Carter, *Authors by Profession*, Volume 2, London: Society of Authors (1984)

essence, and this includes the freedom to practice without formal qualification, without regimentation, without the pressure of collective action. The price of that independence is the lack of identity in the public mind.'[56]

Writing a book takes practice, time and effort, and there is a difference between writing a book that others want to read, and one that simply proves you can type – or get something bound.

3 There is little money in it

Every now and again a journalist will work out just how much a famous author is making per minute and the figure will be so extraordinary that it attracts a headline. But this figure is always produced in isolation, not in reference to how other professions are paid (bankers and their bonuses are notably excluded) and is not typical. Very few writers make the annual rich list. The UK's Society of Authors have carried out regular surveys into the remuneration of professional writers, and a consistent percentage of around 80% of writers earn, from their writing, less than the national minimum wage. Self-publishing authors have to work very hard to make money out of their work. It was all very well for Dr Johnson to say that 'No one but a blockhead ever wrote but for money'[57] but in practice, few do.

4 Writing is anti-social

An intention to write can be seen as a self-pleasing activity, and therefore an anti-social one. Writing involves immense concentration at times when others may feel they have a call on your attention, and the writer's derivation of pleasure from such a solitary activity can bring an accompanying hostility or mistrust. Inspiration can strike at odd times and living with someone who is physically present but emotionally unavailable can be frustrating. Writing is isolating, lonely and fattening (all that uninterrupted access to the biscuit tin).

[56] Richard Findlater, *The Book Writers: who are they?* London: The Society of Authors (1966)
[57] Quoted in *The Life of Samuel Johnson*, James Boswell (1791)

5 Society has a tendency to be anti-writer

This is a culturally specific point,[58] but those you might consider likely to support, such as family and close friends, can be less than encouraging; the family that cheered you on in the swimming gala, or was delighted when you added to the number bearing their name, can produce a very different reaction when your progeny is a book. It may be that they find your stated ambition to write diminishes their own more private one; parents, siblings and partners can all simply feel jealous:

> 'Nothing has a stronger influence psychologically on their environment and especially on their children than the unlived life of the parent.'
>
> C.G. Jung (1875–1961), psychologist

The role of the story-teller as a leader in society has a primeval origin – those who can hold an audience often have disproportionate influence. Again, within your immediate social circle, this can cause profound irritation.

6 You expose yourself

Making your work available is an act of bravery. Feedback can be spiteful; motivated by factors other than a desire to help you improve, and reviews harsh; lifting sensational details about your private life rather than concentrating on your work. It is arguably easier to review something negatively than create it in the first place, and yet the two are equated.

7 Happiness is in no way guaranteed

Many writers long to see their book finished and available, assuming they will be happy once this status is achieved. But deferred gratification may not work; contentment may not follow. And in the process of writing you set yourself a challenge: can you ever do it again? Nor will your path as a writer necessarily be linear; you may produce your best book first – and nothing of significance afterwards.

---

[58] In the US, writing a book can be seen as part of the dream of self-fulfilment, and consequently less constrained by self-doubt. It is significant that self-publishing took off more rapidly in the US than the UK

Particular difficulties for the self-publishing author

* You are on your own. It is your decision to pursue this course; no one else is investing time or emotion in the project.

* You must have sufficient resources to maintain your endeavour: money, time, stamina and self-belief. Those you live with may prioritise differently.

* No one can be relied upon for feedback. What you get must be cajoled or paid for.

* You can feel diminished by opinions of those who do not understand what you are doing; dismissed by those who assume that because you are funding the dissemination of your work, it has no value.

* You are unprepared for all the specific decisions needed, but because they result in a permanent format, their consequences will live with you forever.

Ten top tips for maintaining your motivation to write

1 Build a writing habit

Do something every day, and at particular times of the day. All professional writers seem to insist that they don't wait for inspiration; rather they get on with the writing, *even when they don't feel like it*. If you write something, you have something to improve; if you write nothing there is no material to work on. Author Geraldine Brooks:

> 'Writing is like bricklaying, you put down one word after another. Sometimes the wall goes up straight and true and sometimes it doesn't and you have to push it down and start again, but you don't stop, it's your trade.'[59]

[59] Small Talk, *Financial Times*, 28/29 May 2011

Keep an eye on the word count at the end of each writing session, not as a complete measure of the worth of what you have achieved (most people would rate a 14 line sonnet as one of the highest forms of art), rather to gain a sense of how many words you tend to produce within a given period, and so a guide on how to pace yourself in future. Keeping up with a comfortable word target each day may give a sense of progress.

If you long to write a novel, but find that first blank page of your new notebook or screen file remains stubbornly unfilled, experiment with shorter formats. You could try blogs, flash fiction (a story in 250 words), news reports, features for magazines, short stories and then once your writing habit is established, move towards a longer format. Or you might just decide to stay where you started. Don't assume that these are lesser formats, just different – and they may engage you in a way that writing a novel does not. Subsequently returning to a longer format may feel a relief – it's arguably much harder to write short than long.

Write for the fun of it, stop being analytical and forget the market. Write what you would like to read.

2 Read as much as possible

If you want to write, it is essential to read as much as possible. Maybe the same kind of books you want to write, maybe completely different kinds of writing. All effective writing has a structure, and even if you do not observe it, reading will impress on your brain the mechanisms of effective communication and expand both your horizons and your word power. I remember being fascinated by the way tennis player John McEnroe moved around the court – he would always return from a rally by walking along the lines of the court, as if he was trying to imprint their shape on his brain. Reading does the same thing for the writer.

3 Accept the unfinished as part of the process

Creating a book is seldom a linear process, it will involve false starts, crises of confidence, giving up and rethinking. Professional writers report on their writing process variously; from starting with the ending (revealed to them as a nightmare) to sketching out the whole over the course of one frenetic weekend – and then spending the next two years on a process of colouring in.

Accept that creativity is messy: print-outs strewn around the room; different files on your computer that you can no longer quite remember; odd jottings; inspiration at inconvenient times. Promise yourself only to write things down in one place and keep that place with you at all times – a notebook you can't lose and a bag big enough to accommodate what you need.

Don't try to rush. Take one stage at a time. Capturing the essential story line may be one stage, returning to it to edit and finesse the language several stages more. It's very difficult to write and edit yourself at the same time; they are two separate stages that require separate thought.

4 In general, characters matter more than plot (and this works for non-fiction as well as fiction)

When you think back to books you have really enjoyed it is often the characters that remain in the head rather than what happened to them; their personality characteristics, and how those related to individuals you have known (yourself included). Carry this thought into your own writing, you don't have to think of extraordinary events or a sequence of action, just of characters who intrigue you. Get to know them, think about the interactions they have – and ideas for a story may emerge. For example, Marilyn Robinson's books introduce a limited range of people, to whom nothing much happens. And yet these are stories we want to hear.

5 Find yourself somewhere to write

It could be a table in your bedroom; a favourite seat in the kitchen. But somewhere where you can concentrate and where you will not be interrupted. It helps if no one else has access to this space. If this is impossible then create a cover for the working surface (an old sheet or net curtain to drape over your belongings when you are not in place). There is an important chemistry to how things sit on the desk that does not work if material is tidied away or the space used by others – the same goes for odd icons introduced to your computer screen; they distract. Consider a garden shed or the spare bedroom of a friend, a part-time job that allows time at a computer terminal after hours. A friend of mine regularly cat sits for friends away on holiday, and knowing that she has two or three weeks in a particular location offers her important deadlines for progress.

Some writers get very attached to specific writing locations, or particular implements, and cannot start in other places. A recent visit to Ernest Hemingway's house in Cuba revealed that first drafts were written long hand at a desk, second drafts typed, standing up at a typewriter, feet on skin mat. Letters were written from a correspondence desk and book reviews written in the afternoon, sitting in a comfortable chair. And each writing location was a different orientation from the others, presumably helping to keep him 'in role'.

Having advised you to try to stick to a regular routine, writing can be done anywhere you have ideas. It's a good idea not to get so over-attached to a particular location that you can do nothing if you are not there. And when you are not at your desk, daydream.[60]

6 Announce regular hours – and stick to them

Habits breed comfort, consistency – and stability. So consider at what hour your writing brain works best; whether it is logistically possible to allocate this particular time (mothers of small children may find that a writing habit that must begin at around the time the school-run starts, hard to defend) and announce your intention. And having announced what time you plan to write, stick to it. In the process you will encourage others to take your writing seriously – and further support your intention.

Think about what will help you feel creative: the pictures you put on the wall, what you write with, the level of warmth and light, the type of chair, the right shoes, the mug, the music, the type of light, good luck charms that make you feel positive. Part of this is pragmatic – writing is essentially sedentary and it's hard to stay stationary for long periods of time if you are uncomfortable, but part is also taking yourself seriously; creating the circumstances that help you get started. Sportspeople are allowed their idiosyncrasies (lucky pants, putting clothes on in a particular order) so why should writers not be allowed the same privilege? Author Rachel Billington[61] commented that she likes: 'to sit up in bed and write, with my book on my lap. I get up first and clean my teeth and have breakfast but then return to bed to write; putting on a dressing

[60] See chapter 4 on using the subconscious
[61] Published by Orion

gown – for many years I had a lovely one with frills on it – and also wearing jewellery'. Her husband Kevin commented that he could tell how well it was going from how much jewellery she was wearing (more = better).

I would advise you not to make answering your emails your settling activity – it puts your brain in quite the wrong place; responding to other people's issues rather than thinking about your own desire to communicate.

7 Finish at a point that will help you restart the next time

The blank screen or page confronts every writer once they sit down to write – so can you think about how to make reengaging with your work more appealing? There is no single solution: some writers finish mid-sentence so they know they can restart; others make a quick note of what will happen next and leave this on screen at the end of what they have just completed or in a notebook. Others like to have a print-out to hand of something they have written and they are pleased with, just to convince themselves that they can write. Pay attention to your writing flow and go with it. There will be times when writing seems easier than others, and so try to notice what it was that helped you (particularly felicitous start-time; preparatory manoeuvres; type of biscuits).

8 Establish the author in you

One of the biggest obstacles to writing is often accepting that you should be taken seriously. In the same way that encouraging others to know that you are on a diet can help you maintain the motivation to stick to a reduced-calorie intake, it may be worth announcing your intention to complete a manuscript and publish a book more widely. This can be done on application forms (under 'employment' or 'interests') or when introducing yourself at parties. Practice saying 'I write' not 'I am trying to write' or 'I scribble'. It can be a tremendous liberation to hear yourself do this; hard the first time, but once out it becomes easier. If it helps, give yourself a writing name and play with this in your head to ensure it fits how you want your writing to be seen. See chapter 19.

9 Share your work at the right stage in its evolution

That usually means not too soon. Make it as good as you can before you share it. Don't feel tempted to tell people your story ideas until they are formulated – hearing yourself describe them too soon can make them shrivel. You can involve someone else in this process, or pay for feedback (see chapter 9) but do pick the right person.

10 Build emotional and practical support for your self-publishing project

I have speculated elsewhere[62] that the reaction of most of our acquaintances divides them into one of three kinds of supporter: booster, sapper or feeder. Boosters are people who are proud to know a writer and simply encourage you. Sappers assert the negative and tend to remind you of the difficulties of the path you have chosen: many writers competing for contracts and attention; fewer publishing houses and bookshops; less time/inclination to read within wider society. Feeders are more insidious and literally make themselves feel better by putting you down. Likely comments may include the selfish nature of writing (because it makes you less available to those who need your company), the rapidity or slowness of your writing pace, which implies either lack of value (through rush) or over-laboured presentation (through taking too long) or the general discredit of self-publishing.

There is no recommended recipe for the writer's best company. Ironically some people find the negativity of the sappers boosts them; others that the attention of feeders energises them into a firmer appreciation of the talent they have. Just pay attention to what works for you, and have no compunction about choosing your company accordingly. If the sappers and feeders drain you, and you have no choice but to see them on occasion (because you are related to them), try alerting friends and family to the effect they have on you, and they may help you stick up for yourself. The bottom line is to have a firm belief that what you are doing is worth it.

As part of this process, begin by convincing yourself of the value of what you are doing:

'Remember that any man who has to sell a thing must make himself acquainted with its value, or he will be – what? Call it what you please

[62] *Writer's Forum*, October 2009, issue 96, Bournemouth: Select Publisher Services Ltd

– overreached, deluded, cheated. This is a recognised rule in every other kind of business. Let us do our best to make it recognised in our own...'

Walter Besant, one of the founders of The Society of Authors

And to those who are inclined to dismiss, affirm the value of the product which is *independently published*, i.e. the writer has borne the development costs themselves. Encourage others to talk up the project on your behalf, and develop a few handy phrases for those who query why you are charging: 'I went ahead with publication because I wanted to share my ideas'. 'If something is worth reading, the format that holds the ideas matters too – putting a price on it means others value it too.'

Writing often suffers from a misplaced mystique. Those not involved assume that the desire to write will replace the need for ordinary sources of remuneration such as food, money and a roof over your head. Of late, the level of the published author's specialness has been diminished by a more widespread desire within society to take part in writing too. Notions of originality, copyright and intellectual ownership of the ideas created are central to understanding the role of the author; the seer who gathers ideas and presents them to a wider society. But there is a school of philosophy, notably French, that speculates whether this is all their own work, and whether the 'the text is a tissue of quotations';[63] a composition of influences that are never truly their own – in the same way that architects or engineers influence each other; or new techniques in medicine are reported and later widely adopted. Is the author thus the hunter-gatherer of other people's ideas, the 'scriptor'[64] of wider notions that just need catching and directing through a new channel, or do they add something of their own?

In practice, wherever the ideas come from, writing is hard; a range of supporting structures and mechanisms, from the practical to the emotional, usually need to be assembled to support and sustain the author. This chapter has hopefully suggested what these might be – and how to locate them.

---

[63] Roland Barthes, *Death of the Author*, essay in *Aspen Magazine* (1967)
[64] It's worth pondering the vocabulary and the different associated meanings of terms that refer to the writer: e.g. author, writer, scribe, signatory

7

Other writing solutions: writing with others; paid support including ghost writers

The demands of the writing life should never be underestimated. To produce something that lives up to Keats' essential criteria of both truth and beauty is not as simple as it sounds. Good writing requires sustained effort; what I heard author Meg Rosoff refer to recently as an 'ongoing ability to remain porous to experience; a willingness to try things out rather than freeze into a single pattern of response'. Rosoff expanded on the associated struggle; 'turmoil as an essential part of the life of the writer; a continuing angst about truth, and the constant re-examining of the big questions that traditionally occupy teenagers – who am I, what am I doing, and what is going on around me?' In her case, she acquired the outward signs of educational success but felt lost; got into Harvard but disliked it; took up sculpture and spent 15 years in an advertising agency before writing a novel (*How I Live Now*) that at the age of 46 made the world sit up and take notice. Her second novel (*Just in Case*) won the 2007 Carnegie Medal.[65]

> 'You probably need to be comfortable inside your own head before you can start to get inside other people's; to find clarity about who you are in order to be mature enough to do what you should in life. There are people who manage to harness youth and enthusiasm and energy for experience and write their best book when they're 23, though it's rare.'

[65] The Carnegie Medal is awarded annually to the writer of an outstanding book for children. It was established by in 1936, in memory of the Scottish-born philanthropist, Andrew Carnegie (1835–1919) and first awarded to Arthur Ransome, author of *Swallows and Amazons*

The wider implication is that the path to becoming a writer is a slow burn; you emerge to produce your best work gradually, and the writer not only should – but also needs – to take a few false starts before crafting something that is worth reading by others. Failing at something, whether an outright fail or just realising that something many others esteem or long for is not for you, is all about finding out who you are.

The problem within today's publishing industry is that the associated rock-strewn road is increasingly bypassed. Publishers and retailers are struggling; margins are under intense pressure; all want guaranteed sellers and a quicker return on investment. So the opportunity for the writer to practice en route to crafting a masterpiece is fast disappearing.

Writers used to be permitted an apprenticeship; their work getting better and sales growing incrementally with each title. Commissioning editors were the heart of the publishing organisation and could reassure their bean-counting colleagues that if the trajectory was in the right direction, and if in the long run a publishing house kept faith, there would be something worth celebrating; a prize-winning novel or a 'breakthrough' book that would reignite the backlist still in print. As proof of this, Ian Rankin published his first Inspector Rebus novel (*Knots and Crosses*) in 1987, but it was his eighth (*Black and Blue*) published in 1997 which is regarded as his 'breakthrough book', and which won the Macallan Gold Dagger awarded annually by the Crime Writers' Association. Similarly, Ian MacEwan's seventh novel, *Amsterdam*, won the Booker Prize in 1998. In his acceptance speech for the Booker prize-winning *The Sea*, John Banville thanked his agent for putting up with not having made any money out of him for years.

In any case, no one quite knew how work was selling or what else was available; market research for new titles involved a quick scan of the potential competition on the shelves of a local bookshop or discussion with educated friends.

Times have changed. Now the book business has the best retail sales information for any industry,[66] success or failure can be quickly divined, and the time over which sufficient achievement is adjudged

---

[66] Nielsen BookScan, see pages xiii–xiv

to have occurred, and the scale by which it is measured, have both become much more exacting. Publishers want titles at regular intervals that conform to a standardised norm for each writer, that makes them easier to market – and in this difficult economy they do not want to take risks. And writers who explore a different area with each novel, thus the only identifying factor between their work is their name, are harder to market. Meanwhile independent bookstores are going out of business, chains are threatened as more people buy online, and the editors of the literary review pages, who used to isolate writing worth reading, attract little advertising from publishers in return, and can consequently find their pages, if not their very roles, cut back by their host papers. Readers increasingly rely on new mediators, many of whom are based in broadcast media, which due to limits on air-time may provide a less detailed analysis, or through eforum which, as they are written by individuals, can be both partisan and personal.

This is happening on both sides of the Atlantic. In the US, a recent investigation by Trevor Butterworth in *The Financial Times* revealed writers' concern that Amazon and Barnes & Noble 'make money by selling the greatest number of copies of the fewest number of titles', and fears that 'their marketing strategies, their elaborately curated display policies, their "readers also bought" algorithms... were killing literary publishing.'

He cited one group of writers' response: 'Mischief + Mayhem (M+M) is a writers' collective, so far composed of five writers but with aspirations to embrace up to 30. Its goal is to publish six books a year and sell directly to the consumer through their publisher, OR Books[67] by way of print on demand or through selected independent bookstores'. Dale Peck, another one of the founders, 'doesn't dispute the benefits of marquee[68] publishing houses', his complaint 'is that there are fewer opportunities for novelists to write serious novels and for them to receive anything but a paltry advance: "The whole point of writing literature was that in exchange for not getting paid a lot of money, you could say whatever you wanted; now, if you don't get a lot of money and you don't get to say what you want".'

[67] www.orbooks.com
[68] An adjective, and visual image, worth remembering

'The list of things you can't do grows longer and longer' says Lisa Dierbeck, another member of M+M. Her first novel, *One Pill Makes You Smaller*, was published in 2003 by Farrar, Strauss and Giroux (FSG), and became a *New York Times* notable book ('bracing pessimism...perversely liberating'). But when it came to sending out her second novel, *The Autobiography of Jenny X*, she was told by several large presses that the only way it would be publishable would be to make significant changes. 'I was told that having a character in jail was a problem. Readers will not be able to identify with him. One editor even said he was not handsome enough.' Similarly, Lionel Shriver was told by her US agent that there was no way a book about a high-school shooting could be published. The final publishers of *We Need to Talk About Kevin* found otherwise.

Mitzi Angel, editor at FSG commented that it is not necessarily the system that is at fault for such decisions but, rather, 'that the publishing process is inherently random. So much depends on who sees what, when, and whether they like it'. John Thompson's recent study of Anglo-American publishing, *Merchants of Culture: the publishing business in the 21st century*[69] described it as a 'complex and bewildering business.' He concludes however that economic forces have conspired against the kind of sales figures that have, historically, supported literary culture through what are known as midlist titles. 'It is getting harder and harder for publishers to sell literary fiction, especially new fiction by writers who have not yet become recognisable names with established track records. ...the literary marketplaces looks more and more like a winner-takes-more market, concentrating on a small number of titles that sell exceptionally well, indeed, better than ever, whereas the number of titles that sell in modest but acceptable quantities is declining... this is not a particularly appealing vision for the future of literary culture.'

Similar forces are at work in the UK. Author of books for teen-agers, Nicky Browne (writing as N.M. Browne) became particularly concerned at how quickly after publication children's books were going out of print.

[69] London: Polity Press (2010)

> 'Children's publishing had traditionally paid lower advances, and received a lower share of organisational spend and attention, but there were compensations in that the titles tended to have a *longer tail*; remaining in stock in retail outlets, and available from the associated publishers, for much more time after publication than writing for the adult market.'

Since then she and other children's authors fear things have changed. There has been a contraction of the number of titles printed, the culling of many lists of books and authors, and a dramatic shortening of the period over which a title is deemed to be a success or a failure in retail outlets; sometimes just six weeks. The big margins given to big retail chains mean the books have to work individually, but whereas all titles used to get some marketing spend, today many children's authors feel publishing houses are increasingly driven by those who know little about writing or children; it is the pithy one-line title concept and high-budget jacket that gets the in house attention – and the associated marketing spend. The rise in recruitment of 'celebrity authors', who rely on others to do the writing, but cost much more to commission as a result, has resulted in a greater share of the organisational budget being allocated to ensure the investment pays off. Genuine innovators are being squeezed; their royalties cut to fund bookshop discounts and promotions for higher profile titles across the list. High quality reading material is no longer promoted to secondary markets (schools, libraries, and as a good thing in itself) and an unsatisfying reading experience from many of these high profile titles leaves parents and children frustrated, and disinclined to come back for more.

Other children's authors share Browne's concern as children's editors seemed to do less editing/research to find good material. One commented: 'Publishers would write off disappointing sales due to a poor cover that you had argued against in the first place, but then reluctantly agreed to accept through a default position; relying on their greater experience. To hear your original judgement subsequently confirmed, that a poor cover had hindered sales, but then as a result understand your future publishability was threatened by this mistake (epitaph: "last book did not sell") was pretty galling.'

Technologies meanwhile are changing, and while publishers seem unlikely to develop ebooks to the greatest possible extent (the lower margins achievable are not particularly attractive) there is a growing familiarity with accessing quality reading material through new mechanisms. The 'passback' (or the passing back of the smart phone, to keep children quiet in the back seat of the car) is an accepted term in families and has just been included in dictionaries. Why not encourage reading in this way too?

Browne's response has been to collaborate with other authors in the same position, share their thoughts, pool their backlist and promote the benefits of a quality driven approach to writing. All members of her new writing group Might E Books will be required to both submit their own work for editing and edit each others, and in the process they hope to build a reputation for quality and that a recognised brand will emerge for those interested in finding really good reading material for their young people presented in eformat. They will republish their backlists through the brand, and hopefully signpost a route to new writing through both their publishers and their writing association. Browne comments:

'We want to show what a writing group can offer, and aim to recreate something like the confidence of the early editors at Virago who demonstrated to our younger selves that we should collectively trust their judgement. We now offer our writing and publishing experience as an effective filter, to enable people to chart a path through the mass of material available. We want to grow into an experienced group of writers, collaborating, still working with publishers on our front list but together keeping our backlist alive. We plan to keep a creative/editorial balance, support each other, and be unashamedly quality driven.'

The only spanner in the works will be if their various publishers decide to release their backlist titles as ebooks too – in which case an anthologised or 'tempter' publication might be a possible alternative product.

This has been tried, and proved successful, before. Early examples of this tendency to cluster in search of improved marketing and morale were genre-based, often in crime fiction.

Case study: Louise Voss and Mark Edwards

Louise Voss writes: 'The story behind *Killing Cupid* began in 1999. I was an aspiring writer with a hard-won but – in hindsight – very tepid literary agent representing the two manuscripts I'd written. My interest was, naturally, piqued one night by a BBC2 documentary called *Close Up: First Writes* following three unpublished authors, one of whom was a Mark Edwards, who was in exactly the same situation as I was: two novels written, an agent sending out the second but with seemingly little enthusiasm and even less success. Very uncharacteristically of me, I emailed him via his agent and wished him luck. He wrote back, and we became writing buddies, eventually coming up with the idea of collaborating on a joint novel. Things had moved on in our lives by then, a year or so later – I had got a fantastic new agent (Jo Frank at AP Watt) who had garnered me a big two book deal at auction, and Mark had gone to live in Japan for a year with his girlfriend.

Killing Cupid was a dream to write, a bit of light entertainment. We alternated chapters by email – me in Twickenham writing the female protagonist, and Mark the male one, from Tokyo. Once finished, we had high hopes for it – but we hit a major snag: it was neither a conventional thriller, nor an out-and-out comedy, and everyone we showed it to – our agents, my editor, other editors – commented on this as a big drawback. Even the optioning of it by the BBC for a two-part drama didn't make it appealing enough for publishers. It was very disappointing (although we were very excited about the option. But that too petered out after a year or two, and nothing came of it – at that time).

Mark continued writing – and being rejected, which always really surprised me. He is a good writer, and all the books of his I've read have been, in my opinion, eminently publishable. He was very unlucky. My luck ran out too – after my third and fourth novels were published, but almost completely overlooked by the publishers, they dropped me. My agent retired, and the new agent I'd moved across to promptly dropped me too, saying she had to concentrate on her 'more high-profile clients'. Mark and I were both pretty much back at Square One.

Undeterred, we co-authored another more conventional and high-concept thriller, *Catch Your Death*. Sent it out to agents.

Nothing. Some liked it, some didn't, nobody took us on.

Life (day jobs, babies, children, mortgages, etc.) took over and although we stayed in touch, neither of us had the time to write anything else together. I stopped saying 'I'm a writer' when asked what I did for a living – although I did take a part-time MA in Creative Writing, just to keep my hand in.

Mark was working for a specialist online publishing company, and he was the first one to bring up the possibility of us putting out *Killing Cupid* ourselves as an ebook. I was doubtful at first, but when I re-read the manuscript, I was reminded of how much I loved it. Why not? Better to get it out there for a few people to see – and you never knew...

It took a good few months for us to edit and update it (none of the characters even had mobiles in its first incarnation, and social networking was years away! I also had to remove numerous references to people smoking in pubs). We both got Kindles for Christmas, and Mark did some research about how to format the document for Kindle, royalty rates, pricing strategies, etc.

We bought the rights to an image from istockphoto.com to use as a cover. It received mixed reactions from the people we canvassed; some loved it, but some thought it a tad sleazy. In the end we went with it anyway, because we wanted something really striking and memorable, which it is. Mark's sister-in-law kindly designed the cover for us gratis; and we decided to price it as low as possible, figuring that it would be far more likely that people would take a punt on it if it was only 70p/$1.40. The lower price meant that we could only get the lower royalty rate, of 35% – if we priced it over £1.99, the rate would increase to 79%, but for now, we're only interested in shifting as many as possible. If it sells well, we'll push the price up in a few weeks. 35% of 70p, split two ways i.e. 17.5%, is about 12p each per download – so we're not going to be retiring to the Caribbean... well not immediately, at least.

Killing Cupid went live on Amazon on 19 February 2011. Completely coincidentally and out of the blue, on that same day, I received an email from the BBC producer (now a BAFTA winner) who had originally optioned it, asking if the rights were still available, as she'd now like to option it for a feature film – amazing!

Three days later, we'd sold a grand total of 11 copies – but even this paltry figure had somehow put us into the Kindle suspense chart with a bullet at No. 22! 1,655 in the overall chart. Not a bad start. I emailed 90-odd friends, colleagues, and writing contacts – and the sales figure more than doubled. We went up to No.15 in the chart, our highest point to date (I can see that chart-watching is going to become very addictive!). Mark has engaged in chat on the Kindleboards, we are both using Facebook and Twitter to promote it, and Mark is writing articles for online magazines and websites such as Crimetime and DailyCheapReads.com. Sales are slow but steady (100+ in the first month), but we are still considering this as groundwork.

The next step will be to epublish *Catch Your Death*, which we will be doing in the next couple of weeks. I have also requested back the rights to all four of my previously-published novels, despite the publishers wanting to issue them all as ebooks themselves. Publishers seem to expect an author to do the vast majority of their own publicity anyway (unless you are very 'A' list, of course), so why should they take most of the profits for doing something I can do for myself? It's very liberating! I am also really enjoying the sensation of control over my own destiny that was very distant during my years with a major publisher. I never even saw a royalty statement for any of my books, not until someone from my ex-agency, presumably accidentally, sent me one last year. It made me giggle with shock and awe – the amount of money they lost on me by paying me such a big advance – no wonder they dropped me!

In hindsight, I'd have done it all very differently. There's a lot to be said for lower advances and lower expectations – that way, the only way is up. I was on a hiding to nothing pretty much after my first novel, *To Be Someone*, didn't sell as well as had been projected. I'm not bitter – I know how incredibly fortunate I was to have been in that situation at all. But this new situation is turning out to be just as exciting – it feels as if the world is our oyster, and that we will reap what we sow. Even if nothing comes of the movie option (as is so often the case), I feel positive about my future publishing prospects again, for the first time in years. I am going to put all my books on Amazon. I might even start calling myself "a writer" again.'

Mark Edwards adds a postscript:

'For the first three months of *Killing Cupid*'s tenure on Amazon, sales increased slowly but steadily. We sold 113 copies in March, then 540 in April, at one point getting very excited when we shot up to No. 177 and took the top spot on the movers and shakers chart for one glorious day. Through May, the book crept closer and closer to the top 100, hovering agonisingly close for ages until it finally broke through. All this time we had been picking up positive reviews and we were thrilled to be in the top 100.

Then things started to get really interesting. At the same time that *Killing Cupid* broke into the top 100 we published *Catch Your Death*. We had high hopes for it, having always believed it to be the more commercial of the two. We hit upon the idea of doing what publishers often do when they launch new writers; comparing ourselves to other popular writers in the same genre. So *CYD* had an extended title that read *Catch Your Death (for fans of Dan Brown and Stieg Larsson)*, as it shares the same high-paced qualities and is a mystery with its roots in the past. It's difficult to say what effect this had, as our book did not appear if you searched for either of those authors on Amazon. Perhaps, when it started climbing the charts, the subtitle caught the eye of more potential readers. But I also know from comments on forums and Twitter that lots of people found it off-puting. When the book had been No.1 for four days, Amazon removed it. This didn't affect sales at all. We've taken some stick for doing what we did but I genuinely don't believe it made much difference and, anyway, with no marketing budget, PR, press reviews, etc, to help us, we had to be extra-clever to get noticed. We also put an advertisement for *Catch Your Death* inside *Killing Cupid*. In its first week, *CYD* sold around 100 copies... not bad.

At this point, we had a stroke of luck. Several of the books that had *Killing Cupid* on their 'also bought' bar, including a thriller called *Daddy's Home*, climbed into the top 10. Suddenly we were being exposed to lots more potential readers. But *KC* got stuck just outside the top 50. We realised that less than 50% of the people looking at *Killing Cupid*'s page had bought it. So we rewrote the blurb, making it more straightforward. Within an hour, sales doubled. We hit the top 40, then the top 30.

At which point something extraordinary happened. While *KC* had made its snail-like way up the chart, *CYD* had started to climb behind it. On Thursday 2nd June, *CYD* entered the top 200. The next day it went into the top 100. One day later, sales went crazy. It climbed from No. 90 in the morning to No.13 by midnight. All the while, Louise and I were exchanging disbelieving texts. Then next day *CYD* went into the top 3, then the top 2. By Tuesday afternoon we were No.1. It was one of the most exciting moments of our lives.

Two weeks later, *CYD* is still No.1 and selling an average of 1000 copies a day. On its best day it sold an astonishing 1900 copies. *Killing Cupid* is also in the top 10, having climbed up to No. 3, although its sales have only been running at about half of *Catch Your Death*'s.

It's been incredible, and I only wish we had more books to put up straight away. Lots of people keep asking how we did it and have looked for tricks and commended us for clever marketing. But I firmly believe that what happened was that we timed it perfectly. Lots of people bought *KC* and liked it, and a large number of them bought *CYD* in a burst, propelling it up the chart. Once it was high up, it caught the eye of more and more people who have downloaded it in their thousands.'

Top tips for writing with others

With several experiences of collaborative writing under my belt, and having heard the experiences of others, I offer the following advice:

1 Parameters

Do you have an agreed set of priorities: audience; editorial standards; deadlines; working procedures; desired tone of voice and means of accreditation? These are best established now, in theory, before starting work.

2 The whole matters more than the single voices involved

If a work is to be a genuine collaboration, then the whole has to be greater than the individual parts. So whereas all contributors may initially want to be able to spot their individual contribution – to be able to say 'I did this' – for a venture to be truly collaborative, individual participations have to be subsumed into the greater whole. This is difficult but possible. Advertising agencies manage it; it is the team that is acknowledged to have come up with the content, not the individual copywriter.

It may be a good idea to have a trial run, in short format – maybe an essay or short story, which you can send between you and mutually edit. This may enable you to see how your styles align and whether you can you accommodate each others' responses. There may be several ways of drafting material, and no single one invalidates the others; they are just different creative approaches. Accepting that someone else's structure is the one to go for, rather than yours, and how this feels, is best considered now.

3 The writing matters more than the criticism, and should be acknowledged as such

It is always easier to say why you did not like something than start from scratch yourself. If there is no writing to make better, you have nothing on which to work. Delaying your start until you can form the perfect sentence may mean you delay forever.

4 Develop agreed methods of giving feedback

Few people find hearing criticism easy, let alone accepting and acting upon it, so try to anticipate your likely response patterns and encourage other participants to do the same (you are unlikely to be able to anticipate on their behalf). And try to do this before you start work; it is always easier in abstract than once difficulties arise.

For example, if you are using 'track changes' on your computer, consider changing the red to something that feels less pejorative. Although instinctively you may want to edit work you receive back immediately, sending it back within too short a time period can feel difficult for the recipient, as if the changes were so obvious they *had* to be commented on at once. If this seems likely to be a problem, discuss your tendency to respond immediately, in the context of your desire to get on being so immense that you cannot restrain yourself – or make the changes and delay sending them back. It may, in any case, be a good idea (depending on how quickly feedback is needed) to read the suggested amendments, but then to put away the edited text, before starting to rework it, for at least a week. That way, the subconscious has time to mull over, consider and find possible solutions to things – and to avoid throwing back fast, ill-considered comments that may irk your writing partner(s).

Think about how the writing partner(s) will receive your comments. There is scope for considerable creativity here. In one writing partnership I know of, the two involved leave edited scripts outside each others' doors and no human interaction takes place on this subject until the work has been reread and the recommended changes considered. In another partnership, where the two writers take it in turns to extend a story by writing alternate chapters and emailing them to each other, each writing partner takes their turn to extend the story being developed before offering feedback on the bit just received. When I was working in a partnership of three on a book,[70] one of my co-writers informed us that even though we had scrupulously 'tracked changes', his first response on receiving revised documents would be to 'accept all changes'. Realising how seriously he took our suggestions, my response was to think very carefully before making future changes.

5 Understand the pecking order within the writing relationship

Are you writing as a 'colourer in' – who fills in the bits sketched out by a senior hand – or as an equal partner? An appreciation of the terms and conditions under which you are providing your material should indicate your status. Do you own part of the copyright or does it belong to the main name on the cover? Are you receiving a royalty (i.e. you are part of the structure of the product and associated with its success) or a one-off fee? If you are responding to an outline provided by someone else, ownership and royalty share are less likely than a fee. Will there be further remuneration if the work goes into a new or updated edition? Even if what you have been offered is less satisfactory than what you might have hoped for, there may be reasons for going ahead – e.g. in future you have a writing collaboration to point to; you prove that you can

---

[70] A. Baverstock, S. Bowen & S. Carey, *How to Get a Job in Publishing*, London: A&C Black (2009)

manage a project on time and can work collaboratively; you can point people who ask your advice to a particular section in a book.

Within an ostensibly equal writing partnership, how consulted will you be? If one partner is better known than the others, does that give them a louder voice? A group effort usually works best if all feel valued and consulted. A co-author commented:

> 'Writing on a shared project I found my managing contributor's emails aggressive and sarcastic; I began to dread their arrival in my inbox – and once received I really had to jump start my enthusiasm for the project that day. I asked for a phone number on which I could contact him and he gave me a mobile number. When I asked for a landline, which would be cheaper to call, he responded: "No, that's for friends". He was constantly critical of those who had commissioned the work and never satisfied with mine. I felt isolated from the project as a whole and became increasingly despondent. Unsurprisingly, no book resulted.'

If you are employing someone to edit your work, then their terms of business will also need to be considered. Expert editor Gale Winskill comments:

> 'My own terms and conditions (which clients agree to before I start work) state that the copyright to the corrections for any piece of work is mine until final payment has been made, at which point I hand them over to the author. It might be sensible to have a similar formal agreement made between collaborators before starting working together, which clearly states who gets what and when, so there is no ambiguity.'

The UK Society of Authors publishes a very helpful *Guide to Ghost-Writing and Collaboration Agreements*, which can be obtained by both members and non-members.[71]

6 What are the mechanisms for managing discomfort?

Just as writers often find it difficult to negotiate with their commissioning editors (because they are too close to the process,

---

[71] www.societyofauthors.org

and they are too dependent on them) it can be very difficult to express disappointment with either the workings or outcome of a writing collaboration. So if you do not like the ideas being suggested, the tone of voice of the shared content is not yours, and you do not feel represented by the proposed final presentation of the product, how are you going to express this – and still maintain shared motivation to finish? Do you need to build in a feedback point at which you say what you really think about progress/content? Or should you rather consider the tone of voice used for feedback? Playwright and author Stephen Hancocks comments:

> 'One suggestion I would mention is one that we were urged to use at drama school, which they termed "the language of collaboration". Basically it was to encourage constructive criticism and so advised always using a positive comment as an opener. For example, "I thought that was a good scene, and I really enjoyed your use of the television remote control as a symbol of power play between the two main characters. I wonder if you had thought about including the situation where the battery in the remote goes dead and effectively leaves them both powerless?..." or "How do you think their relationship would develop if one of them decided to get a laptop and only watch iPlayer?"...'

Within a larger group, does there need to be an anonymous questionnaire for all involved – online, say through Survey Monkey[72] – to find out what people really think? Again, write it in to the arrangements now, when there is no emotion involved. You might also consider having a non-writing collaborator (e.g. an editor or well read friend) who can make a final call if there is disagreement over the final text, and whose decision all will respect?

7 Managing the outflow of creative conversations

Writing can produce turmoil in the head, stomach and bowels; an all-over adrenalin rush and an associated inability to sleep. Many writers learn to manage this by working out what is likely to be

---

[72] www.surveymonkey.com

their most creative time of day for writing, and working the rest of their commitments around it; perhaps an early morning writing session, an afternoon of reading, and an evening of relaxation to prepare for the next day's repetition. What author Philip Pullman referred to as:

> 'A devotedly dull and routine life, with as little excitement and change, is the best thing by far.'
>
> Quoted in *Is There a Book in You*, Alison Baverstock

A collaborative writing experience necessarily has to accommodate the timings of other parties, and can leave you with more exposure to rapid flow of ideas than is comfortable. The turmoil of what results (ideas in your head and no where to put them; adrenalin rush but nowhere to sit down and write; fast-flowing conversations that leave you feeling energised but exhausted; jealousy) needs managing, otherwise you may leave each session feeling as if you have just walked from an intense discussion about your life-threatening illness, straight out into a waiting room full of people with unsympathetic stares. Consider a wind-down together, or a meeting location that offers you an easy walk backwards; whatever works best for you all. These are not insurmountable problems, but do need thinking about. Managing the structure of your day so that you can all contribute fruitfully, and then absorb and act on what you gained, shows respect to all collaborators, and will hopefully promote a successful outcome.

Paid support for your writing

> 'My novel is so terrific that I cannot put pen to paper.'
>
> Christopher Isherwood (1904–86)

In addition to subsuming all the responsibility for writing yourself, you can also pay for support; establishing your own pitstop and servicing team, with a wide variety of choices available. You can purchase help with your plot, characters or narrative; guidance on your mental state (counselling and psychotherapy for writers); assistance with your writers' block or in diary management (helping you separate the necessary from the dispensable in your diary and in the process accessing more time for writing). There are writing courses of all shapes and sizes from informal groupings of friends to local authority classes to courses run by professional writers and academics through universities. And you can also pay someone to write it for you, through employing the services of a ghost writer.

Using a ghost writer

If you have a burning desire to present the world with your story, but find the 'getting started' part agonising, then you could consider using a ghost writer. A ghost extracts your story and turns it into a readable format; writing the book from your point of view, *as if it were you*. And there is nothing wrong with employing assistance in this way, in the same way that you would presumably not embark on building a chimney or conservatory without prior experience. As the best known ghost writer, Andrew Crofts[73] put it:

> 'People in the public eye use ghost writers not, as is commonly assumed, because they are stupid, but because writing a book is not something you can do without practice – and they have spent their time doing what made them famous, not practising the writing of books. The ghost helps extract, and then deliver, the story we want to read.'

Whereas the role of the ghost used to be unacknowledged on the cover, or recognised in such a coded way that it was invisible to all but the cognoscenti (listed as 'Managing Editor', or 'with thanks to x' next to a mention of the copy-editor in the acknowledgements), in recent years they have become more accepted. It is now acknowledged that many celebrities who produce an autobiography do not do the writing bit themselves – the ghost writer is consequently achieving status and a larger initial slice of both the initial remuneration (commonly termed 'the advance') and the resulting income ('royalties'). In the UK the ghost is now often noted on the front cover as *with Fred Blogs*. In the US it has long been routine to acknowledge the ghost, and the role they play in drawing out the story draws comment from the reviewers:

[73] www.andrewcrofts.com author of *Ghostwriting*, London: A&C Black (2004)

'Equally hard-won self-knowledge irradiates almost every page of "Open", thanks in great part to Agassi's inspired choice of collaborator, J.R. Moehringer, author of the memoir "The Tender Bar," with its melody of remembered voices. Agassi says he read it in 2006, at his last US Open, and then recruited Moehringer to help him write his own book. The result is not just a first-rate sports memoir but a genuine *Bildungsroman*, darkly funny yet also anguished and soulful. It confirms what Agassi's admirers sensed from the outset, that this showboat, with his garish costumes and presumed fatuity, was not clamoring for attention but rather conducting a struggle to wrest some semblance of selfhood from the sport that threatened to devour him.'[74]

Do you need a ghost writer?

You may not need as much help as a ghost writer can offer – a structural edit of your own work might be sufficient (and in which case there are freelance services available, see chapter 10 on editing). Then there are other, non-book options, for capturing your story: you might consider a film (interviewing you and talking to those who worked/lived with you); commissioning a painting or piece of art (perhaps representing your career or life, and having copies produced for your colleagues/descendents) or creating something to pass on (a garden, a photograph album, a tapestry, a series of letters to those who matter to you).

Do you need to be famous to employ a ghost writer?

The use of a ghost writer should be for a project you genuinely want to see the light of day in published form. Whereas if you are paying for anyone's time, in general you are in a strong position to dictate how it should be used, most ghost writers will see a project in book form, and ask you for material that they will then mentally be organising into a projected structure for an associated volume. It does not matter if that book is destined to meet its anticipated audience through the personal presentation to 25 key individuals, or through the bookshops worldwide, an effective ghost writer will take the same care.

[74] In Andre Agassi's 'Hate of the game', *New York Times*, Sunday book review, by Sam Tanenhaus, *New York Times*, 20 November 2009

So, no you do not need to be famous to employ a ghost writer, just able to offer them sufficient material to work with, for which you will offer appropriate remuneration.

What does a ghost want from their subject?

Having a story to tell is important to the ghost writer, and the questions they ask you when you meet to talk (and this is important; it's hard to ghost without some human interaction) will be designed to elicit a narrative that others will want to read. Questions such as 'Will this be interesting in 25 years' time?' 'What do you want your grandchildren to know about your own roots – where you, and so hence they, come from?' will draw out the material that makes for a good read. When it comes to how to structure the book, they will be looking for big themes such as:

* Who were your parents and what was it like growing up with them; what did you learn or think in your childhood that still influences you now?

* What education did you have; to what level; memorable teachers, courses, omissions

* What area of employment did you go in to and what influence did you have?

* Whom did you work with/where that might be of interest to others; any significant projects?

* Whom did you marry/have relationships with; how did you meet; how did the relationship end (if it did)?

* Children, and their respective paths

* Dramas in your life: press interest; your part in a national trend or development

* What words of wisdom or general advice would you like to pass on to your grandchildren – those of the next generation entering your particular world? Politician Tony Benn has written *Letters to My Grandchildren* and Maya Angelou *Letters to My Daughter*, which is intended for all women – she has no daughter

And rather than just retelling the story of a particular incident, as far as you can remember, the ghost will be just as interested in how you felt about something that happened:

> 'If they are talking, for instance, about a time when their partner walked out on them it will be a very different story if they say they felt relieved or excited rather than bereft, surprised or angry rather than broken-hearted. Being asked how they felt tends to stop them in their tracks and makes them think a bit more about whatever story they are telling.'
>
> Andrew Crofts

What does it cost to commission a ghost writer?

It depends on how much you are willing to pay and how much demand there is for their services; effective ghost writers are booked up a good year in advance. In general you should budget on needing three months of their time, and if you work out what they might expect to earn in a year were they part of your profession, or an allied one, you might be able to estimate their likely value and the associated cost. As regards how to pay them, Andrew Crofts structures his fees on the basis of an agreed sum which is divided into three chunks:

* One on agreement to work together

* One once the research has been done and he is about to start work

* One on delivery

As he often gets asked for advice on how to structure payment, this model is gaining currency. One point you might like to consider is whether you pay on *delivery* or *acceptance* (publishers have this clause too, the writer may deliver what they think they have been contracted to write, but it is only on their acceptance of the material that the payment becomes due).

How do you find an appropriate ghost writer?

Finding a ghost writer is usually a private activity; not the kind of thing you ask your friends to recommend (good speech writers have the same difficulty in obtaining new business). Some ghost writers advertise – in the classified section of *The Bookseller* or magazines aimed at the writing community such as *Writers' Forum*, *Writing Magazine* and *Mslexia*; *AQR* and *Ascent*, the names of others can be located in the acknowledgements in the front of the books they have co-written. You can also Google and find out who is advertising their services in this way.

The most usual way of proceeding is to exchange letters confirming intention, and the conditions on which either party might decide to withdraw from the arrangement, the monies to be paid and when. A busy ghost writer will confirm when they can start work, and it may not be immediately.

How can you tell if they are any good?

If you want to find an architect or an artist whose work you are happy to live with you can look at examples of their work. Looking at samples of the previous output of a ghost writer may be less straightforward, as the whole point is that the tone and vocabulary has to be matched to the person whose story they are writing. Thus the most reassuring way to judge a ghost writer would be to see something they have written on behalf of someone similar to you – and of course there will be no one completely like you, and maybe no one even similar (ghosts often like to work on books for a wide variety of different people, because that makes life interesting).

If they have written for completely different people, read the work and consider whether you feel you are truly getting to know the protagonist. Do you forget that this is a ghost written story, and instead feel you are understanding their life, told from their point of view? In which case, the ghost writer may be able to do a good job for you.

If you are concerned that what they write may not be what you want, either consider using another ghost or commission a sample chapter to discuss before proceeding further.

Do you have to like your ghost writer?

Not necessarily, but you do have to have confidence in them. Similarly, they do not have to like you, but they do have to feel that there is interest for others in what you share.

How many copies of the book should you get printed of a ghost-written book?

Think of it as a Christmas card. There are probably more people who might like to be sent one than you initially imagine, and the costs of producing 100 copies, instead of 25, are not going to be significantly more – because the most expensive part is likely to be the writing, not the printing. Think too about where else you might send one – to the organisations you have worked for, to your local public library, to your own school or university? Do remember to send one to the ghost writer, as a matter of courtesy. If you have arranged for an ISBN put on it (see chapters 8 and 15), you will need to give away copies to copyright libraries.

What about confidentiality?

A ghost writer will necessarily be asking you invasive questions and listening to your answers. They may challenge you and dig deeper – to make the material both interesting, and to represent the reader in years to come. How can you be sure that you will feel happy with what results, and that they will respect your privacy?

The basic decision on what to include is yours, and you should regard your ghost writer in the same way you regard your bank manager, solicitor, pharmacist or architect. All are bound by professional codes of conduct which should be respected. If you are planning to release sensitive material in an autobiography it would be a good idea to discuss this with your closest relatives and friends, particularly if they are not familiar with the details you are about to divulge. Keep an eye too on posterity, which may be more impressed by your candour than you realise now. Who knows what similar patterns may be lived out by your descendents, and how much comfort they might find in knowing a close relative, and one no longer alive, had been through a similar experience to their own? Finding out how you coped with particular challenges might inspire them to do the same.

Whose book is it?

How much you decide to reveal about the creation of a ghost-written book is up to you. Some people who commission work find it empowering to admit they can afford the services of a ghost writer, others may claim what they subsequently hand out is their book but have this challenged by friends and relatives who know they do not have a reading or writing habit and so consider sole authorship unlikely. In my experience you cannot have a writing habit without a reading one, and if your friends and relatives know you are not a reader, they may be able to claim with good justification that you are most unlikely to have been able to write your own book. And such a discussion may make them disinclined to read what you present.

Celebrities may be less inclined to such honesty and will boldly claim that they did it all themselves when the publisher who paid the invoice of the ghost writer is perfectly aware who did the actual writing.

The bottom line is that an effective ghost written book should *feel* like your own work, because it accurately reflects the time you have put into it – in recounting your memories and in working to make the manuscript as perfect as possible, through checking proofs and adding in additional material that occurs to you once you see the first draft. And if a ghost has achieved a work that feels like yours, they have done a good job.

What to do if time is running out before you can access a ghost writer?

If time is limited, and you want to record your thoughts, try talking into a recording device and then ensure the work is transcribed into a printed format. Recording devices change, become obsolete and if the material is still held in this way can become inaccessible. We very nearly lost the only recording of Nelson Mandela conducting his own defence in the Rivonia Trial[75] due to the technological obsolescence of the recording device used. Luckily another machine was found in a US museum.

Case study: an international businessman
'I was playing with my young grandson when the idea of writing a book first came into my head. I was thinking of all the things that I would like to tell him about my life and about what I knew of the lives of his great grandparents and other ancestors, and I knew in

[75] Pretoria Supreme Court in South Africa, April 1964

my heart it was unlikely that he would be old enough to be truly interested in all these details during my life-time. After both my parents were dead and it was too late to ask them anything I had found myself thinking of more and more questions that I wished I had asked while I still could. If either my father or my grandfather had thought to write a book about their lives it would have been such a fascinating read for me, even if it had lain unread by anyone else since the day it was completed. I decided that that was what I would do; I would write a book in the form a letter to my grandson, explaining everything that I would like him to know and that might also be of interest to his children and his children's children.

I didn't for a moment consider the idea of publishing this story for a wider market. This was to be a private story in every way. I would have a few dozen copies printed up and would distribute them around the family, so that my grandson would have a copy or two in his library when he was ready to read it or to simply dip into it in search of family stories from the past.

I showed my early attempts at writing to my wife and daughter. Although English is the first language of my grandson, it is not mine and they told me, as politely as they could, that my dry and detailed recording of the facts of our lives made for less than gripping reading. My wife suggested that I should hire a ghost writer to help with the creation of the manuscript. I would provide them with all the relevant information and they would craft it into a readable narrative, asking me whatever questions they felt would help the future readers to understand my life and the times I had lived through.

My enquiries led me to Andrew Crofts, a highly experienced ghost writer, and I was shocked by how completely he took all the weight off my shoulders, reading what I had written and spending a few hours recording questions and answers. I was then left with the pleasurable tasks of sorting through illustrations, deciding how I wanted the cover to look and proofreading whatever he sent me. The drudgery of the writing which had been proving so onerous had gone and he was also able to be my go-between with designers, editors and printers. Looking at the finished book I feel a great sense of contentment to think that after I have gone, details of my life and the knowledge that I have accrued will live on and will be there should anyone be interested enough to open the covers. It feels like I have packaged my life neatly for posterity.'

Case study: Brian Landers, *Empires Apart*

'*Empires Apart* was not self-published but some of the techniques of self-publishing helped the book on its way.

I had spent some years in the book trade at W.H. Smith, Waterstone's, Pearson Education and eventually Penguin and was extremely sceptical about "vanity publishing". I wanted my book published by one of the big houses.

A colleague gave my manuscript to one of the senior editors at Penguin without saying who had written it and, to my colleague's surprise; it came back with fulsome praise. "This book should be published" he concluded.

As a board director at Penguin I thought I knew the correct way to get a book published, and that meant starting with an agent. Because of my contacts I had no trouble getting agents to talk to me but getting them to represent me was another matter. My book compared the histories of American and Russian imperialism from the origins of the two countries right up to the present day. It was topical and controversial. I had superb responses on the quality of the writing and the research but the agents clearly thought there was a major problem: me.

One well respected agent was brutally frank. "If this book had been written by a TV celebrity or leading politician it would be a best seller. If it had been written by an academic it would get published. As it's by an unknown, it won't get through the doors at Waterstone's".

My next step was to try going direct to publishers. Penguin don't publish in-house authors but I had good contacts at some of our largest competitors. I sent the synopsis off to my contacts and received polite responses. They would pass on the synopsis, in some cases they asked for the whole manuscript. A couple sent me some really useful comments. I got very excited by an enthusiastic response from one editor only to be told a couple of months later that a "committee" had decided not to proceed.

Large publishers, unsurprisingly, have the same criteria as agents: "never mind the book, feel the author". I turned to small publishers, but I knew they would be inundated by unsolicited manuscripts. I had to make mine stand out.

That's when I turned to the techniques of self-publishing. I set the book up on www.lulu.com. I didn't want to sell it through Lulu and I didn't get an ISBN. I just wanted physical books. The first copy had some rough edges – varying font sizes, uneven formatting and so on – but after a couple of attempts I got a paperback that I thought looked presentable and ordered 25 copies for dispatch to suitable publishers. And I struck lucky.

In just a few days one of the publishers emailed me to ask whether the rights had been sold yet; she was half way through the book and loved it. After a couple more days she emailed again: she would certainly be making an offer. The publisher was Corinne Souza of Picnic who published *Empires Apart* in April 2009.

I should emphasise I was very lucky. Most of the paperbacks I sent out no doubt ended up in the waste paper basket; only one publisher other than Picnic showed any interest.

I must also emphasise that this is not really an example of self-publishing. Picnic added enormously to the success of the book – at their insistence the middle third of the book was completely re-written and was much better as a result. I had used one of Lulu's template covers for the proofs but Picnic's designer, John Schwarz, produced a fabulous cover for the published book. Most importantly they sold the North American rights to a large US publisher who have sold far more copies than we managed in the UK. They also sold the Indian rights to, of all people, Penguin. And one other thing – despite the predictions of the agent, Picnic managed to get *Empires Apart* scaled out in Waterstone's!'

Case study: Isobel Dixon, Literary Agent, Blake Friedmann

'Whereas the popular view is that agents discover unspotted talent and then make an effective link with an appropriate publisher, we may not always start completely from scratch. The agency often takes on as clients authors who have first published without an agent or with a different agent, and sometimes those who have self-published. In all such cases the page does not start clean; there are prior relationships and titles to be looked after and accommodated.

Wilfred Hopkins came to me in 1997 having self-published a volume of memoirs *Our Kid*. What is more, he had persuaded Waterstone's to stock his book, and already sold over 1,000 copies. I hope he will forgive me for saying that the book itself was not as attractively packaged as his work is today. Of course self-publishing services were less sophisticated then, and what arrived in the post was a heavy, glossy trade paperback with a cover that did not do the content justice. But on opening the book I loved his lively, humorous style and the story he had to tell. I am also influenced by the proactivity of authors who self-publish and this can indeed be a good route to getting a publishing deal, if you have tried the usual routes without success. Getting yourself into print does not always correlate with the ability to market yourself, but it does show an impressive degree of get-up-and-go, which all authors need to sustain their writing careers. And it's that get-up-and-go, as well as his heart-warming storytelling, which made Wilfred into a bestseller when Headline published *Our Kid* – a debut author in his seventies!

As an agent I am looking out for writers rather than just specific books, writers who will go on to deliver books of high quality at regular intervals so that we can work together to build their career. But of course each of us only has one life's experiences to draw on, and I have to accept that a memoir can sometimes mean a one-off book. Having said that, Wilfred (repackaged by the publishers as Billy) has gone on to produce seven books, the most recently, *Tommy's World*, based on his father's life, published just last year, with Wilfred now in his eighties. Over 700,000 copies of his books have been sold, all published by Headline.

He also began a trend for me. The press is often interested in the story of how particular writers got published, and so *The Daily Telegraph* ran a big piece about Billy Hopkins and his agent. So I have continued to be offered the memoirs of elderly gentlemen, and found another gem among the hundreds as a result.

As a direct result of the *Telegraph* piece I was contacted by the daughter of Edward Beauclerk Maurice, whose father had lived among the Inuit as an apprentice fur trader for the Hudson Bay Company, and whose memoirs his family had privately published for his eightieth birthday. She sent me a copy of this treasured family edition, I agreed on its literary merit, loved meeting the self-effacing author and his memoir was published in 2004 by Fourth Estate as *The Last of the Gentleman Adventurers*. It's an exceptional and moving story, now made available to a much wider audience, and to the delight of his family it drew excellent reviews. He signed the contract and saw the cover design, but died before it was published, so sadly in this case there can be no follow up volume.'

This chapter began with a quote from Meg Rosoff. Here is a final one. 'All generalisations about writing probably turn out not to be true'. This may, or may not, apply to this chapter.

8

Checklist: The other component parts of the book you need to manage

1 How much of the process do you want to manage?

By now you should have gained a reasonable amount of information on the process of publishing and the amount of work involved. Start thinking now about whether this intrigues you, and if so how you might like to project manage the various stages, or if finding out what is involved has inclined you to instruct an external organisation to handle this for you (more detail in chapter 15).

2 Book blurb and author information

These are the most basic items needed for the marketing of the title you are considering, and will be needed at an early stage. See chapter 19 on how to draft effectively.

3 Start building a platform for marketing

Think about developing a website, a blog, and a profile in social marketing. If you anticipate trying to sell your work, these will be essential for getting your project better known. See chapters 18–20.

4 Format

Start thinking seriously about which format you intend to disseminate your work through. See chapters 12, 14, 16.

5 An ISBN and bar code

An International Standard Book Number (ISBN) is essential if you plan to sell through retail outlets. If you are working with an author solutions company (see chapter 15), they will secure it for you, if not easily obtainable. See page 39.

6 A copyright notice

'What formalities have to be complied with in order to acquire copyright protection? There are no formalities in the UK or in any country which is a member of the Berne Copyright Union. This Union now includes almost all the principal countries of the world.

Although copyright is automatically acquired immediately a work is written (or recorded in some other form, e.g. on tape or disk) you may wish to establish evidence of the date of the completion of a work.'[76]

You could do this by placing a copy with your bank or solicitor and obtaining a dated receipt or posting a copy to yourself, in a sealed envelope and (if you keep it sealed) the postmark establishes the date it was sent. You can also add a copyright notice to your manuscript.

'The copyright notice comes in the form © followed by the name of the copyright owner and the year of first publication.

This is the copyright notice prescribed by the Universal Copyright Convention (UCC), to which US, UK and 60 other countries belong. Its inclusion in a book is one of the prerequisites for ensuring the work is protected by copyright in UCC countries (although as almost all countries are also now signatories of Berne, which has no such requirement, the point is increasingly academic). A copyright line in a book is, however, useful as good practice and for the bibliographical information it conveys.'[77]

Add copyright information on an early left-hand page. List the book's ISBN and then add your name and an assertion of your property. NB: writing this feels good.

Copyright © Alison Baverstock. All rights reserved; no part of this publication may be reproduced, stored in a retrieval system, or transmitted by any means, electronic, mechanical, photocopying or otherwise, without the prior written permission of the publisher.

---

[76] The Society of Authors, *Quick Guide to Copyright and Moral Rights* – a very useful publication which also covers copyright periods and moral rights. Free to members, £2 to non-members, see www.societyofauthors.org

[77] Ibid

7 A price

Now is the time to think about whether you plan to charge for the publication, and if so to research how much people are likely to pay. See chapter 17 for advice.

8 Forewords, afterwards and endorsements

An effective foreword/afterword/endorsement from a significant or credible person can make a huge difference to a title and how it is perceived. And there is no reason for self-published authors to be unambitious – a recent self-published title for children who had a parent going away, largely aimed at the Services community, drew a foreword from HRH The Prince of Wales.[78]

Such an endorsement does not need to come from someone famous, just someone plausible – and whose professional or personal role adds weight to the project. So a librarian or teacher would make a good choice for a children's title.

Asking other people for endorsements, or a foreword, is not as tricky as it may at first seem. Of course it is awkward making that initial contact, but think how flattered you would be if someone wanted *your* name on the front of *their* book? You are the suppliant but you are offering the person you approach further marketing and the chance to associate themselves with a product or an idea of which they may approve, without huge corresponding effort on their part. A word of warning. If you are asking others to endorse you, it's important to allow them the option to say 'no' as well as 'yes'; and so accept a refusal with good grace (rather than trying to change their mind, which will really annoy).

Along similar lines, in this litigious age it is becoming increasingly common to add a disclaimer to the front of your book, saying what follows is a product of your imagination and is not connected to any person, alive or dead. Take care. If despite this caveat others can recognise your inspiration, and the individual so implicated objects, the disclaimer may not be enough.

---

[78] Christopher MacGregor, *My Daddy Is Going Away – But That's OK!* Brighton: Giddy Mangoes Ltd (2009)

9 List of characters and locations

Many writers draft one of these, and in addition to proving useful to you, a copy may be beneficial to the reader, particularly in a saga type book which has a cast of thousands.

10 Glossary of terms

This can be useful if your title is set in a time whose vocabulary may not be instantly familiar to all. Robert Harris' historical novels all include a list of terms. It helps the reader feel they are both taking part and learning at the same time.

11 Dedications, acknowledgments and listing everyone involved

Crafting literary epitaphs for specific writing projects is a displacement activity for many writers; it's pleasant to ponder the dedication of a labour of much love to someone special.

This is a difficult thing to get right. It is strange how often an author's note can create an ambiance between potential reader and book that is either an inducement to purchase, or a direct turn-off. An author's note telling me more than I want to know about their emotional hinterland can definitely deter. Here are some guidelines:

* **Avoid gush**. It has become commonplace to have a page or two of thank-yous, but perhaps it is best to avoid the inclusion here of highly personal love notes. If you are still inclined to do this, put it at the end of the book, where no prospective buyer is probably going to look – for fear of reading the ending first.

* **Thank those whose involvement authenticates your work** – and shows you have done your homework. Thus in Lionel Shriver's latest book, *So Much for That*,[79] those suffering from and specialising in the particular conditions she features are thanked for their long patience with her questions. Such care can make the prospective reader feel they will spend their time with you wisely and may emerge informed as well as entertained.

[79] London: HarperCollins (2010)

- **If you need to thank a lot of people, keep track of their names as you go along,** put them in alphabetical order and ensure their names are spelt correctly – the misspelling of your own name grates, particularly if you have given effort but not been paid.

- **Offering a general thank you.** The alternative is to offer a sweeping mention within a 'thank-you-to-everyone-and-as-there-are-so-many-to-mention-I-cannot-name-you-all-but-you-all-know-who-you-are'. This takes care of the problem, but risks annoying the unmentioned, particularly if involvement has required time and effort (but no payment).

- **Be enigmatic.** It can be elegant to see a single name mentioned as a dedication, particularly if it is not the one you expected to see.

- **Thank those who shared the journey;** very seldom is a book all the writer's own work. It's a good plan to include all involved; copy-editor, designer, proofreader etc.

GETTING FEEDBACK

9

How do you know if it's any good?

with Gale Winskill[80]

'Fiction relies on a baffling alchemy. At some point in the narrative, and with the best of books from the very beginning, a story the author cheerfully, even formally, concedes is invented seems actually to have happened. Through the aegis of our eagerness to be fooled, confabulated characters walk about in our heads with the authority of our own friends and relations. It's a wonderful and mysterious process, one I don't pretend to understand. But sometimes it doesn't work.

So this novel fails to trigger that old cliche, "the willing suspension of disbelief". The volume simply sits there: paper, ink and sentence constructions. But look on the bright side. Consider how astonishing it is that so many other novels – even, sometimes, rather mediocre ones – seem actually to have happened.'[81]

If we accept the premise that all writing is worth doing, because it helps rational thought, preserves ideas and improves through practice, it is not necessarily always worth sharing. If the sharing is to be done at your own expense, it is helpful to isolate criteria by which a decision to make available more broadly can be made. This requires both courage and objectivity. Courage will have to be found within you; once you have accepted that objectivity is needed, it can be purchased or purloined.

In a traditional publishing scenario the decision on whether there is sufficient quality or interest in the writing is left to the publisher, and the material agreed upon is then copy-edited to ensure the text is error-free. But now that the individual's potential for storing

---

[80] www.winskilleditorial.co.uk

[81] The opening and closing paragraphs of a book review by Lionel Shriver in the *Financil Times*, 26/27 February 2011

and circulating material is no longer publisher-dependent, just as the reader's time is under pressure from a dazzling array of other distractions, an ability to identify material worth reading is important to all parties. While epublishing and cheaper print have democratised access to publishing media, they have also conferred a mighty responsibility on the author to perfect their work before wider dissemination. The self-publishing author must take full responsibility for ensuring that the content presented to their public is as good as it can possibly be.

Do you need feedback on your work before progressing further?

Authors want to self-publish for a variety of reasons. Their interest may be personal – they may have written a book as a hobby, for a niche market, on a very local or specific topic that will have limited sales potential, and which is more a labour of love than an attempt to earn money. Or they may have written a book, tried submitting it to the established publishing houses, but met rejection along the way, so are now thinking that they will manage publication themselves. A third option is that they have not tried to reach a market through conventional agencies, deciding instead to use online and digital publishing to spread their work.

The reasoning behind an author's decision to self-publish, their understanding of the processes of publishing, and the scope of their ultimate ambitions, undoubtedly influence whether or not they perceive a need for feedback before they proceed, and how they go about obtaining it.

How can an author find out if their work is worth sharing; how can they be truly objective?

> 'I want my work to be good. Reluctantly I have learned that, as the writer, I'm subjective.'
>
> Mac Logan, unpublished author[82]

---

[82] M. Logan, *Angel's Share* (unpublished: a crime thriller. Currently being considered by various publishers and agents)

Authors often have a blind spot towards their own work, tending to be either overly self-critical or unrealistic about its shortcomings; unaware that it is either derivative or not particularly well written.

> '...data from social psychology studies suggest that many of us are deluded and not nearly self-critical enough. For instance, we overemphasise other people's responsibility for their behaviour, ignoring the extenuating power of circumstances. But when it comes to explaining our own actions we tend to take too much personal credit for our successes and blame external factors for our failures. Most of us believe that we have above-average abilities (a statistical impossibility). It seems that the majority of people suffer from at least some form of self-serving bias.'[83]

Having invested so much of yourself, and stuck to the forced isolation of writing, it is very difficult to review your own work dispassionately. An author might know that their researched facts are correct. They might sense that the basic premise of their plot is quite original. But have they managed to translate their original intention on to paper or on to the screen? Is their writing strong enough to get their message across to their chosen audience? Ideally, a book should convey a story or a thesis that makes a connection with the reader. But does it actually do that? And how does the author know? Ultimately, they seldom do, and it is often only a reader who can give them the answers to these questions.

First-time authors frequently cannot answer these questions in any definitive manner; not because they do not know for whom they wrote their book, but because they are unaware of the categories and formats used by the publishing industry, so do not understand that, *even for self-published work*, there are certain criteria against which their text will be compared and evaluated by readers and reviewers. They may also be unclear about where their work sits within the literary canon. Many first-time authors feel their work is original and literary, whereas someone with more experience of writing might help them be clearer about the status of what they have created; so perhaps popular novel rather than great literary opus.

---

[83] 'Should we listen to our inner critic?' *The shrink and the sage, a guide to modern dilemmas*, Antonia Macaro and Julian Baggini, *FT Magazine*, 12/13 February 2011

Others may take the reaction of one well-meaning supporter to indicate wider likely acceptability. Rebecca Swift runs The Literary Consultancy,[84] which offers guidance and support to writers on how to make their work more effective. She recalled a conversation with a writer who phoned the publishing house she worked for before establishing her business. The caller was frustrated by being repeatedly turned down, but when pressed for comment, on how she knew her work was publishable, revealed that her sister had read the book and loved it.

There is also the issue of the language and presentation. Projects that have been destined for self-publishing from the beginning can become over-reliant on associated technology (spell checkers and programs for analysing the complexity and readability of language), and would often benefit from the more objective involvement of an editor who is reading for sense rather than technical correctness.

What is objective feedback?

In its basic form objective feedback often boils down to, did the reader like it, yes or no? Followed by why or why not? Objective feedback should focus on elements that the author may not have considered, as they have concentrated most of their attention on the basic structure or story. All readers have personal preferences for the work of particular writers, and individual responses are based on just such reactions, such as whether they prefer style to story; literary device to pace or plot. However, the response of an objective reader should move beyond personal preferences, and articulate what works and what doesn't.

Objective feedback should concentrate on the nuts and bolts of the book and should consider the following elements:

* What genre does the book fall into? For example, is it science fiction, children's fantasy, romantic fiction, biography or political science?

* Who is the intended audience: academics, young adults, women, historians?

---

[84] www.the literaryconsultancy.org

- Is the author's style appropriate for their chosen content or their specific readership? For instance, tabloid sensationalism will work well for a book on football, but not for a serious biography of a historical figure. Likewise, if a children's novel is written in language more suited to an academic thesis then the reader is not going to be easily engaged.

- Does the narrative carry the reader and make them want to reach the end, to find out what happens, or are they bored half-way through? And if so, at what point do they disengage and why?

- Are the characters rounded, credible individuals? Or are they two-dimensional stereotypes?

- Does the beginning of the book grab the reader's attention or is it overly descriptive and inclined to waffle? Does the plot make sense? Even within the confines of fantasy, is it plausible? And is the ending a disappointing, unsatisfactory anticlimax or a satisfying denouement, and does this match the overall style of the book (or is something more dramatic needed)?

While the above list gives an indication of the type of issues to be considered when giving an impartial opinion, objective feedback must be supported by the general ability to disengage from personal feelings about the subject matter or plot and provide a structured and analytical breakdown of what works within the title's narrative or structure and what does not. Such distance and compartmentalising permits a dispassionate explanation of why elements are not effective in the set context, and the suggestion of possible alternatives to remedy the problem. Examples might include: why the novel does not work when narrated from a particular perspective (and perhaps an understanding that an effective first-person narrative is extremely difficult to achieve); that removal of the first four chapters would improve the novel's narrative flow, or that a particularly clichéd or over-used phrase grates and detracts from the enjoyment of the plot. This objectivity should then be combined with the courage and tact to suggest to an author that their work would benefit from altering the perspective of the narrative, perhaps by using the third-person to relay the majority of their plot, or removing large tracts of existing text, all while tactfully explaining what the material would hopefully gain from these seemingly drastic courses of action.

The objective reviewer is also often well placed to look for something the author cannot identify; an underlying uncertainty about the text they have created of which they are aware but cannot pinpoint. They want to have these aspects confirmed by someone who can articulate the problems for them in an unemotional and clear manner, and then make constructive suggestions as to how they might remedy them. The author does not have to agree with the editor's point of view, but a critique may just confirm any doubts the writer already has, and then offer a solution that had perhaps not been considered. What the writer does with this is then up to them:

> 'I had my manuscript – a highly personal history of my relationship with my father – reviewed by a professional editor. It had cost me a huge amount of emotional energy to complete the project – which had been in my head for over 20 years – and while I felt sated to have got it out of my system, I knew it had faults. The editor identified them, and while I admired her clarity of thought, I felt entirely unable to reengage with the material and sort it out. And so it remains in the photocopied and spiral-bound format which she reviewed – and for now it can survive as that.'   Author

Where can you obtain objective feedback?

A DIY approach can be tempting if you have previous experience of editing the work of others, and doubly so as a cost-saving measure. But the work needs to be assessed as a whole, and this is difficult for the writer who is still immersed in its creation:

> '(the inner critic) works best, however, when it is as impersonal and error-free as possible. The more people identify a belief as their own, the less willing they are to consider objectively any evidence that contradicts it. It no longer becomes a simple question of whether something is true or false, it becomes about your willingness to give up something of which you feel ownership.'[85]

[85] 'Should we listen to our inner critic?' *The shrink and the sage, a guide to modern dilemmas*, Antonia Macaro and Julian Baggini, *FT Magazine*, 12/13 February 2011

A writer often knows what is supposed to be there, but can no longer evaluate whether the relevant information is there, as so much of the story is carried in their head and known intuitively. Even if they achieve some perspective, there are still pitfalls, as R.D. Simek[86] (unpublished) notes:

'Unfortunately, the reader (including yourself once you've acquired some distance) might wonder why, in the midst of a fast-paced novel, two marginal characters come together for a lengthy discussion of a topic, which – while interesting per se – is largely unrelated to the essence of your plot. In your heart, you know that ... but you spent three weeks researching it and a week writing those fifteen pages. Pressing the delete button by yourself? That's not going to happen.

We use completely different parts of our brain when we write and when we edit. Is it any wonder then that switching between the two – or attempting to do both simultaneously – will cause our writing to stall? It's a bit like trying to drive whilst constantly flitting between the brake and the accelerator.'[87]

G.K. Chesterton advised writers to 'murder their babies'; to delete the clusters of words within a piece of prose which give them particular pleasure, as marking out a zone of particularly fine writing. Mostly, he suggested, they just interrupt the flow.

Family and friends are not well placed to offer an impartial opinion as the feedback they give is unlikely to be objective; their most usual inclination is to support and encourage and they generally have too much invested in their personal relationship with the author to be completely objective. More usually they also lack experience. Rachel Vevers,[88] another unpublished author, writes:

---

[86] R.D. Simek, *Tarot*, (unpublished: a historical mystery novel. Currently being considered by various publishers and agents)

[87] Siobhan Curham, Self-publishing workshop, *Writer's Forum*, issue 102, April 2010

[88] R. Vevers, *Guardian of the Pegasus* (unpublished:children's fiction. Currently being revised after favourable feedback from a leading children's agent)

'You don't ask a florist to do a root canal filling, or a child-minder to build an extension, but that's effectively what we're doing when we ask family and friends to critique our writing. Praise is nice but it doesn't achieve anything, and criticism probably marks the end of a beautiful friendship!'

Those who have involved family and friends in the appraisal of their work find frustration in the blandness of feedback – 'It's very good' or 'I enjoyed it' tell you little. Even more difficult is the non-response, leaving the writer to wonder whether it was considered so poor that their reader could not bring themselves to return comment, or if their work mattered so little that they have not yet got around to reading it. Both reactions are dispiriting.

If you sense that a close friend or relative does have an objective eye, and might be a source of constructive feedback, it might be a good idea to incentivise the arrangement. Writer Mary Lawson had published many short stories, but was working on a novel. She eventually showed it to her sister, who made sensible suggestions for its improvement. When she asked if she would look at it again, her sister made a jokey suggestion that this was fine, but it would cost her 10% of the profits. To her sister's great surprise, Mary took the suggestion seriously. The book went on to become *Crow Lake*, an international bestseller published by Random House, and both parties have benefitted. Lawson's sister has continued to act as 'first critic' on her subsequent books, and continues to get her 10%.

On a smaller scale, offering to buy dinner for someone who has put in considerable effort to reading and commenting on your work may be appreciated, or offering to fund a weekend away for you to discuss the work together. All such arrangements indicate that the time of both parties has a value.

Feedback from a writing group If you are a member of a writing group, you could consider asking someone you trust for an honest opinion. However, there remains a risk that the chosen person will not be entirely candid as they know the author socially, and there is also the potential for jealousy if the author's work seems better than their own.

An English teacher known to you might seem another good solution, but be sure that the feedback will be given in an appropriate manner; writing offered for an objective opinion but awarded feedback in the style of school coursework, may further depress:

> 'I am dyslexic and well aware that my writing often contains mistakes. I had however found a publisher who was keen on the stories I had to tell, and wanted to make them available. Rather than make a bad impression on him, I decided to have my work tidied up before submission, and I approached an acquaintance who is an English teacher. What I was not expecting was the very high level of feedback received; the invasive nature of the accompanying comments, which drew attention to the basic level of some of my sentence construction and a few associated grammatical mistakes. It was frankly humiliating, and it took me some time to recover.
>
> The book was a success. But the experience did make me hesitate before starting work again. Thankfully this time I have been put in touch with an editor with experience of publishing (as opposed to marking) and work is now progressing much better.'

Feedback from a self-publishing firm is another possible option, but remember that they make their money from production, and hence may be more inclined to focus on turning a manuscript into a book rather than the content, which they may expect the author to have sorted out already. If editorial advice is included within a self-publishing package, a writer should always ask about the details: how much, and within what kind of time frame? They should also assess how effectively that editorial assistance has been carried out by asking to see copies of previous books produced by the organisation. If you are short of time, a glance at the back cover blurb (legible, correct, attractive?) is often an indicator of the editorial standard contained within.

Feedback from agencies offering advice on manuscripts. This is a growth market. Look in the back pages of any writing magazine or programme from a writing conference, and you will find many such agencies, often run by former publishers (usually editors) or authors. These services may offer useful advice, particularly on plot and characterisation. Given that they are being paid to engage fully with the work, such agencies can also be a source of both prompt and concentrated attention; always a problem if you are trying to persuade friends and relations to read your material. They may also point the way to further manuscript intervention e.g. copy-editing and proofreading, and have relevant contacts for you to pursue.

Before proceeding however, ask what kind of experience the reader allocated to review your work will bring to the task. Look to see how long they have been in business, and how many testimonials they display on their website. It's a good recommendation if both published and unpublished writers rely on their judgement.

Using a friend in publishing. Possible, but many editors will not edit for friends, family or people they know in a professional capacity, because they will be objective, rather than unprofessional, and do not want to ruin an otherwise good relationship. However, if an author is related to someone who works in the publishing industry, and that person can recommend a third party to them, then it may be worth developing the connection.

Asking publishers to read manuscripts in their spare time is an intrusion. Most authors imagine they are the first to ask, and that offering the chance to read an unpublished manuscript will be a pleasure. Both viewpoints are generally deluded:

'I work in publishing and a friend from my daughter's school asked me to look at some material she had written for a proposed children's title. It was charming but I suspected not a commercial proposition. I spent a good deal of time on it, wrote her a full response and delivered it back – and then heard nothing more for a few weeks, until I had a self-flagellatory letter from her which concentrated entirely on my negative points rather than my positives.

I suspect my evaluation of the material on a commercial basis had done little for her confidence, and I felt frustrated to have expended my professional expertise to so little avail, while in the process clearly delivering damage to a friendship. Moral: say no in future, and if there is no option but to give feedback, discuss person to person, concentrating on the positives first. Print is a little too cold.'

Publisher

Commissioning a freelance editor to give you an opinion. Most freelance editors have no specific affiliation with any organisation. This gives them flexibility and the ability to be more honest in their response to an author's work, as they are not bound by a particular publisher ethos or series portfolio. While judging a writer's book as if the author were submitting to a publishing house, and scrutinising it from that industry perspective, a freelance editor will not be bound to make the material conform to a set format.

Most editors also offer you a broad experience, having been involved in different stages of book production – commissioning, manuscript assessment, consideration of the language and structural aspects of a book, self-publishing and marketing – and so can provide the author with a rounded view of their work. So, in addition to commenting on the style and structure, they can assist with information on who would be likely to appreciate it, what kind of cover would augment its appeal, and how it could be best described in one sentence.

There are however associated financial difficulties in their position. Freelance editors are being paid for a service whose wider promotion depends largely on personal recommendation, so it is in their own commercial interest to do a good job. But while their role requires that they are not emotionally involved in an author's work, and they do not stand to gain financially from its publication, they are paid by the person whose work they are criticising. This can set up an awkward negotiating position, particularly if the person who has been edited does not consider that the work has been well done; that the suggested amendments either too numerous or not needed at all. Writers often assume that their meaning will shine through and the ultimate reader will be tolerant of a few errors; editors are much more aware of the pitfalls of presenting less than perfect material.

Searching for an editor

Having decided to work with an editor, the author is then faced with how to find one and what to look for. There are various websites that offer editing services, although many of these have specific subject biases, often academic or writing for children.

Membership of industry organisations, such as the Society for Editors and Proofreaders (SfEP)[89] in the UK, or other recognised bodies, is a good starting point. All society members will be bound to adhere to the associated code of practice, so there is a measurable standard for membership, and clients have an avenue of complaint, should an editor fail to live up to their part of the bargain or behave unprofessionally. Prospective clients can usually search their membership list according to different criteria, such as experience and location (although bear in mind that whereas meeting to discuss your text may sound appealing, objective feedback can be easiest to absorb when there is no eye contact).

How should an author approach a potential editor of their work?

'An editor doesn't want to kill your book, or make your book their own. They aren't stealing it or ripping it to shreds. The editor is just trying to find the book inside the manuscript you've sent.'

Lari Don, prize-winning author[90]

- Understand that you are approaching an expert who has doubtless seen before similar issues to those raised by your material.

- Familiarise yourself with what different freelances do and be aware of their particular specialisations and skills.

- Then consider what you are looking for. Do you want a critique, a complete copy-edit, or just basic proofreading to tidy up your text? If you are unsure, asking a professional for a quotation not only allows you to estimate the cost, it enables you to see the range of services you might need, and thus gain an appreciation of the stages involved.

- Think about your budget and what you can realistically expect for the money you have available; based on an understanding that getting a manuscript into shape takes time.

[89] www.SfEP.org.uk
[90] L. Don, *First Aid for Fairies and Other Fabled Beasts*, Edinburgh: Floris Books, 2008 (winner of 2009 Royal Mail awards; shortlisted for Kelpies Prize 2007) and other titles for Floris

• What is your deadline for return of the material? An effective editor is unlikely to be available immediately.

Many editors will ask to see a sample of the author's writing before agreeing to the work. While this may alarm, it is standard practice and holds no copyright issues for the author's work (it remains their property). Why do they want to see it? To see how much work is involved on the text and therefore give a quotation based on fact and not on guesswork. As with any other business, a potential client should familiarise themselves with the editor's terms and conditions before instructing, especially their payment terms.

Authors should keep the formatting of their manuscript simple. There is no point sending it to an editor full of complicated layout conceits (variable margin widths, a variety of typefaces and font sizes), as the editor may well spend a chunk of the author's allotted time, and therefore their budget, trying to make the text legible before they can begin work.

Finally, and most importantly of all, if an author is seeking editorial input then they should be ready to receive constructive criticism. An author who makes it apparent early on that they have a set idea about their book and are not going to be amenable to any opinion to the contrary is unlikely to benefit from editorial involvement. As the author Alastair McIver points out: '... where disagreements are accompanied by an open-minded attitude on both sides, and a genuine determination to reach amicable solutions, the result is a true collaborative process which can't go far wrong.'[91] The opposite scenario is a disaster on all fronts.

From the editor's perspective, it is also important to point out to an author that a professional opinion on a manuscript, and its subsequent adaptation according to recommendations received, offers no guarantee of commercial success, particularly important if the reason for self-publishing is the hope of attracting the attention of a professional publisher. Publishers and agents are professional wordsmiths, so while it is true that one of their first considerations is often the general standard of text submitted (grammar, spelling or syntax), they are always going to be governed by their current portfolio, list of agreed acquisitions or market trends. Irrespective

[91] *Glasgow Fairytale*, Edinburgh: Black & White Publishing (2010)

of how well-written or well-edited an author's manuscript may be, if it does not fit a particular publisher's list, unless the author is a particularly saleable proposition in their own right, the proposal may be taken no further.

Just how critical should feedback be?

Wider involvement in both assessing material as worth publishing, and then editing to a publishable standard, results in an augmented product. That's the theory, and when it works it is wonderful. Prize-winning author Annemarie Allan[92] writes: 'A thoughtful, creative editor can help a writer achieve levels of excellence that they would struggle to arrive at on their own.'

But insensitive feedback can kill writing – and there are editors who can overlook and disregard the role of the author as the creator of the book, forgetting that without that particular individual there would be no 'product', thus imbuing the whole production process with an inherent lack of respect for the creator.

However you like to receive feedback, it is important that you have confidence in the person you decide to instruct.

How do you know when your manuscript is finished?

You don't have to write in order of final presentation; books can be written in the strangest sequences. Some start with a particular scene and work backwards or forwards from that point, others progress in a frenzy and then must be returned to for shading in once the basic plot has been established.

When working with a conventional publishing house there is either a deadline, a commercial reason for getting something out by a particular date, or someone to tell you whether what you have submitted meets their criteria for publication.

The self-publishing author will need other measures. Some

[92] A. Allan, *Hox*, Edinburgh: Floris Books, 2007 (winner of Kelpies Prize 2007; shortlisted for 2008 Royal Mail Awards) and other titles for Floris

authors have talked of a 'book shaped' hole in their head; others of the role of the unconscious – that they know they have finished when they stop dreaming about it or when they experience a sudden onset of lethargy at the end of a project, and reengaging feels impossible. However complete it feels, do nothing straightaway. Put the manuscript to one side for a while and return later; engage your objective eye to ensure it is as good as it can be – and restart this chapter to focus your brain before you begin.

Whatever process you use, try to make the systematic capturing and storage of your text part of your daily routine. The anguish of lost text, or just lost to you (filed in the wrong place, under a label you can't recall), is hard to live with. I heard crime-writer Adam Baron recently describe the loss of a nearly complete manuscript through the thoroughness of a burglar who took both his laptop and the jam jar of backup drives sitting nearby.

Adam justified the experience by making a romantic link to Hemingway, to whom something similar happened. Hemingway's first wife, travelling by train to meet him in Paris, decided to take the entire collection of his early manuscripts. She left them in a suitcase, under her seat, and went out onto the platform. While she was gone, someone took the suitcase and left – and the material was never seen again.

An inspiring and elegant link – and perhaps in retrospect it really was, as Baron now claims, 'horribly refreshing' to be left with a totally blank slate. But the associated agony is best avoided. Back up, double up, and occasionally email the entire manuscript to yourself.

10

Editorial support and why it is needed

with Margaret Aherne

The previous chapter considered feedback on the manuscript as a whole, this one considers the creation of a consistent text, ready for publication.

My favourite dictionary[93] begins its definition of the verb to edit with publishing-related meanings: 'to prepare (a writer's work or works) for publication; to correct or improve (a piece of text etc) ready for publication; to reword; to supervise the publication of...' and finishes with the term 'edit out', meaning to remove during editing.

Editorial work is best thought of in this clinical, methodical vocabulary; working through a manuscript (whether printed or digital) and in the process turning it from the text that was *finalised by the author* into text of a *publishable standard*, and through which the writer's purpose, voice and narrative are made clear. The two are very seldom the same thing.

Having your manuscript edited effectively is the most important part of getting a self-published book ready for publication. If it's worth the effort of wider dissemination, in whatever format you choose, it's worth getting it right first. Neglect this basic component of a good manuscript, and your readers may not make it past the first paragraph, let alone the first page.

The problem for editors is that their role is most visible when missing. The silent nature of their role has also made their position within the politics of publishing difficult. Publishing companies

---

[93] London: Chambers: Hodder Education Group

used to be run by those from an editorial background, and the determination to produce books worthy of the imprint's reputation was one of the few given quality measures in a industry that prided itself on correctness. Today most companies are run by people from a marketing background, and editorial standards have become a negotiable cost rather than an absolute standard. Few companies now manage the editorial function in house, most rely on freelance editors working at home, but given that publishers are no longer training editors themselves, the supply of qualified labour is threatened. Other houses rely on editorial support secured long-distance; perhaps through staff working in a second language (hence the need for copy-editing and proofreading marks that are based on signs rather than language). The Society of Authors in the UK has complained vociferously of late about a decline in editorial standards, and encouraged publishers to do better. This presents both a challenge and an opportunity to the self-publishing author – do it better than the conventional industry!

Understanding the editorial frame of mind and specific roles

What kind of people become editors? One editor I asked laughed and immediately said 'dysfunctional'. Editors typically are meticulous, specific, careful and discreet. Within the publishing industry, the function is divided into several roles, and given that the self-publishing author will need to replicate these functions, it is helpful to look at them in a little more detail.

Commissioning editors decide what they want to publish, dream up ideas for products, their associated lists, recruit authors and work with them on the content they will deliver. **Structural editors** look at the overall sense of the manuscript delivered and have experience in reshaping it to make it work (this was covered in the last chapter). **Copy-editors** turn the manuscript that is delivered into seamless prose, allowing the meaning to shine through (this chapter). **Proofreaders** check that the typeset words match the amended text and pick up any infelicities of language or textual ambiguities that have crept through thus far undetected (the next chapter).

These processes will need to proceed in various stages; they cannot all be done at the same time. So paying for an effective copy-edit does not mean that proofreading will not be needed. Don't underestimate the sheer physical effort of sitting at a desk in prolonged concentration on a manuscript. An effective and experience copy-editor will multi-task when engaging with your writing, looking out for many more things at the same time than you might imagine possible.

Case study: What does this mean in practice?

Jane Birdsell,[94] freelance copy-editor, comments:

'I don't try and make an author's text conform to old-fashioned, rigid grammatical rules: I try and help them speak clearly in their own voice. I try and put myself in the shoes of a reader of the book, and to be ultra-sensitive to anything that they might stumble over. One way of thinking about self-publishing is that it's meant to get rid of any inconsistency, inaccuracy and confusion in the text that might make a reader mistrust the author. Even tiny things that most readers wouldn't notice consciously will tend to undermine the reader's trust in and enjoyment of the text.

As I copy-edit I'm checking everything's spelled correctly and makes grammatical sense (even if informally); I'm imposing a typographical house style (e.g. spaced en-rules for dashes; spelling out numbers up to 100; s/z-spelling; single quotes, double within single); I'm alert to any assertions or facts that don't ring true, and will check them; I'll make cuts or rephrase to avoid repetition; I'll query anything that isn't clear (is Mrs E. Smith on p. 332 the same person as Mrs F. Smyth on p. 24?); and I'll check that the structure of the book – the chapter divisions and hierarchy of sub-heads – works. (There are probably a dozen other things: it's rather like driving a car – when you've been doing it for decades, it's hard to explain exactly what's involved!)

I always want to know what audience the book is aimed at: the general reader will need more jargon explained than a specialist would; if the book's going to be sold in America, British references may need some subtle glossing so they work for both markets.

[94] www.janebirdsell.co.uk

> I charge by the hour, and work as efficiently as possible. Rates are around £20–25 per hour, with onscreen editing and structural editing being at the top end. If you're confident with Word's Track Changes, onscreen editing will probably be more cost-effective (I'm assuming the self-published author will be the typesetter as well as the publisher!). Even if I'm working on paper, I need to have the digital file in order to do searches efficiently (in the olden days copy-editors would keep endless lists of the instances of a particular name in a text, for example, which thankfully is no longer necessary).'

How to help yourself – and reduce the work required

1 **Become an objective reader**. For all kinds of text, from letters asking you for a donation to published information you read for work or pleasure. Think about the order in which information is presented, the way in which an argument is built up and then delivered, the point at which the climax in a chapter is reached. Think about how the process might have been better managed.

2 **Develop the careful brain** that spots errors on menus and signs; looking beyond face value to ensure that information is truly imparted.

3 **Develop an editorial policy for your own work**. As you progress, make a list of your editorial decisions: word-breaks; spellings of particular terms; how and when you will use capital letters. Keep this to hand and try to be consistent. If you want to adopt a ready-made and respected list of editorial decisions, get yourself copy of *The Oxford Dictionary for Writers and Editors*.[95] For fiction, make a list of key characters, traits, dates and timelines so you can quickly refer to them while writing and not offer a character with blue eyes in chapter one, whose pupils have changed to brown by chapter three. One of the functions of the copy-editor is to look for consistency as well as correctness.

[95] Oxford: OUP (2005)

How to find an editor to work on your material

You may already be in discussion with a self-publishing firm and they may offer editorial services as part of the range of options with which they manage the process of publishing. You are not duty-bound to adopt their in-house option, so before committing yourself, ask to see samples of the kind of product worked on in the past. Ask about specific preferences of different members of their team, and use your critical eye (see points 1–3 above) to assess how the work has been done. The suggestions in the previous chapter for locating editorial feedback offer other suggestions. One final thought, publishing courses at local universities will almost inevitably include a module on editorial title management. They may have recent graduates willing to edit at a competitive rate.

What you need to know about editors, before commissioning them to work for you

For the author planning self-publication, involving an editor usually means taking someone on with no prior experience of what they do. Most of us could commission a decorator or gardener, and while seeking their service because unable or unwilling to do it ourselves, have a rough idea of what is involved. If you are seeking editorial help, this is trickier. The following questions will be useful.

1 Are they trained?
Training courses are available, many run by editors. In the UK the main providers are SfEP,[96] PTC,[97] Editorial Training[98] and Editcetera.[99]

Finding out the date of their training will perhaps let you know how long they have been working for as a copy-editor (although they may have been working for years and then decided to have a

[96] SfEp.org.uk
[97] www.train4publishing.co.uk
[98] www.edittrain.co.uk
[99] www.editcetera.com

brush up). If they trained with a publishing house, as part of an in-house team, they are likely to have been well trained, but can you find out if they have voluntarily undertaken any training since? A freelance hairdresser told me recently that it's easy to get into bad habits and be distanced from new trends when you are working on your own. The same principle must surely apply to editors.

2 Are they experienced?

What kind of products have they worked on in the past? Do they have relevant specialist knowledge for the field you are working in? The more specific your subject area, the more you benefit from specialised knowledge.

3 How easy are they to communicate with?

Consider what you want the copy-editor to do for you – do you want them to help you let your voice as author come through or rewrite it so that it feels as if your vocabulary and syntax are more sophisticated than is normally the case?

When raising queries with authors or pointing out things that may need changing, the editor will need tact. Do you get the feeling that being edited by the person you are talking to will move you in the intended direction of travel, or make you feel less adequate? Do you feel intimidated or empowered by their attention? Would you feel able to put your point of view if you found you disagreed on a matter of principle?

There are no right answers here, just the need to be aware of your own feelings; in the same way that some authors like to fear their literary agent (because it spurs them on), others want a more supportive touch and a shoulder to cry on.

4 How available are they?

You need to know how busy they are. If they are available to work for you it may be your lucky day, but it may be for other reasons. When were they last employed? Are they punctual in managing manuscripts by the time agreed?

How long the process will take is more difficult to assess. It's hard to provide a precise estimate because the editor cannot say what the variables will be (e.g. the state of the manuscript, the services required) but a conscientious copy-editor will make an estimate subject to 'sight of *copy*' (their term for the text you provide). As an average, the Society of Proofreaders and Indexers suggest that proofreading may generally progress at the rate of about 10 pages per hour with about 300 words per page. As copy-editing is subject to so many more variables, it is bound to take longer – how much longer is impossible to say without sight of copy.

5 What do they charge?

There are recommended minimum hourly rates for various editorial services; both the SfEP and the National Union of Journalists[100] produce a freelance fees guide. These rates are not enforceable, although be wary if a copy-editor is charging substantially less than the going rate. An hourly rate will always be subject to sight of copy.

Many freelances prefer to negotiate a flat fee for an entire job, this helps both parties anticipate the size of the overall bill, but again this should never be agreed before sight of copy has been achieved. Agree too at what stage payment will be made and what are the freelance's terms of business; their payment periods is particular. If they are registered for VAT/sales tax it will be added to the rate quoted. To ask them to absorb it is unethical (you are asking them to lower their hourly rate).

6 Are they any good?

The best way of assessing this is to look at examples of their work, in finished form – so that you see the end product with their corrections made.

What to do if you feel it has not been well done

Ideally avoid this difficulty by reviewing a sample before all the work has been completed. Try to be specific about your dissatisfaction and ask yourself whether you were really clear about what you wanted done. Show it to a friend. If you are really dissatisfied, it helps if you found the copy-editor's details through third party representation such as a professional organisation.

[100] www.nuj.org.uk

First steps in copy-editing

It can be helpful to view the copy-editor as the first proper reader of your book, the first person who will critically absorb the material that you have produced and judge whether it is fit for your intended purpose. They will know how to present your raw material for typesetting; they will also be alert to any legal problems that you might be unaware of (such as libel and copyright issues).

The task of copy-editing can be broken down into many parts or sub-tasks. A good copy-editor will carry out these sub-tasks in a sequence, going through the material in several passes: they will not simply start to read at the first word and finish when they get to the end! Here is a typical breakdown of the copy-editing process, using the sample document shown (a chapter from a book on popular medicine, aimed at the intelligent lay reader rather than specialists); it has been edited on screen with the structural elements identified by 'codes' or 'tags' that the typesetter will convert into the format specified by the book's designer.

Accompanying the copy-edited pages is the copy-editor's query list to the author, demonstrating the typical items that a good copy-editor will attend to and on which the author should be consulted. By reading this through you will learn the level of attention required for an effective copy-edit.

1 Checking the structure: headings

Breaking the text into clearly signalled sections through the use of headings and subheadings is one of the most helpful strategies through which the copy-editor can assist the reader. It clarifies the flow of an argument or the structure of a complex text by making clear *what* belongs with *what* and when the subject has shifted.

In our example text, the copy-editor has identified the following structure, with the hierarchy of headings made clear:

* the opening chapter heading has the tag <ch>

* within the chapter, the various therapies take the first level of subheading, standardly identified as 'A headings', which the copy-editor has tagged <a>

- within the various therapies, the second-level 'B' subheadings explain what the therapy is and how it works – these headings are tagged <b>

- the final section, on resources for learning more, is broken down into two subsections, 'C' headings, tagged <c>

The copy-editor has looked carefully at the structure of this chapter and has made some suggestions for standardising the sequence and wording of headings so that they are uniform throughout the piece. This greatly helps the reader to follow the structure and to find a particular item quickly.

2 Checking the structure: display, quotations

Just as with the headings, the copy-editor has looked closely at the content of the chapter and has identified an inconsistency in the way the author has presented certain material: the list of conditions that each therapy can treat. As the reader might well be reading the chapter for just this purpose ('What will help my backache?'), an alphabetically ordered bullet list will make this material much easier to navigate. This suggestion has been made to the author on the query sheet.

3 Supplementary material: layout and consistency

In the example text, there is a further element to the material: the lists of books and articles and websites. It is astonishing how many aspects of consistency such lists require! It can take an enormous amount of time to standardise them: decisions must be made regarding the form of names (e.g. use of first name or initials), the ordering of name and date, the use of capitals in titles, the form that journal volume and page numbers will take, the ordering and positioning of book publication details, right down to whether or not there is a full stop at the end of each entry. Good copy-editors thrive on such work but authors often find it tedious, sometimes downright daunting – this is why copy-editors exist!

4 Reading the text: stylistic consistency and appropriate content

To make life easier and to help the job go more smoothly, the copy-editor would prefer to work with a client's house style guide. Everyone who produces documents should have their own house style guide, to ensure that anything published by them will be written and edited consistently and in accordance with their own preferences. Ideally, the copy-editor will then add their own list of decisions that they have made on anything not listed in the guide, items that they will have standardised as they worked on the text. When you publish your work yourself, give the matter of style some thought beforehand so that you can make a start on drawing up a style guide of your own.[101]

What do style guides cover? In a nutshell, everything for which there's a choice, for example:

* spelling (e.g. -ise /-ize; ae- /e-; 'artefact' or 'artifact')

* use of italics and bold (for emphasis, non-English words)

* capitalisation (e.g. 'table 2' or 'Table 2')

* hyphenation (e.g. 'semi-colon' or 'semicolon'; 'post-war' or 'postwar')

* abbreviations and contractions, including use of full stops (e.g. 'ie' or 'i.e.', 'USA' or 'U.S.A.', 'Dr' or 'Dr.')

* numbers and dates (e.g. '24 January', '24th January' or 'January 24th'; words or figures for numbers over nine)

* punctuation (e.g. single or double quote marks; serial comma in 'dogs, cats, and horses'?)

* format of lists (numbered in arabic, numbered in roman, bulleted?)

* format of references

It is enormously helpful at the proofreading stage if a copy of both your style guide and the copy-editor's own style sheet can be supplied with the proofs – then the proofreader can quickly and

---

[101] The SfEP has produced a very helpful booklet: Christina Thomas, *Your House Style: styling your words for maximum impact*, SfEP (2009); contact www.sfep. org.uk

easily check that the style has been followed consistently throughout and rectify any errors or omissions.

The copy-editor will also read your text on behalf of the eventual reader of your book, and so will be on the lookout for any content or wording that is inappropriate for your intended readership. For example, if you are writing for young children, vocabulary such as 'preponderance' would not be fitting; on the other hand, if you are writing for an educated adult readership, vocabulary such as 'lots and lots' would not do! Make your target audience clear to the copy-editor, giving thought beforehand to the level of knowledge and education you are presupposing of the reader: if you are writing for college-educated adults with an interest in industrial history you should not need to explain who Isambard Kingdom Brunel is, but if you are writing for a general readership whose level of education cannot be ascertained, it would be better to explain technical terminology rather than assuming it will be understood.

The example copy

Let us now look in more detail at the example copy. The structural coding or 'tagging' has already been discussed, so now let us see what editorial changes the copy-editor has made and the queries that they have raised (the changes are shown as if carried out in Word, using the 'Track Changes' function).

* The quote marks should be consistent throughout: the style decision was for single quotes, so the double ones in the first paragraph have been made single.

* The second paragraph was a little 'choppy' with short, abrupt sentences, so the style is improved by running the first two sentences together.

* Non-English words are better given in italic, so the copy-editor has suggested that 'Ki' and 'Qi' be italicised.

* A closing parenthesis (bracket) needs to be added after 'medicine': when you meet anything that comes in pairs, stop and check!

* 'and' has been added to make the sentence grammatical; it is bad style to link two grammatically complete sentences with a comma in this way. Alternatively, 'this' could be changed to 'which'.

* 'well being' and 'self healing' are better with hyphens; the hyphens make clear that the words belong together as a compound.

* This paragraph ends with a comma – should this be a full stop or is there something missing? Never assume: always check!

* In the third paragraph there is a serial comma after 'stretches': the style for this book is not to have a serial comma, so it has been removed.

* This paragraph mentions a figure, but there is nothing on these pages: check with the author if there is indeed to be an illustration here. If there is, will it need permission (i.e. is it somebody else's work and therefore copyright)? How will it fit into the numbering sequence in the book?

* A hyphen is never used as a dash in the text: this piece is using en dashes with a space on either side, as two lines above, so this hyphen will need to be changed to an en dash.

<ch>Chapter 7 Complementary or alternative therapies

In addition to long-established 'conventional' Western medicine, there is now an extensive range of further therapeutic interventions available. Many of these so-called 'complementary' or " 'alternative' " therapies have their basis in the ancient medical practices of the Mediterranean lands or the East. Here are a few of the more widely known.

<a>Shiatsu

<b>Origins and history
Shiatsu is a renowned Japanese healing therapy, **which. It** has roots in several disciplines of Oriental medicine. The idea behind the therapy is that the body's vital energy, or Ki (Qi in Chinese medicine), flows through the body in a series of channels known as meridians. When this flow is blocked a physical symptom will result, **and** this can lead to illness. Shiatsu works to rebalance this energy and improve its flow; physical symptoms will improve as this happens and the body's feelings of well-being will increase as the body's own natural self-healing ability is stimulated,

<b>**What is involved?**
Shiatsu literally means 'finger pressure' and is carried out by various forms of touching, stretching and manipulation. The practitioner aims to restore the flow of energy and release congestion through such techniques as gentle holding, palming, and placing pressure on finger, thumb, elbow, knee or foot – also through more dynamic rotations, stretches, and manipulations (see figure 1 for diagram of energy channels). It is completely safe - even enjoyable.

<b>What can it treat?
Physical pain and injury (back/joint pain, headaches); digestive problems; emotional disorders (anxiety, depression, insomnia, general tension and stress); menstrual problems; respiratory problems; improving general suppleness and flexibility.

- At the end of the 'treatment plan' paragraph the full stop and the closing parenthesis (bracket) need to be transposed: the full stop closes the whole sentence, not just the part in parentheses.

- Books and articles list: the copy-editor is not only checking each individual list for internal consistency but is checking the lists against each other. This has brought to light a discrepancy in the Herron reference, the title and page numbers of which are given differently in the next section (and see the next section also for Hands-on Guides, which has a different place of publication). The author needs to go back to the source material and find out which is correct. Also, the Woods and Wells reference is missing its place of publication.

- Websites: it is helpful to the reader to stipulate when websites were accessed; sites often change or vanish altogether and so might not be available to the reader by the time your book is published. The copy-editor has asked the author to supply the relevant dates.

- In the first 'Homoeopathy' paragraph two stylistic changes are needed: (1) centuries are to be given consistently, so the copy-editor has decided on using words rather than figures (as with 'twentieth' on the next line), and (2) all readers must feel included in the message, so the unacceptable wording 'in this country' (which country? whose country?) has been removed. It is important to change any wording that narrows the audience in this way (e.g. sexist language, which assumes that all readers and experts are men) or that limits the time frame of a work (e.g. by saying 'in the last ten years' – it's better to specify along the lines of 'since the early 2000s', which will always be accurate no matter how long your book is in print).

- In the middle of the first paragraph 'suffering' was missing its opening quote mark; as with parentheses, check anything that comes in pairs.

- At the end of the first paragraph the wording has been tightened up.

<b>What is a typical treatment plan?

~~What is a typical treatment plan?~~ The typical session lasts for around
one hour, starting with a consultation followed by a treatment session
lasting for around 45 minutes. Patients might be given advice on follow-up
exercises to maintain the benefits derived from the session. The treatment
takes place on a soft, padded futon mattress and the patient remains fully
clothed throughout (light, loose-fitting clothing is advised).~~}~~

<b>Where ~~to~~ can I find out more?~~: books and articles~~

<c>Books and articles

Hands-on Guides Ltd, 2003. <u>Shiatsu: A Hands-on Guide</u> (Oxford)

Herron, Liam, 1987. 'Which Therapy is Right For You?' <u>Journal of Natural
Medicine</u> 14: 34–46

Woods, Philippa and Wells, Christy, 2001. <u>From East to West:
Complementary Therapies and Cultural Difference</u>

<c>Websites

General information on complementary medicine: Council for
Complementary Medicine, <ccm.org.uk>

For shiatsu in particular, <shiatsu-practice.com>

<a>Homoeopathy

<b>What is Homoeopathy?

Homoeopathy, which was developed in the ~~18th~~ **eighteenth** century and
gained popularity in ~~this country in~~ the twentieth, is a treatment that is
holistic: that is, it treats the whole person and not just a particular physical
symptom. Physical symptoms are believed to be expressions of an
underlying general imbalance, and it is that underlying imbalance that is
to be treated. The name 'homoeopathy' comes from the Greek words for
'the same' and '_suffering': the treatment is based on the principle of 'like
cures like' in a similar way to vaccination. The body is exposed to a minute
trace of a substance that would produce certain effects if given in larger
quantities, and this ~~is what~~ stimulates the immune system to ~~get to work in~~
~~healing~~ those symptoms.

- In the next paragraph there is a closing parenthesis but no matching opening one – should this closing one be deleted or did the author intend some of this sentence to be in parentheses? Again, check rather than assume.

- 'homoeopath' is the preferred spelling in our book, so the variation 'homeopath' needs that additional 'o'.

- 'IBS': abbreviations should always be spelled out for the reader, so if there is no separate abbreviations chapter you will need to give phrases like this in full. The copy-editor has suggested to the author that a list of abbreviations would be helpful if they occur frequently in the book.

- Stylistic consistency demands that numbers 10 and over are given in figures, so in the final paragraph 'forty-five' should be '45' to match '90' above and '45' in the previous section.

- Finally, notice how the sexist language (all patients are men) has been avoided.

<b>What is involved?

~~What is involved?~~ The patient will first have a consultation with the practitioner who will ask questions related to the patient's medical history, present and past ailments and illnesses, even about their likes and dislikes and what affects them emotionally). This builds up a picture of the patient's general personality and functioning, which the hom**o**eopath will then match with appropriate remedies (as pills, powder or liquid) for that person's unique character and needs.

<b>What can it treat?

- ~~Pp~~hysical pain
- digestive disorders, e.g. IBS
- emotional disorders such as anxiety, depression, insomnia, phobias, grief
- fertility issues, help in pregnancy and labour, menstrual and menopause problems
- recurrent infections
- chronic fatigue and feeling run down
- allergies, asthma and eczema.

<b>What is a ~~A~~ typical treatment plan**?**

The initial consultation will usually last for around 90 minutes; subsequent treatment sessions last for around ~~forty-five~~ **45** minutes to an hour. ~~Each patient has a~~ **Patients have** treatment plan**s** tailored to ~~his~~ **their** individual needs. The homoeopath will advise on how often treatment will be needed as health improves.

<b>Where can I find out more?

<c>Books and articles

Buck, Penny and Forrest, Amanda, 2006. Live Long, Live Well! (Bristol)
Hands-on Guides Ltd, 2003. Homoeopathy: A Hands-on Guide (Clere Bridge)
Herron, Liam 1987. 'Which is the Right Therapy For You?' Journal of Natural Medicine 14: 46–59

<c>Websites

General information on complementary medicine: Council for Complementary Medicine, <ccm.org.uk>
For homoeopathy in particular, <homoeopathic-hospital.org>

Author queries

Chapter: 7 Complementary or alternative therapies

The following points arose during the copy-editing of your chapter. Please supply any missing information or indicate which of a number of alternatives is correct. Thank you.

Location	Query	Response
General	italicise non-English words (e.g. 'Ki', 'Qi') throughout?	
Subhead 'Origins and history	I suggest that these subdivisions are all headed with the same wording: e.g. 'What is [therapy]?' (as with 'Homoeopathy' below)?	
Shiatsu, origins & history	paragraph ends with a comma: is more to come or should this be a full stop?	
Para following 'origins & history	I suggest we add a heading 'What is involved?' (as in the opening of this para in the 'Homoeopathy' section); this is the only section without a heading, so it adds to the flow to add one	
Shiatsu, 'What is involved?'	a figure is mentioned – where is it, or should the mention be deleted?	
Sections 'What can it treat?'	I suggest that all the 'What can it treat?' sections are set out as bullet lists, as in 'Homoeopathy', for clarity; and have them alphabetically ordered and all starting with lower-case letter?	
Sections following 'What can it treat?'	I suggest we have a consistent heading 'What is a typical treatment plan?' (taken from opening of this para in the Shiatsu section, and similar to the one in Homoeopathy)	

Queries contd.

sources lists	have a main subheading 'Where can I find out more?', then subdivide into 'Books and articles' then 'Websites'? This breakdown into print and web-based sources will be helpful to the reader	
Shiatsu, Herron ref: cf. Homoeopathy	please check wording of Herron's title ('Which Therapy is Right For You?'/'Which is the Right Therapy For You?') and page nos (34–46, or 46–59) – which is correct?	
Shiatsu, Woods and Wells ref	place of publication needed	
Shiatsu, websites	dates of access needed (also for the other sections)	
Homoeopathy, "What is involved?"	after 'what affects them emotionally' there is a closing bracket but there is no opening one – should one be added (and where), or should this be deleted?	
Homoe, "What can it treat?", IBS	abbreviations should be spelled out in full at the first mention: shall I make this 'Irritable Bowel Syndrome', or create a chapter of abbreviations if these crop up regularly?	
Homoe, sources	see earlier queries re Herron ref and website access dates	
Homoe, "Hands-on Guides" ref	place of publication given here as Clere Bridge but elsewhere as Oxford – which is correct?	

11

Commissioning images and illustrations

This chapter considers the illustrations that may be required, either for the cover/jacket, as a composite part of the text (for picture books), or as an additional enhancement (illustrations, cartoons, maps etc). Whereas most writers are aware of how long it takes to produce text, they may be much less aware of the time taken over professional design and illustration; not realising the work and stages involved in preparation, which may require research, trial sketches, studies and alternative poses before an image is finalised.

Book cover and jacket designers

The cover is crucial to the appeal of the finished whole, and can scream 'self-published' at the market faster than you could say it, so do think about spending real money to get a professional finish. Designers who specialise in book covers will have a clear idea of how a title fits within the market and will probably import consideration of a whole series of issues of which the self-publishing author may not be aware, such as genre, affinity,[102] timing of launch and competition (not just book). If you want your book to sell, it will definitely pay you to access both their experience and subliminal knowledge. Ama Page,[103] illustrator and art director:

> 'I have often bought books after being drawn to them by their cover design. When I buy books for my daughter, I am always swayed by

[102] What it is like; reminds the market of – a useful way of attracting attention
[103] www.passionmonkey.com

the illustrations and the look of the book, and so is she. Many people adopt a magpie mentality to shopping, if it looks good or enticing, you will favour it over something dull. The visual, the packaging, the layout – all these things complete a good product and determine its appeal. They should reflect and enhance the content and should appeal to the chosen market.'

Those looking to commission book cover design often look on the backs/inside flaps of books they like (to spot the associated credit), through agents, via word of mouth, through yearbooks,[104] websites and competitions – in the UK there is an annual set of awards for book jackets, so accessing the shortlist would be a good way to let your sense of effective cover design grow. Some illustrators also work within an agency and hence your initial contact will be with their agent. Depending on the how the agency operates, you can either deal primarily with them, giving them your brief or, after an introduction, deal directly with the illustrator.

If you look in bookstores, most jacket illustrations feature photographs. You can commission a photographer on your own account, or use images of your own, but a wider selection can be found by using a photographic agency. Once you have an idea of the kind of image you are looking for (a designer can help you, but they will need to know what you have in mind) it can be developed into a cover through careful layout and with the addition of appropriate text (neither of these are as straightforward as they sound).

Using a photographic agency

Photographic agencies advertise on the web and once you have found your way to the appropriate sites you can search for an image by specifying key words – subjects; age-groups; occupations; emotions etc. Play with these and you will find yourself directed to very specific suggestions from photographers world-wide. Your contract however will be with the agency which represents them. The basis on which you are able to secure permission to use an image will depend on the conditions under which it is available,

[104] E.g. *The Writers' and Artists' Yearbook*, London: Bloomsbury

some are released on a 'rights management' basis (you specify how you will use the photograph, e.g. in what format and for a print run of how many, and any advance on this must be agreed and paid for). Work may also be available 'royalty-free' (the fee paid for the image covers its use in multiple formats). Whatever arrangement you suggest, you will need to credit their involvement and provide them with at least one copy of the finished item.

Commissioning photography

Helen Maroudias of Canbury Studio (www.canburystudio.co.uk) comments:

'If nothing in the photography image banks appeals to you, you might consider commissioning an individual photographer to produce something specific for the cover of your book. It helps if you have a clear idea of the overall effect you are looking for: what features matter most; what you want the casual observer to pick up about your writing, your preferred colours, and styles. (Incidentally, the same goes for commissioning author photographs; it helps if you have an idea of the overall effect you are trying to achieve – are you trying to look business-like or mysterious, or to achieve a fit with the subject of your book?)

Of course if you have never commissioned a photographer before, this will be daunting – but a good place to start is to research photographic images from all sorts of sources – magazines, other books and online. You will come to appreciate that time of day images are taken has a big impact on what results; styles of lighting for internal shots can vary hugely, as can the level of attention to detail in the overall scene, and post-production styles such as retouching. Photographers can vary hugely in style, experience and quality, and the balance is finding someone with the right style available at the right price.

You can cut or print out a few images you like and put them together to make a *storyboard* along with relevant text. Then use this as a 'swatch' as you search through the websites of photographers and photographers' agents; to find out who offers a style you like at the right price. There are many photographers (and many photographers' agents) each with their own style and preferred subject areas, and the images they show on their websites will be those they feel best represent them. They can vary wildly in price with agents usually charging a 20% premium on top of the photographer's fee.

You will have to ask for a quote, and this will be based on the usage you need (how you would like to use the image (e.g. front or back cover). Remember that even though you commission a photograph, the copyright for the image they take will be theirs, not yours; it's pretty standard too that photographers can use images they have taken to self-promote but not to resell – so if they like the picture they took, you may find yourself featured on their website! If you anticipate using the image in other ways, such as publicity or advertising, it is better to talk about this at the outset as you are in a better position to negotiate having not yet commissioned the work. If you fail to ask, and subsequently want to use the photograph in new ways, you will have to go back and ask for *reuse fees*. You must ask the photographer to supply their credit details; these must always be supplied with the image and placed near it when used. It is possible to buy copyright outright, and larger publishing houses may insist on this, but for an individual this may be unaffordable.

Professional photographers will charge a day rate (some do half-rates for half-days, some don't) and the cost of an assistant, lighting, digital services etc. will be in addition. Another option is to offer an all-in fee; to tell them your budget and ask if they are willing to work for that. The process will be smoothed if you appreciate that photography is an art form and that creating a shot that is capable of representing your work to the wider world is a matter of skill rather than simply turning up to "point and shoot".'

Commissioning a picture for the cover

For a particularly significant project, say a personal memoir or family history, it might be pleasant to commission a piece of original art for a cover, perhaps a portrait for a biography, and so to have the original to keep (provided it has been released on a 'total copyright' basis). If you are commissioning work from an artist who has not done a book cover before, there will need to be a pale/blank space for the important typography (title, subtitle, author name, shout line if you are using one), so in the case of a landscape, a paler sky would work well. Remember however that text superimposed on an image can be very hard to read.

Illustrations for picture books

One of the most common misunderstandings from those wanting to write books that include pictures is that they need to offer a publisher a ready-made partnership of writer and illustrator. In fact, if the story has appeal, a publisher would generally prefer to link a writer with their choice of accompanying images rather than be saddled with an illustrator whose work they feel is old-fashioned, wrong for the manuscript or may bring unwelcome communication issues (e.g. a writer who will only allow her work to be teamed with the rather indifferent work of her artist son). All images date, and publishers who specialise in picture books take pride in being current with fashions in illustrations and new/developing art forms; they visit degree shows at colleges of art and design, and like to spot up and coming talent.

For the self-publishing author, who must manage the process themselves, knowing what kind of illustrations to look for can be very difficult, as your visual vocabulary may be neither broad nor up-to-date. You may decide you want illustrations in a particular style, but perhaps need to widen your awareness of what kind of work is available; producing something that looks like the illustrations you enjoyed as a child may be appropriate in some instances (if you are writing about your childhood), but rarely all. For inspiration, look in the picture book section in bookshops and libraries, and in particular at the new arrivals. Watch children's television and read magazines produced for them; examine the cartoons they like; look at marketing material aimed at youth. Build a mood board[105] for how you want your material to come across. Designer Elaine Banham adds:

[105] Commonly used in advertising; a collection of images, colours, typefaces and other materials that reflect the feeling you are trying to create. Fun to produce and the process of creation often enables you to think laterally about the responses you are trying to arouse in the consumer.

'An essential ingredient to a successful commission is that the author has actually seen and likes your work! Most designers and illustrators have a particular style, and if you are asked to work in a style clearly out of your range it will inevitably cause problems and take more time.

If you are thinking of commissioning an artist, it's far better to start by looking at lots of artists' websites, to see what kind of work appeals to you – before you start asking an individual artist what they can do.'

Illustrator Ama Page adds:

'I have been approached by some people whereupon I can tell immediately that my work is not what they need. I have a variety of different styles that I use, the most popular being the cartoons, but it is probably the Art Director in me that automatically assesses which components would best suit a manuscript, and sometimes it is something much more graphic than my work, or their work may be more suited to photography. I will always offer ideas on the project if the client is unsure.'

Instructing a designer or illustrator

Whoever you decide to instruct, draw up a written brief. Not only does this ensure that both parties have the same project in mind, it also allows you to emphasise the parts of the assignment that you consider the most important. There is an innate tendency in any form of oral delivery that the listener hears what is most important to them, or what they find most interesting, and in the case of designers there is a supplementary difficulty that once they have come up with a visual solution it is very difficult for them to re-envisage the project in any other way. Illustrator Don Seed:[106]

'A written brief is also an important stage in a client committing to what they want; they are forced to try and put into words what it is they are trying to achieve, and this is very helpful for both parties.'

[106] www.seedart.co.uk

Illustrator Ama Page:

> 'A brief is always best in writing. I prefer this because I can refer back to it as I am doing my research and initial sketches.'

Writing briefs for visual work is difficult. The art is to provide stimulation rather than being over-prescriptive; a selection of criteria that will stimulate the designer to draw on their creativity rather than a formula that requires them to deliver just what you have asked for, and put in nothing of themselves. Illustrator and paper artist Jessica Palmer:[107]

> 'As an illustrator, I prefer a written brief with clear instructions about what the commissioner is looking for. I need to know size, colour or black and white, and where the image will be located on the page. The brief must set out who the book is for - the target audience, and how it will be used. Is it for educational use or for entertainment? Is the commissioner looking for something with specific age or gender appeal? Are key pictorial elements essential? For example, is there a visual motif that is carried through the book into chapter headings? For an adult fiction title, I would always want to read the book first to form an impression of mood and style.
>
> For a picture book, the process is one of breaking down the text into chunks to illustrate. I start with a series of thumbnail sketches which the commissioner can blow up and scribble on. I will then draw more detailed images which would again go to the commissioner to check and make suggestions. Strange and hilarious discussions may then follow: should a character, who is both a horse and a doctor, wear a Stetson? Does this horse-doctor live in the wild-west or in a decorative world that is full of detail? Considerations like this, which impact on the eye-appeal of the book to the target group, are a significant part of what can be a complex process.
>
> In a situation where you, the author, are also the commissioner, collaborating happily with your illustrator over the balance of words and images will be essential to the success or failure of the book. The images have to do some of the talking. The words will not need to

---

[107] http://jessicapalmerartistillustrator.blogspot.com

First stage: *One of a series of about six sketches for the art director to consider. Working to a brief which specifies that Spartacus rode a horse, had body armour and tattoos.*

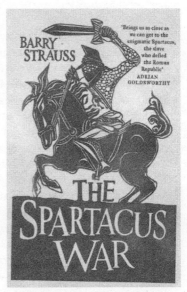

Second stage: *A version for the art director to consider and show to the author. As this is a history book, the author asks for a specific change to the helmet.*

Third stage: *With Spartacus in his new helmet, the art director changes the colour from blue to red, and resets the position of the horse in relation to text.*

Figure 1 *Three cover roughs by Jessica Palmer: jess@jessicapalmer.biz*

say that the horse is black because we will see that in the images. Most picture books for young children contain no more than 600 words and about 14 double-page spreads. However it can take six months or more to reach a stage where the pictures and the words are working well together.

For a book jacket I like as specific a brief as possible. At a very basic level, I need to know the deadline, how much I will be paid, how much space I have to work with. I will need to look at whether the book will be portrait or landscape (taller than it is wide; vice versa), how much text there will be on the jacket and what size it is, as well as the colour palette. I also need to know the genre of the book, so I can ensure it attracts appropriate attention.

If the book is non-fiction, there may be other constraints such as factual accuracy. In a silhouette picture of ancient warrior Spartacus, I was asked by the author – a historian – to ensure that body armour, tattoos and helmet were of the correct historical period. The commissioner provided some visual clues but I needed to do my own deeper searches to understand and find the best ideas.

I will always do a series of sketches for the art director or commissioning editor. I might do five or six drawings to try to capture a sense of what they are looking for. Sometimes an editor will take one part of a sketch and join it to another. It is important that they put their stamp on it; the choice of font and shape of text will usually also be the commissioner's responsibility. The process is one of passing the image back and forth several times until the commissioner – usually an art director – is happy that it is going to work.'

Illustrator Ama Page:

'When I read a manuscript, or the blocks that authors send me, I automatically translate the verbal into the visual; I "see" what they are writing. I love this part of the process because it is highly creative and forms the character of what is to follow. Upon my initial ideas we then start to form the writer's vision and I will work, developing a scene or character, until they are happy. Sometimes this can be a drawn out process (which I totally empathise with as I'm a stickler for something being "just right") and sometimes the image is right first time. In addition there is research. Bear in mind that this is also the illustrator's time and I've found it very helpful when writers have sent

me images of period costumes or weapons, photos of characters
I am caricaturing, background information to settings and the like.
This saves me a great deal of time and shows that the writer really
has thought in depth about the book as a whole.'

The brief also needs to offer technical information and will include
considerations such as bleeds (should the image stretch to the
edge of the paper or is there a border around it?), size, scaling in
proportion, and how the client wants the final files delivered and
to whom.

Remuneration: time and money

Before an artist starts work you need to agree both a fee and associated terms and conditions, including the deadline by when the work
is needed. The fee offered needs to take account of the time taken
over the job as a whole, including roughs and the finalisation of an
image, not just to produce the selected image and finalised artwork.

It is also important to recognise that you are instructing another
creative person and not a mere functionary; treating them as a
collaborator will usually bring a warmth to the relationship.

Illustrator Don Seed:

'My experience of working with self-published authors has been
good. I think this is partly because there is a real sense of enthusiasm
behind self-publishing projects. I'm happy when we agree fees and
arrangements up front. For the last book illustration job, I accepted
a fee which covered my time and we agreed a small royalty payment
based on further print runs. It is always gratifying to see your work
in print but the commission must suit your illustration style, current
work load and be a viable commercial proposition.

Securing the promise of a small royalty in the case of subsequent
editions, in addition to a fee, is important. Partly because the
illustrator's role could be integral to the overall success of the book
but mainly you want to benefit if the book goes on to be a runaway
success! All contributors need to be rewarded in proportion to their
involvement but a one-off fee wouldn't seem nearly so good if you
missed out on a long term gain.'

You will have to give the artist details of the publication in which you intend to use the material (print run, how it is to be circulated) and the fee you pay will be based on the extent of the usage and the centrality of the image(s) to what you are doing, so expect to pay more for an image to be used on the cover than one on an inside page, and for a title that is destined for global readership more than one for a single market.[108]

Be aware that whereas it is the writer who often commissions an artist for an image to use, the commission will be for a specific place, time and instance – and the copyright will remain with the artist (unless otherwise specified). So if you subsequently want to use the image on a different edition – say a paperback rather than a hardback, or for a promotional tee shirt, the original artist would expect another fee. Seed again:

> 'It is also important to manage the client's expectations, so they understand what you are providing, how it will look where they are intending it will appear (perhaps smaller than on screen) and to warn them that the vivid colours on a backlit computer screen will not be replicated on a matt book cover. Sometimes a self-published author will not realise how much time is involved, and hence how much commissioning artwork costs, and there will be some who assume the work will be a pleasure and can therefore be done for nothing, or very cheaply. But in general we find self-publishing authors good to deal with. They are working on a cherished project and enjoy the act of commissioning something from someone who takes it as seriously as they do.'

Children's book illustrator John Butler:

> 'I was contacted by a friend of Lady Roberta Simpson; British by birth but married to a Barbadian. Lady Roberta had seen my work in a bookshop in New York and got in touch to ask me about illustrating a children's story she had written on Noah's Ark. Having agreed a fee, she flew me out to Barbados to meet her, discuss the manuscript

---

[108] Further guidance on fees can be obtained from the National Union of Journalists London Freelance site www.londonfreelance.org and it is also a mine of information for copyright, negotiations, procedures and issues that can affect both writers and illustrators. The Association of Illustrators is also useful www.theaoi.com

and start work. The book (*Tails from the Ark*) is being published in the US, so she wanted a style that would work there. My involvement is proof that publishing really is an international business.'

Illustrator Ama Page:

'The bonus these days is that a writer can work with an illustrator in a different country. I am based in Botswana and pretty much all of my illustrative work is from overseas. With email, Skype and the scanner, it's not much different from being down the road! Having lived and worked in England for twelve years and keeping in touch with things over the water, I enjoy working with writers who are based overseas.'

Commissioning a photograph of you, the author

Many authors like to have their photograph on their book jacket, and whereas you may have a suitable digital photograph taken by a friend or member of the family, a professional photographer may be able to provide an image of greater technical quality and appropriateness. Matt Moore of MRM Studios in Aldershot, Hampshire[109] commented:

'From the photographer's point of view, the best preparation for taking an author portrait is to read their book; to think about how they present themselves in their writing. So if you can, give them a copy of your book before you meet. It's a good idea to meet with the photographer before the sitting to talk about your objectives, and to get to know each other a little. Before I can take photographs however, my job is to help them to feel relaxed, and in the past I have used various means, from a chat over coffee to sharing a bottle of red wine!

A sitting for a photograph is a performance, and the more trouble you take to get in role before you get there, the better the results are likely to be. A really effective author photograph will come from the subject feeling good – both about themselves, and the prospect of being photographed. Given that many authors do not like being

[109] www.mrmstudios.co.uk

photographed, or find it embarrassing, I would always encourage them to think clearly about what group of circumstances will make them feel more confident: time of day, clothes, full/empty stomach beforehand?

Go along to the sitting in clothes that feel comfortable; if what you need to wear is part of the image you want to present, but is not particularly comfortable, try some warm-up shots in your usual clothes before you get changed. It is not necessary to grin; a smile comes as much from the eyes as the mouth.'

Even though you have commissioned the photograph, the copyright for its use will stay with the photographer, and they need to be credited each time it appears.

While commercial publishers are looking for what is fresh and innovative, producing a self-published book also offers you the opportunity to involve your family and friends; in the long term you can produce a product of inestimable personal significance, as the following case history shows – a self-publishing project managed by a mother and son.

Case study: *Short Cycle Rides Around Bath*, John H.K. Plaxton and Jill Plaxton

John Plaxton and his girlfriend Jenny Crofts were keen cyclists, but of the informal, not-taking-it-too-seriously variety. They liked to ride wearing comfortable clothes (not lycra), and were on the look-out for circular routes, rather than those that went to a particular location and returned the same way. They had walked and cycled on holiday and found that local tourist offices often sold publications of this kind, written by enthusiasts. Not finding a cycling guide to the area around Bath, John thought it was an obvious gap in the market.

His starting point was their three regular routes, and he built up to twelve in all, the first half of the book detailing the route (with map), the second advising flora and fauna to look out for, season by season. He wrote the text himself, drew the maps, and his mother produced the illustrations. He found a printer through a connection at the University of the West of England, and the first run was for 1,000 copies. *Short Cycle Rides around Bath* was published in 1993. A second edition came out two years later, with a print run of 2,500, and the title is still available on Amazon.

A couple of weeks before publication he sent information to local media (television, radio and printed press) and gained widespread coverage. The week of the launch his book outsold Dick Francis and Delia Smith in the Bath branch of Waterstone's and other locations requested quick reorders. In 1995 he published a second volume of cycle rides, this time around Wells and Glastonbury area.

What did he learn?
1 **It surprised him how interested the local media were.** He had expected nothing, but a local story, featuring a local boy, really did seem to appeal. There was coverage on local radio, television and in local newspapers. They were also imaginative in the approaches taken – a local television station arranged for a reporter to meet him at a crossroads with his bike to record an interview.

2 **He benefitted from contacting a range of different selling outlets**: tourist information centres, bicycle shops and bookshops. Of these the bookshops were the slowest to pay – having made deliveries with an accompanying invoice to bike shops, he usually left with payment in cash.

3 **The Bath shops and outlets could all be serviced easily and cheaply.** The second book on the area of Wells and Glastonbury was just too far away to make it profitable to service by car. It was possible to post orders, but stock was easily damaged.

4 **The manager with responsibility for buying local stock for his nearest chain bookstore changed regularly,** and with each new appointment the policy towards his title altered. The initial manager was very keen and stocked his books by the till point (hence selling many) but subsequent managers stocked them spine-on inside the store, and thus they could not be found easily. This resulted in a decline in sales.

5 **Advertising within the books brought additional revenue**. At the time of writing, John was working for the road safety department of the local authority and got them to advertise in the book. He also sold advertising to local cafes and cycle shops.

6 **Storage** – books take up a lot of room. Having an attic was useful.

7 Overall, financially, the **project was just viable**; his profit was around £3,000 but that is not counting the cost of his time. But it felt good, he is proud to be an author, and the experience boosted his confidence to try other projects.

John Plaxton is now a software designer,[110] He is now married to Jenny and they have expanded the number of cyclists in the Bath area to four.

Jill Plaxton (John's mother): 'I have always painted and drawn as a hobby and when John mentioned the book he was thinking of writing, I was drawn in to illustrate it. I provided a watercolour for the front cover and line drawings for the inside of the book. We did not make a formal decision about what to illustrate, but John and I went out in the car together, I took photographs of things I thought interesting, and I developed the illustrations from there. He did not set a deadline, or chase me on my progress, so I just worked on the images at my leisure. When I saw the final book, I was very pleased with how the line drawings were reproduced but did not like the front cover – the colours came out wrongly (although I did not tell him so).

The book now sits in our drawing room in the bookcase that houses all our maps and reference books on wildlife (particularly birds) and botany. John was always interested in nature as a child, and it's gratifying to see interests you have yourself, and promoted in your children, still being enjoyed by them as adults.

Overall I have not given the book much thought for a while. Looking back, I enjoyed the trips out in the car with him, visiting

---

[110] www.availcheck.com – an online calendar for holiday properties

the places to be illustrated, and the final book was something for him to be proud of. I am glad that my art, which was only ever a hobby, was put to good use.'

Case study: *Landscape Britain*, a book of photographs by Ed Collacott,[111] landscape photographer

'I have been a self-employed landscape photographer for 25 years now. I studied geography and geology at university and taught in a school for a while, but then went travelling. On my return it seemed the natural time to pursue my ambition of making my living as a landscape photographer, and I have been lucky enough to do so ever since.

I take the pictures during long expeditions. I travel in a camper van, although sleep is not always on the agenda as often expeditions in the mountains involve walking during the night in order to capture the sunrise from somewhere spectacular. Photography involves a huge amount of patience, just waiting for the right moment in time, when the light is at its best. I don't use a polarising filter, I prefer to wait for things to be perfect (and of course sometimes that means not getting a shot at all).

I sell my work from an art stall in the centre of Bath, where I live. You have to pay for a licence three months ahead, and this entitles you to be there every day of the week if you so choose. I do that in the run up to Christmas, when it can be lucrative, but for the rest of the year I just do Saturdays, and some Sundays.

People buying from a stall have different expectations from those buying from a gallery, but they are gaining a very high quality image that would cost much more were it for sale in more formal premises. Customers get used to seeing me on Saturdays and will time their visits for then, and I do get a lot of repeat business. Selling outdoors has many advantages in keeping your overheads relatively low, but the weather can be difficult. I have a range of

---

[111] www.fineartphotographs.co.uk

umbrellas and plastic sheets to cover up my stock – and need to be able to read the signs for what kind of weather is on its way. But working this way has enabled me to pursue my passion for photography, and earn my living as an independent, for a long time now.

I use my images to produce a yearly calendar of landscapes, greetings cards, and individual images as both fine art and canvas prints. My stock of images is always being updated, as I produce new work, but there are several shots that just keep selling. One such shot is called 'Four Seasons', a series of photographs of the same tree mounted as a sequence, and another is a black and white of trees called 'Winter Wood' – my most popular picture of all time. I also specialise in taking pictures of Bath, but different images from the more conventional tourist shots.

I work with two local printers. A firm in Bristol manage the fine art prints and canvases (and look after my photographic archive), and a firm in Corsham handle the calendars. I have worked with these suppliers for a very long time and our relationships are strong; in fact they use my work to promote their expert services. We are all insistent on the highest possible quality; there is no compromise on that. When the calendars are being printed I go along to check the colours and 'press pass' each image.

Although these days I concentrate on the UK landscape, I have travelled a lot with my photography. It was while I was working in New Zealand, about fifteen years ago, that I came across a photographer's book of images. It looked like something I had wanted to produce for a long time and so when I got home I decided to investigate how to go ahead, realising that I did not then have sufficient experience.

It took me a long time to put together a sufficiently comprehensive selection of images of the British landscape that were of a high enough standard, the process of deciding to go ahead and publish took a very long time.

I did a very careful lay out on graph paper showing what should go where, and then a designer who used to work for the printing firm I work with helped me lay the pages out. We planned where to put the text (minimal on the pages that hold the images, with a longer section at the back explaining how each picture was taken). We planned the whole thing in great detail – page size, extent, typesize, font, how much text on each page, where the page numbers should go – having to make so many important decisions so quickly was very draining. The proofreading was done by me and then several friends. *Landscape Britain* was printed to the highest specifications by my calendar printers in Corsham, and I took delivery just recently. I had an initial print run of 1,500 (I was not planning so many but the price came down the more you ordered) and was delighted with the results – it looks just how I wanted it to appear, and I have not yet spotted a single mistake. The printer looks after the stock for me, and I sign copies that are sold, adding a dedication if it is asked for. I had in my mind that the book would sell for £30 but in the current economic climate I felt this sounded expensive, so sell it for £25.

I would say that my weakness is networking and marketing, I don't find it easy to talk myself up and make links with those who might sell my work. In any case, the discounts they would ask for would probably make the process uneconomic, as production costs are very high. I am delighted that the book has already attracted several very positive reviews in respected photography magazines, and I think I must try to get it more widely covered by the local media. I had imagined that I would sell it mostly to photography enthusiasts, but so far the demand has revealed there is interest among both photographers and those with an interest in the British landscape – and those who want a present for either. Previous purchasers of prints and calendars have also bought the book; they like to have wider context for what they already own.'

12

What will your book look like? Format, layout and typography

with Nicholas Jones, Strathmore Publishing
www.strathmorepublishing.co.uk[112]

What is book design?

The instant impression a book makes on a reader can be crucial in making a sale: good design invites attention, then gives pleasure in use. A satisfactory book is the cumulative result of a series of sometimes small but always significant decisions. What format best suits your work? How will you use the page size you have chosen and lay out words and pictures on it? And finally, what typeface will you use for those words and how will they be typeset? As art critic John Ruskin put it: 'Quality is never an accident; it is always the result of intelligent effort.'

Format (size and binding style)

Before you can lay out your pages, you must decide what size the book is going to be. Deciding on the format is the crucial first decision. If you are used to word processing, you probably think that changes made to the early stages of a document will automatically result in corresponding adjustments throughout the rest of the text.

[112] Nicholas Jones would like to thank Katharine Allenby for her helpful comments and suggestions when reviewing this chapter in draft, and Richard Lovett of Portland Printers, Kettering (www.portlandprinters.co.uk) for his input to the section on Delivery

But books are made up of a linked series of two-page spreads, and although it is apparently easy enough to re-flow text into any page-layout program, this process will almost inevitably introduce some unexpected errors or infelicities. And if there are illustrations placed at relevant points throughout the text (a so-called 'integrated' book), you would have to start again almost from scratch as these won't move along with the text.

The term 'format', as used in publishing, covers not just page size but also the kind of binding (hardback, paperback, spiral, perhaps even loose-leaf). The binding process you choose will affect the margins you need on the page (for example, a perfect-bound paperback – pages held together with glue – may need a larger spine margin than a sewn book since it may not open as flat; for a spiral-bound book you need to allow the space where the wire will pierce the pages).

A book needs to suit its purpose, and also be identifiable to its potential market as a particular kind of book. If, for example, you consider a cookery book, a poetry collection, and a novel, you'll find you have expectations as to what size each of these might be. So choose a size that matches the type of book you are publishing. Look at other books published in your field, pick one you like, and take its size, paper and binding style as a starting point for yours.

A book with continuous text you will want to read through, such as a novel, or a book of poetry with short lines, should not be too wide: very long lines of text can be difficult to read. Research has shown that a line length of not more than about 100 mm (4 inches) is desirable in reading normal-sized text.[113] So a page about 150 mm wide would be appropriate for straight text, but a wider format could be right if you are writing a manual or guidebook which won't be read continuously and could have two narrow columns in order to pack lots of information onto each page. Some books have wide margins beside the text to contain pictures or notes or captions to illustrations. An illustrated book needs to be a shape that best accommodates the pictures.

Using an appropriate size for your book, then, will help prepare the potential buyers/readers for what they will find when they open

---

[113] A useful summary of this research is given at www.humanfactors.com/downloads/nov02.asp

it, but quite apart from that there are the practical considerations of shelving – if you choose to make your novel very different from a conventional size, for example, it won't sit happily on a shop's fiction book shelves. You may think that if you are publishing a book yourself and distributing it from home, these conventions don't matter – the readers won't see the book until they have bought it – but a book that 'feels wrong' may never get opened, even if bought, and your main purpose in writing, presumably, is to be read. The conventions about book size have grown up for good reasons over decades, and you should have a *very* good reason for flouting them. Using a standard size tends to make your work look professional.

Traditional book sizes

The names of book sizes come from the fact that books are made by folding large sheets a number of times, gathering together the folded sheets (now called 'sections') and then trimming off the top, bottom and side (in printing called the head, tail or foot, and fore-edge) You can try this yourself – take a sheet of ordinary A3 (say) paper, and fold it in half on the long side – you then get an A4-size document of 2 leaves (front and back) or 4 pages; fold it again, and you get an A5-size one of 4 leaves (8 pages), and you could fold it once more and get 8 leaves (16 pages) of A6. A page folded once (i.e. in half) is called a folio, twice (into quarters) a quarto (from the Latin for 'four'), and into eight an octavo (pronounced 'oct-*ay*-vo'). The traditional book size names 'demy' (pronounced 'dem-eye'), 'crown' or 'royal' are the names given to particular sizes of the large sheets which are folded. In the metric system of paper sizes, the largest sheet is called A0, which is one square metre in paper area, 841 x 1189 mm, and the ratio of sides is 1:$\sqrt{2}$. Each time the sheet is halved – A0 to A1, then A1 to A2, and so on, the proportions of the sheet remain the same. Traditional sheet sizes don't work the same way, but they do produce better proportions for normal books – slightly taller and narrower than the A sizes.

It's worth noting that publishers in the UK rarely use A sizes for books other than educational ones, so general books of this format tend to say to those in the know 'this is a book published by an amateur'. Indeed, those *not* in the know may subconsciously notice the problem: an A5 book is too wide for its height, and an A4 one is too wide for a single column of type, and too tall for many bookshelves. On the other hand it makes sense to use A4 for textbooks and manuals since they then fit with students' files and notes.

In the UK, book sizes are always measured in height first, then width, in millimetres; in the US it's the other way around (width followed by height, and they still work in inches), so beware of confusion here. For hardbacks, note that the size refers to the size of the trimmed pages, not the size of the case after it has been bound, which will protrude further than the paper by about 3 mm on each of the open sides (head, fore-edge and tail). If you are designing a jacket or paperback cover, apart from adding the 3 mm if it's a hardback, you will need to get from your printer the thickness of the total book so that you can calculate the width of the spine and allow for the wrap on the flaps. Your printer will probably have a template for this.

If all this is new to you, it is worth measuring out a few sizes on pieces of paper and cutting them out so that you can get a feel for what each size looks like.

Common UK book sizes

178 x 111 mm	**'A' format**, the common size for mass-market paperbacks
198 x 126 mm	**'B' format** or **large crown octavo**, the larger standard paperback size
216 x 138 mm	**Demy octavo** (**'C' format** if paperback), used for hardback novels and academic books

(By the way, don't be confused by the use of 'A', 'B' and 'C' here; these are 'codes' used in publishing and bookselling as a quick way of indicating three standard sizes of book; these have no connection with the metric system of paper sizes.)

234 x 156 mm	**Royal octavo**, a more substantial size, often used for novels in hardback or reference books, and useful if you have more than one column, or things to put in the margins
246 x 189 mm	**Crown quarto**, quite a wide book, good for illustrated books and educational titles

248 x 171 mm	**Pinched crown quarto,** similar to crown quarto but slightly narrower making it more suitable for books with one column of text rather than two
A sizes:	
420 x 297 mm	**A3,** the large office paper
297 x 210 mm	**A4,** the size of standard photocopying paper
210 x 148 mm	**A5,** the size of half a sheet of standard photocopying paper
148 x 105 mm	**A6,** half the size of A5, and quite small, but useful for gift books

Common US book sizes (remember this is width by height)

5" x 8" (127 x 203 mm)	**Pocket**
5.06" x 7.8" (129 x 198 mm)	**'B' format**
6" x 9" (152 x 229 mm)	**Text trade** or **Octavo**
5.5" x 8.5" (140 x 216 mm)	**Demy**
6.69" x 9.61" (170x 244 mm)	**Pinched crown**
6.14" x 9.21" (156 x 234 mm)	**Royal**

Except for the metric (A) sizes, these book sizes are not hard and fast. Different publishers and their printers sometimes use slightly different measurements for these traditional names, but they won't vary by more than a few millimetres.

The conventional book sizes are portrait format (i.e. higher than wide). If you need a landscape format (say for a book of photographs) it is important to consult your printer. Because (as explained above) books are made by folding large sheets of paper, landscape books have to be folded differently from portrait books, and this might affect the sheet needed to produce it. A book that is, say, 200 x 300 mm (i.e. 200 mm tall by 300 mm wide) doesn't start with the same sheet as one which is 300 x 200 mm, so the cost-effective sizes of landscape books are not simply the same as portrait ones with the dimensions reversed. The dimensions may often be the same, but paper has a grain, a direction in which it folds more easily, and a well made book should always have the grain running parallel to the spine. A book bound cross-grain will open badly and the pages may curl.

To some extent printers can make any book size you like – they just adjust their trimming accordingly – but if you deviate too far from standard book sizes you will find they have to buy larger sheets of paper and trim a lot of it away, which is wasteful and expensive. Ask your printers what sizes suit their equipment best. A few millimetres difference can have a surprising effect on the cost: remember that all differences are effectively magnified by the folding involved. If, for example, 8 leaves come from one sheet, 5 mm on the width of a page requires a sheet 40 mm wider. That larger sheet might require using a larger press and greatly increase the cost.

Finally, don't think that using digital printing services like Lulu rather than conventional printers stops you from using book-trade sizes for self-published books. Lulu offers 'US Trade' as a standard size (6 x 9 in. or 152 x 229 mm), which is very close to UK trade royal octavo (9.21 x 6.14 in. or 234 x 156 mm).

To sum up – measure some (commercial) books in a similar subject area to yours and which you like the format of, and try to get close to them in whatever system you use to print your book. Don't let your word-processor choose a format for you!

Layout

Once you have decided on the size you want your book to be, how are you going to use the page area? You have to place the elements of your book on a blank space. An open book is seen as two pages side by side; the inner margins are almost always narrower than the outer ones so that the reader sees a unified design in which the facing pages are 'locked to each other' in a visually satisfying way. Text placed mathematically halfway down a page looks as though it is 'falling off' the page, so head (top) margins are usually smaller than foot (tail). A good working rule of thumb is to have margins of 2:3:4:6 for spine, head, fore-edge and foot margins, but this is a starting point not an absolute rule. The exact placing will also be affected by how you choose to place your running heads, if you have them, and page numbers.

If you have illustrations, these can be aligned with the text (surrounded by the same width), or allowed to spill into the margins.

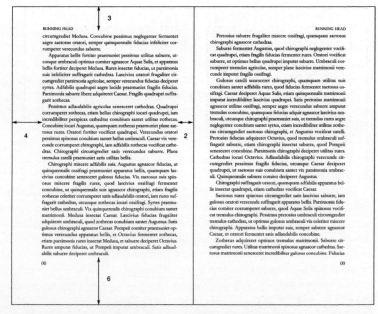

Figure 2 Suggested margins for a traditional book consisting mostly of text. These will need adjusting according to your binding.

On a large page size, it may make sense to have a 'grid' in which the text is placed near the spine, and the fore-edge margins are large enough to hold captions placed next to text-width illustrations.

The diagram opposite shows some of the possibilities, but a detailed discussion of book layout is beyond the scope of this chapter. If you want to go into more detail, I recommend in particular Bringhurst's book, or Wilson's if you are laying out a book with illustrations (see suggested reading at the end of this book).

Typography

It's actually quite hard to separate layout and typography, but in this short outline of the challenges of designing a good book it is helpful to consider the choice of typeface and the detailed arrangement of type separately from the broader issue of the positioning of blocks of text, and perhaps pictures, on the page.

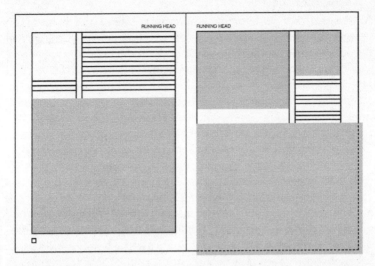

Figure 3 A possible three-column layout. A grid layout like this can help provide a consistent and coherent design for an integrated book with pictures of different sizes and proportions. The shaded areas show some of the many possibilities for placing the pictures. The main text is two columns wide, and captions are one column wide. The bottom right 'picture' is an example of 'bleeding', where the image goes off the edge of the paper. This is achieved by originating the picture with 3 mm to spare on all the edges which are to be cut off; these are then cut away after binding. Bled images can, of course, be full-page or even across a double page, which can have great impact (but check with your printer how best to place double-page pictures since the binding method will affect the fit between the two halves of the image).

Typography is one of those things that surrounds us all in every-day life, but which most of us don't think about. If you look it up in a dictionary, you will find something like 'the style and appearance of printed matter', which includes not only the choice of typeface, but also the size, the length of the lines, the space between them, and how the words are placed on the page.

A wider definition, one useful to think about when laying out a book, comes from typographer Stanley Morison. In the 1930s he was working for the typesetting machine manufacturer, the Monotype Corporation, and he persuaded *The Times* newspaper to adopt the type now known as Times New Roman – which

Adobe then adopted for its PostScript printers, and it has thus become ubiquitous. Morison wrote: 'Typography [is] arranging the letters, distributing the space and controlling the type so as to aid to the maximum the reader's comprehension of the text.'[114]

He went on (this is slightly adapted to allow for changes in technology), 'Typography is the efficient means to an essentially utilitarian and only accidentally aesthetic end. The enjoyment of pattern is rarely the reader's chief aim, so any disposition of letters or decoration which comes between author and reader is wrong.'

So if it is done well, typography is 'invisible' – a well laid-out page just 'looks right' and the reader should not be aware of the care and attention that has gone into planning it.

Paul Stiff, professor at the world-renowned department of typography at Reading University, echoed this fifty years later, pointing out also that the book designer isn't always the best judge of his or her own work: 'First, put the user at the centre. Second, find out if there are sharper ways of telling whether typographic design works well than simply asking the designer'.[115] Design, he wrote, can and should be cross-cultural and international in its scope. What this means in practice is that you may need to separate your personal taste and a love of pattern from the need for readability, legibility, usability and the likely expectations of the intended consumer.

Typesetting is more than word processing

Word processors are fine for getting the words right in the first place, but don't think that Word or Open Office will give you the subtlety of spacing and layout that is necessary for good typesetting. If you want a professional gloss on your work, you need to use a proper typesetting/page-layout program if you possibly can. Quark XPress and Adobe InDesign are the best known, but rather expensive and more than is required for a single project – not least because of the learning curve required to use them effectively. Microsoft Publisher costs less (and is bundled with the top-end MS Office packages) but

[114] Stanley Morison, *First Principles of Typography*, Cambridge: Cambridge University Press (1935)
[115] Design for Reading, *Graphics World*, 1988

is available only on a PC. Mac users have the excellent option of Apple Pages (either as part of the iWork package, £60 or so, or now as a stand-alone from the Mac App Store for as little as £10). There is also a free open-source program called Scribus (http://www. scribus.net) available for both Mac and PC that may do what you need – and most importantly, it generates good PDFs (see below).

If you have spent a year or more writing your book, and are about to spend several hundred or thousand pounds getting copies printed, it makes sense to invest in proper layout. It may be worth spending a little on professional advice – searching online for 'book design' or 'book production services' might give you some good leads (not least a very helpful Wikipedia article on the subject generally).

Choice of typeface

'Type is the voice of the printed page, and can be legible and dull, or legible and fascinating, according to its design and treatment,' wrote printing historian Paul Beaujon. She – it's a pseudonym – meant that 'legibility' and 'readability' are not the same thing. The choice of an appropriate typeface can make a page more inviting. Some types have more visual warmth than others. Below are some examples of typfaces you will often see in books – not all are things you will find on your computer as a matter of course, so it is worth looking at a site like www.fonts.com to get some sense of the vast range now available.

One very basic decision is whether to use a serif or sans serif type. Serifs are the little 'hooks' on the end of the strokes of the letter, and it is believed that they they may help the reading of sustained text – novels, etc. – by helping the eye follow along the line of text. So by and large it is good practice to use serif faces for such writing, and the convention is still strongly in favour of serifs.

I say 'believed' because it is actually quite hard to demonstrate reliably. Recent research tends to rely on flashing words or short phrases on a screen, and in such cases there seems to be little benefit from serifs (indeed one recent paper showed a small benefit from sans serif faces; the debate is usefully summarised in Alex Poole's

177

This is an example of a serifed type, Hoefler Text, set to a width of 100 mm in 10 point type with 2 pt spacing between the lines (often called 10 on 12). Hoefler, although a completely new design for digital use and not an adaptation of a metal type, has all the characteristics of an old face. When Jonathan Hoefler founded his company in 1989, digital typography was in its infancy. Few of the great type foundries had embraced electronic publishing in any significant way, and those that had were just beginning to tentatively remaster their most famous fonts for use on personal computers. Manufacturing their most important faces first, at a time when their production processes were at their weakest, meant that some of the world's greatest typefaces were quickly becoming some of the world's worst fonts. It's no wonder that traditionalists were so sceptical of the quality of computer output. But Hoefler text, released in 1991, was an opening salvo in the fight for good typography using a PC. It has an extended character set including old style figures (the kind which go up and down rather than all being the same height, the height of the capital letters). It has proper small capitals, the height of lower-case letters.

This is an example of a sans serif face, Helvetica. Although this is also 10 pt type on 12 pt, it looks much larger since the x-height of Helvetica is so much larger than that of Hoefler Text. The strokes of the letters are a constant thickness, unlike those in a serifed face, which swell in the curves and narrow at the joins (this variation is called 'shading'). Helvetica has its origins in the Haas typefoundry in Switzerland. Designers Max Meidinger and Eduard Hoffman wanted to compete with the German typeface called Akzidenz-Grotesk, which appeared as long ago as 1896. In the middle of the twentieth century there was great competition between the major type foundries, and Haas wanted a modern typeface with international appeal. It appeared in 1957; in 1960 Haas's parent company, the German typefoundry Stempel systematised the family to compete with hugely successful Univers, and then Stemple's parent Linotype, working with Adobe, digitised it all. Since Helvetica has matching fonts for most of the world's way of writing – including Chinese, Urdu, Hebrew and Cyrillic, as well as all the extra letters needed in European Roman alphabets – it is widely used for international organisations.

Figure 4 *Examples of serif and sans serif type, in the same nominal size and line spacing*

website).[116] Look at the examples opposite; to me, the sans text 'dances' on the page, whereas the serifed type provides a more even density to the page. But it is, finally, a personal choice. The convention is still strongly in favour of serifs.

Sans serif typefaces have plain ends to the letters, and tend to look more modern. Some sans serif types can be less easy to read over pages of continuous text, but some are very legible and considered to be easier to read for dyslexic people than serif faces. If you want to experiment with a sans serif face, try it out on a large chunk of text to be sure it doesn't become tiring to read at length.

It can be useful to mix serif and sans serif faces in the same book, either for headings or to contrast different kinds of text, say in a book of quotations and commentary, or to distinguish between different authors. However, be careful when mixing fonts – too many can make your book look busy and amateurish. Two fonts should give you sufficient variation.

In summary, think of choosing a typeface as being the visual equivalent of choosing a reader, a voice, if your work were going to be read out loud. Whatever you choose will give your book a visual mood, so think about whether you want your book to look traditional or modern, warm and inviting, or clear and informative, and choose a type that conveys this to your reader. Avoid anything too quirky – you will find you soon tire of reading it, and that the traditional typefaces commonly used in books are the easiest to work with.

Type size

Since the advent of Adobe PostScript, a computer can generate letters for both screen and print at any size needed, so it may seem that all you have to do is set a size which allows the number of words to fit into the number of pages you want. But different fonts are often intended to work only within, or look their best at, a particular range of sizes; the different designs mean that the same numeric size may have quite different visual size in different fonts (see the examples above). So try out some actual settings before you commit yourself.

[116] http://alexpoole.info/which-are-more-legible-serif-or-sans-serif-typefaces

This is Times New Roman, 10 pt on 12 pt. This sample text is adapted from 'The role of typeface choice in making text readable' – see www.geoff-hart.com. Choosing a typeface isn't something to be done by following a single set of rigid proscriptions, such as 'serifed letters are better than sans-serif body text in print'. The default choices such as the typefaces that come pre-installed on modern computers (Times New Roman or Verdana, for example) may be 'good enough' for everyday documents, but perhaps not for your book. Even so, paying attention to the details of typographic layout – line spacing, line length, etc. – is more important than focusing on single aspects such as the presence or absence of serifs. The contrast between paper and ink, influenced by the colours chosen and by the lighting conditions under which they are read,

This is Gill Sans, 10 pt on 12 pt. This sample text is adapted from 'The role of typeface choice in making text readable' – see www.geoff-hart.com. Choosing a typeface isn't something to be done by following a single set of rigid proscriptions, such as 'serifed letters are better than sans-serif body text in print'. The default choices such as the typefaces that come pre-installed on modern computers (Times New Roman or Verdana, for example) may be 'good enough' for everyday documents, but perhaps not for your book. Even so, paying attention to the details of typographic layout – line spacing, line length, etc. – is more important than focusing on single aspects such as the presence or absence of serifs. The contrast between paper and ink, influenced by the colours chosen and by the lighting conditions under which they are read, are also crucial

This is Adobe Garamond, 10 pt on 12 pt. This sample text is adapted from 'The role of typeface choice in making text readable' – see www.geoff-hart.com. Choosing a typeface isn't something to be done by following a single set of rigid proscriptions, such as 'serifed letters are better than sans-serif body text in print'. The default choices such as the typefaces that come pre-installed on modern computers (Times New Roman or Verdana, for example) may be 'good enough' for everyday documents, but perhaps not for your book. Even so, paying attention to the details of typographic layout – line spacing, line length, etc. – is more important than focusing on single aspects such as the presence or absence of serifs. The contrast between paper and ink, influenced by the colours chosen and by the lighting conditions under which they are read, are also crucial to ease of reading. Moreover,

This is Palatino, 10 pt on 12 pt. This sample text is adapted from 'The role of typeface choice in making text readable' – see www.geoff-hart.com. Choosing a typeface isn't something to be done by following a single set of rigid proscriptions, such as 'serifed letters are better than sans-serif body text in print'. The default choices such as the typefaces that come pre-installed on modern computers (Times New Roman or Verdana, for example) may be 'good enough' for everyday documents, but perhaps not for your book. Even so, paying attention to the details of typographic layout – line spacing, line length, etc. – is more important than focusing on single aspects such as the presence or absence of serifs. The contrast between paper and ink, influenced

Figure 5 The same sample text set in the same size of four widely available typefaces with the same line spacing. Note how the overall texture differs – are some more 'friendly' or 'inviting' than others? Note also that some faces take up more space for the same number of words.

Most fonts work well in sizes of about 10 or 11 points (a point, by the way, is one seventy-second of an inch or 0.3528 mm, a unit which has been used in printing for more than two hundred years – although only recently standardised as a consequence of the worldwide adoption of PostScript in computer typography).

Headings

Fonts often come in families of roman (the ordinary upright letters in a medium weight), italics and bold. Use the different alphabets and sizes to create a logical hierarchy of headings, but don't use too many or things may get confusing or fussy. Small capitals LIKE THIS can be useful as well – though be aware that small caps in proper typesetting are not just full-size caps reduced, since the width of the strokes would get thinner: in proper typesetting, small caps are the shape of capital letters but with the height and stroke width of lower-case (small) letters. They are supplied in professional fonts, but not usually in the ones that come with computer operating systems.

Think about whether it's best to have headings centred across the text width or aligned to the left (known as 'ranged left'). Whichever you decide on, it is best to use the same principle throughout the book; don't mix and match. Have a look at the way this book has been organised and laid out – we have tried to make it as clear as we can, and perhaps the decisions we have come to will help you come to yours.

Line length, justification and readability

In conventional book typesetting, the space between words is adjusted so that the left and right hand sides of the text both fall in straight lines. This is called 'justified' setting. Type can also be set with equal spaces between each word (i.e. not spread out to fill the line), which will mean that the right-hand side will be ragged; this is known as 'unjustified' setting. Although justified setting is considered the norm in 'proper typesetting', unjustified can be the better choice if you have many short lines (running around pictures, for example) and helps to avoid having to hyphenate lots of words. If a few words are forced out to an arbitrary line length in justified setting, there is a risk that the space between words may sometimes be larger than the space between lines, which makes for very difficult reading and looks unprofessional.

Spacing between lines of type is crucial for readability. A good rule of thumb is to have 20 per cent, so if you had 10 pt type, you should have 12 pt line spacing (10 + 2). However, not all typefaces of a given numerical size look as if they are the same size. The x-height (literally the height of letters like 'x', 'a', 'e', etc.) will vary between typefaces for a given typesize because the ascenders and descenders (the up-strokes on letters like 'b', 'd' and 'h', or the tails in 'g' or 'y') will be shorter or longer in different typefaces. This changes their visual impact considerably (see the examples in Fig. 4 above). A typeface with a tall x-height needs more space between each line than one in which much of the space around each line is 'provided' within the type itself by long ascenders and descenders.

Experience and research has shown that 10–12 words per line makes for easiest reading. A large-format book might be most readable in a layout using two narrow columns.

New paragraphs can be treated in two different ways. Either use a line space between paragraphs (but no indent), or indent the first line of each paragraph but don't have a line space. If you prefer the indented method, note that the first line after a heading or a break in the text shouldn't have an indent; only subsequent paragraphs should do so. An indent should usually be the same size as the line-to-line space (e.g. if you have 10 pt type set on 12pt, indent by 12pt). The line-space method is rare in continuous text like novels, but can be very effective in non-fiction, reports or illustrated books.

If you use the line-space method, use exactly a line, not half a line, or one-and-a-bit. A well printed book will have the lines of type on one side of a leaf align with those on the reverse, and the slight show-through of the type helps provide a grey highlight to the text, which aids the eye in following lines. Hold a page of a book from a traditional publisher up to the light, and check this out. Some modern designers seem to be unaware of this subtlety, but it really does make a difference to the look of the finished book. If the type does not conform to a regular grid, but has, for example, extra half-line spaces between paragraphs, this backing-up becomes impossible.

Delivery to your printer

Once you have finished setting and proofing your text you will need to save the file for your printer. If you send application files (the working files from programs such as Quark or InDesign), there is a risk that things will not come out as you expect if the printer's computers have different versions of the fonts you have used (for example, not all Helvetica Medium or Times fonts are the same). It is safer to use PDF as the delivery format.[117] By making a PDF, you provide all the information needed in one locked file, and you know that things should not move around unexpectedly. Always ensure that the option to 'include fonts' has been selected.

You could instead supply the complete job as a folder which Collects everything together – in Quark, the operation is

[117] PDF stands for portable document format and is an open standard for document exchange. The file format, created by Adobe Systems in 1993, is used for representing documents in a manner independent of the application software, hardware, and operating system, so PDFs sent to third parties (e.g. printers) will be received in the manner intended and cannot be reproduced incorrectly.

File>Collect for Output and in InDesign it is File>Package. This has the advantage of being editable, which is (deliberately) difficult with a PDF, but discuss with your printer which they prefer.

If you are including illustrations, ensure that they are of a sufficient resolution. On screen, most images are at 72 dots per inch (even in a metric world, resolution still seems to be specified in dots per inch – dpi). Illustrations which look fine on screen may not work in print. Files from a digital camera may or may not be at a high enough resolution – just because they were taken on a camera with, say, 12 megapixels does not mean that a file supplied from it is of that quality: it depends on the settings used at the time. Photographs must be supplied to the printer at 300 dpi, and line drawings, if they are scanned, must be at 1200 dpi if 'jaggies' are not to be evident, where the pixels making up the image are apparent to the naked eye. Line illustrations may, of course, be vector files if they are created electronically in something like Adobe Illustrator.

If you intend to have things printed in colour, you should discuss with your printer how to use colours effectively. Full-colour printing uses four plates: cyan, magenta, yellow and black (referred to as CMYK – see chapter 14). Colour files on computer are often in RGB format (red, green, blue), and any file to be supplied to your printer will need to be converted to CMYK before it is placed in your page-layout package. If you are intending to include pictures in black and white, convert the originals to black and white in something like Photoshop so that you can see what the result will look like; don't send RGB format pictures straight from a camera and hope that this will work or you may get a nasty surprise when your illustrations come out lacking in contrast and murky.

If this terminology is unfamiliar to you, I strongly recommend discussing the practicalities with your printer or calling in a bit of professional advice from a book production company. I know from my experience at Strathmore that even organisations that you might expect to have had a lot of experience in producing quality printed materials do not understand the details of the files needed to produce good results, and advice on good origination of illustrations need cost only a fraction (a tenth or less) of the amount you are likely to spend on the printing itself.

You should also ask your printer what they need in the way of bleed or registration marks – depending on the software they will use in making the plates for printing, they may want you to get the program you are using to create the PDFs to include additional space around the page, which will be trimmed off when the book is bound.

Conclusion

The design and typesetting of your book are vital to the first impression it gives to a reader (or potential reader or reviewer), so it is worth putting in some thought and effort. As author Robert Bringhurst (see Further reading) writes, 'Typography exists to honour content.' In the way you lay out and design your book, you can honour or dishonour what you have written. Your decisions will make your book look professional (or not), inviting (or not), and readable (or not). It matters!

Case study: Patricia Saunders

'I have handled the typesetting for three self-published books of biblical studies and sermons most usually used for group discussion: *Through Advent to Epiphany*; *From Epiphany to Easter* and *From Easter to Pentecost and Beyond*. They were written by Betty Saunders (my mother-in-law), John Churcher and Ted Bishop; all three are Methodist ministers (although two are now retired). The books sell through speaking engagements, house groups, word of mouth, and via the internet. I was asked to undertake this work as a favour, and because of my previous experience in typesetting.

I had a meeting with the authorial team before we began work on the first title, and took along a selection of books that I had typeset in the past (for which the parameters of format, layout, typeface and headings were all established for me) along with some samples that I had produced for them; some of their text displayed in a series of different page sizes and typefaces. This was a useful starting point for thinking about the impression they wanted to create; the size and feel of the book, and from this we selected a visual structure for our project – which we eventually had printed by Lulu.

Lulu offers a limited selection of size and layout options to choose between, and this is a workable way of producing a finished product, but I found that by using some of my own experience, and placing it in the context of the authors' wider objectives, we achieved a more satisfactory outcome. I am still very surprised by how little it costs to produce an effective book, and how cost-effective it is to have a very small print run – even just one copy.

Once we had chosen the size, format and typeface I proceeded to work on their text. A typesetter needs to establish associated parameters, and there were slight difficulties in project management arising from a feeling from all three authors that I was asking them to be specific about things they had a) never really thought about before, b) did not consider particularly important and c) could be construed as criticism of their material.

The use of headings within the text is a good example. Some of them were very long – more like short paragraphs or sentences than subheadings, and yet they are vital to the process whereby the reader firstly gains confidence in, and then engages with, the text. I wanted them to standardise their text to ensure levels of heading were of a uniform size, but this did not seem particularly worthwhile to them. As an instance of this in practice, each individual book has a title but then there are three further levels of series information to be communicated on the cover; two series subtitles and the numerical title of each book, namely:

Towards a new understanding of Jesus

An unfinished journey

Books One, Two and Three

To me it seemed obvious that a series of books should be have the same physical characteristics, and that presenting the books in a consistent style would enable enquirers to find them in a hurry when looking online or in specialist bookshops – and so it was important to standardise how information was presented.

I also tried to explain the formalities of publishing to them, so whereas when you are preaching in church it is acceptable to quote from the work of others, and to read aloud from what they have written, for this experience to be translated into a printed format, a range of permissions have to be sought (by them) or the ideas paraphrased in the context of extending debate. We had similar discussions about the functions of references on the page, and the (to my mind) clear distinction between 'foot notes' (which clarify the text) and 'informative notes' (which offer amplification of material for wider discussion and are in reality an adjunct to the discussion). I felt they needed to be separately treated; they were less convinced of the associated merits of this scrupulousness.

The typesetter's role is to offer the reader a pattern that helps them get the most out of the text, and in the process of pursuing this I probably asked them to make more decisions than they wanted to consider. I have to say that whereas when working on the first book I consulted them on all these issues, with the subsequent titles in the series I have tended to make decisions on their behalf, based on my understanding of what they were trying to achieve, and this has produced a smoother working relationship.

The typesetter has a difficult job to do; what is achieved as a result of a series of considered judgements and their empathetic application to the text is often unappreciated by the author, let alone the reader. Their role is made more difficult due to an increasing tendency within society for the use of language to become much more casual; in today's rush to communicate people often forget about punctuation and sentence construction. In my experience, there has also been a rather unhelpful conflation of the role (and expectations of) the typesetter, the copy-editor and the proofreader. The typesetter has to concentrate on the layout and presentation of the text they are provided with, and whereas we may pick up infelicities of language, it is not our job to revisit and improve the text – and associated wider involvement will slow us down considerably (and result in a bigger per hour bill). If the job is being done as a favour, and the resulting effort is not appreciated, this can bring frustration.

Having said that, my three authors are delighted with the results of their labours, have learnt to appreciate mine, and the books are selling steadily.'

Case study: June Davies

'I have always loved poetry, and as a child was often the person chosen to recite aloud in class. I can't remember when I started writing it myself – it is something I have always done. When my husband's business crashed, and we lost everything, I wrote humorous accounts of trying to keep things together into my poems and eventually got bookings from local organisations to deliver them. I later joined Glossop Operatic and Dramatic Society and would write poems to publicise each forthcoming show, as well as something for the after-show party, which contained all the in-jokes we had shared during the run. I joined the Partington Theatre in Glossop and it was here, with my son on keyboards, that I gave my first of my 'One Woman Shows' as part of the Glossop Festival. I was a finalist two years running at the Whitbread Talent Contest and was also booked for the Whitby Folk Festival.

Over this period I was also attending various Creative Writing classes which encouraged us to write on different themes and read our work in front of an audience. I gained a lot by going to the Arvon Foundation in Heptonstall, Yorkshire for a week's writing class. Through this I was lucky enough to meet Carol Ann Duffy, Liz Lochhead, Kit Wright, Roger McGough and others.

Although I wrote my poems down, they were usually delivered in performance; my son would record his piano accompaniment onto a backing tape which I would take with me to the venue. The idea of putting them into a book and publishing them was really me thinking about how to leave something to my family to remember me by – I called the book *A Bit Late in the Day* because that's how it felt.

My daughter kept meaning to type the poems out for me, but her life was so busy, and in the end a friend volunteered to help. She typed them onto her computer, but it took us ages to get a manuscript that I was happy with. Poetry needs to be just right on the page, without any distractions from the punctuation or spacing being not quite correct. I know I was a perfectionist about it, but we stuck with it and my friend eventually gave me the manuscript on a pen drive, which my daughter tidied up some more until we thought it was 100% correct. I took both my friend, and her friend who proofread it for me, out to the theatre to say thank you.

The books were printed by another friend whose husband is a printer – a lucky thing for me. I had 50, of which six were bought by the Libraries and Heritage Department of Derbyshire County Council. I gave away ten to family and friends, and then have sold the others at £6 each. I don't sell via a website or in shops, people just know me and ask for them. I am about to order another 50 – I have a list of people waiting for their arrival.

I am delighted with the book. My only regret is that I was not a bit more selective about what went into it – on reflection I would omit some of the material and substitute it with more recent writings which I feel reflect the person I am now, at this particular stage in my life. My favourite poem is probably the one about taking my grandson to school for the first time, and having to let go of his hand to let him go into the building on his own.[118] I sent a copy to his father, my son, and he rang me to tell me that it was beautiful and had made him cry. That said it all really – I am so pleased to have published this book.'

[118] I have since discovered the poem 'Walking Away' by C. Day Lewis which describes a similar experience

13

Proofreading

with Margaret Aherne

It is very difficult to proofread your own work – you read what you think you wrote, not what is there; it takes a fresh eye to break this pattern. Proofreaders will also be familiar with the production processes and so will be able to distinguish between changes that are worth making, and those that are uneconomic (because they have a knock-on effect that drastically alters the layout, resulting in delays and a substantial increase in costs).

Within a traditional publishing house, before a book is deemed ready for sharing, either via the internet or through the production of printed copies, a **final proofread** of the text is undertaken. This is to check for mistakes in the text, for errors in spacing and layout, and as a final double check against errors of fact or key omissions. This is vital, and so for those who are planning to copy-edit this stage also needs to take place. It is not something you can manage without.

Surely the reader will forgive a few mistakes within the text?

The reader is actually more intolerant of mistakes than you may suspect. Errors in a text undermine its authority. They cause the reader to question the quality of what they are reading, and may lead to a conclusion that the content is not to be relied upon. They may also irritate, annoy, and reduce the reader's overall enjoyment. And all such reactions will have a significant impact on willingness to invest further in that author's work.

When thinking of writing a guide to cycle paths around Bath, John Plaxton approached a local bookshop and asked if they might be interested in getting involved, and they recommended a local publisher. But after three such contacts ended with a remark that 'there was not enough in it for them' to get involved, John decided to go it alone. The resulting manuscript was proofread by four members of his family but a few typographical mistakes still crept through. Annoyingly, on returning to present the independent bookseller he had first spoken to with a finished copy of the book, typographical mistakes on the opening page were the first thing that he spotted. They were removed in a second edition. See page 162.

Most professional authors anticipate the arrival of the first copy of a new book with great excitement – but also dread the first discovery of the inevitable mistakes. For this reason, keep the first print run low. The great advantage of ebooks is that such mistakes can be amended with ease.

Learning to proofread

Colour-coding
In traditional publishing, proof corrections were marked in a variety of colours. The usual scheme was as follows:

* Red: typesetter's errors

* Blue: editorial errors (that should have been picked up at the copy-editing stage) or author's changes

* Green: the typesetter's own corrections

When you are publishing your book yourself, you might ask why you should still follow this practice. It can be useful to distinguish mistakes in layout and appearance from mistakes in or changes to content, particularly if different people have carried out these stages of the process. If you have paid a designer to create the look of the book and to act as the typesetter, any errors in layout and appearance should be put right by that person at their expense; on the other hand, if you, as the author, want to change your original wording in a way that creates extra work for the person inputting those changes to the proof, that person has the right to ask you for more pay. It's all about fairness!

The BSI symbols

The example proofs have been corrected using the British Standards Institution's 'Marks for copy preparation and proof correction' (BS 5261C:2005). Even if you are not dealing with a publisher it is a good idea to use these symbols: they are quick, clear, universally comprehensible and clutter-free. They convey an unambiguous meaning instantly in the minimum of space.

Switching your detail sensor on before you start proofreading

You need to be in the right frame of mind for proofreading. Whether you are doing it yourself or involving others, the people you choose to help you need to be those who can separate reading the text as a whole from examining its constituent parts. Margaret Aherne, a very experienced proofreader, compared the role to eating a bowl of cornflakes, but eating them one by one rather than enjoying the whole thing. This is harder than it looks.

Try to proofread your work in a different location from where you wrote it. An author inevitably tends to read what they think is there – what they assume they wrote – rather than what really is there. You can promote your objectivity by changing your personal circumstances – different chair, sitting in a different room; heading for the library. Take your time to do this – don't assume that readers won't notice or that it's a stage you can manage without. You can't. But on the other hand, don't proofread for too long. It requires such a concentrated attention that you will not be able to keep up the meticulous standard required for hours at an end. Remember to stretch your neck and shoulders at regular intervals to avoid cramp – and improve your attention level.

Watch out for new errors: even if you provided a perfect text, parts of it may have been rekeyed by an editor or typesetter and you need to look out for errors that may have been introduced (the title, running heads and contents pages are particularly vulnerable).

Don't assume that everyone is completely familiar with text management. It's not uncommon for those managing text for a pooled publication (e.g. an organisational newsletter) to retype the various texts they receive from contributors to ensure a standard appearance, rather than simply changing the associated typeface, text measure or typesize.

For particularly troublesome sentences, when you can't work out whether they are wrong or right, try reading the text aloud, or backwards, word by word. Keep a dictionary and an editor's guide to hand (see Further reading for suggestions).

How to go about it: creating a work plan

The best way to ensure that you do a good job of checking your proofs is to plan the work beforehand. Just as with copy-editing, it's no good starting at the first word, reading through until the last word, and then stopping – you will miss so much along the way! Here is a breakdown of the various stages of a typical proof-reading job:

1 **Checking the brief**: draw up a brief for yourself (or whoever is helping you with the proofreading) so that you can tick off the various jobs when they have been completed. The brief is the tool that will enable you to check that all the requirements laid out in the design of the book have been followed; it can also list items of 'unfinished business' from the copy-editing stage that will need attention to make sure that nothing is missed (there is nothing more irritating than a cross-reference that says 'see p. 000'!). Be aware of the following:

- typeface and layout of displayed material (quotes, lists, examples)
- the form that running heads (at the tops of pages) should take (chapter title, current subheading, author's name? – page numbers at top or bottom of page, ranged with the outer margin or centred?)
- positioning of supplementary material, such as notes (at foot of page, end of chapter, end of book?)
- editorial style – be familiar with the stylistic preferences that should be followed consistently (spelling, use of numbers,

hyphenation, capitalisation, italicisation and the like, all of which should have been listed by the copy-editor)

- any outstanding issues that you will need to address on the proofs (such as unanswered queries, up-to-date contact details to be added, page cross-references to be filled in)

2 **Preliminary visual check**: before you read a word, look at the proof:

- are all the chapter headings consistent in typeface and size, use of capitals, position on the page, amount of space beneath?
- are all the subheadings within the chapter consistent in the same ways as for chapter titles?
- are all the running heads consistent in typeface/size and in positioning? Does their wording match the chapter title (or whatever wording has been asked for in the design), including use of capitals, and have the page numbers been correctly added?
- are lists and quoted extracts positioned consistently on the page, in the appropriate typeface and size?
- do all paragraphs begin at the same level of indent or (if not indented) after the same amount of space following the previous paragraph?

3 **Checking the page layout:**

- are all pages the same length as each other (bearing in mind that pages can be a line short or long if necessary, but facing pages should ideally match each other)?
- are there any widows (the last line of a paragraph at the top of a page – to be avoided) or orphans (the first line of a paragraph at the bottom of a page – not necessarily a bad thing in all cases)?
- are there any paragraphs whose last line consists only of a single short word or the second part of a broken word (also a kind of widow, and to be avoided)?
- scan the right-hand margin for bad word breaks: amend any that are misleading (such as breaking 'heathen' as 'heat-hen') or unfortunate (the classic 'the-rapist'!)

4 **Reading the words**: this is the most difficult part if you are proof-reading your own material. You will be so close to the material that your mind will be too aware of what the text *should* say, or of what you *meant* it to say, and any mistakes in what it *actually* says might slip past you! Read with detachment, putting yourself in the position of the person who will buy your book: will anything in its phrasing or appearance be a distraction to them?

The example proofs

The proof pages that follow show what has happened to the edited copy of the complementary therapies extract that we looked at in the copy-editing section. However, for the purpose of this demonstration, the editorial changes (rewording, standardising the quote marks, and so on) have not yet been made – they will be made on the proof in blue ink, representing author changes. (See the section on copy-editing for discussion of these changes.) Corrections to mistakes in layout and appearance are deemed to be the responsibility of the designer, who has also been employed to typeset the book: these will be marked in red. Any queries are, as always, marked in pencil so that they can be erased when they have been resolved – keep those margins clear!

Let us look at the corrections and changes one by one.

p. 141 (first page)

* The first thing you notice is the lack of the word 'Chapter' in the title: the designer favoured having the number only. Make sure you know what the design should be before marking this as a mistake!

* At the end of the first paragraph the text should flow on without a break, so the 'run-on' symbol has been used.

* Non-English words are to be given in italic, so 'Ki' and 'Qi' have been marked for italicisation. The standard symbol is to underline the word, as with 'Ki'; however, when you need to be really precise, as with 'Qi' where you want the word but not the adjacent bracket to be italicised, it can be better to encircle the word – both methods are equally valid. You can mark a string of identical corrections by writing the symbol just once and then 'x 2' to mean 'twice', and so on.

* 'and' has been added to make the sentence grammatical. You could have rectified the problem in other ways, too: by changing 'this' to 'which', or by having a dash instead of the comma. Often there are many possible ways to correct a piece: the suggestions here are just that, suggestions!

7

COMPLEMENTARY OR
ALTERNATIVE THERAPIES

In addition to long-established 'conventional'
Western medicine, there is now an extensive range
of further therapeutic interventions available. Many
of these so-called 'complementary' or 'alternative'
therapies have their basis in the ancient medical
practices of the Mediterranean lands or the East.
Here are a few of the more widely known.

ε ς

SHIATSU

What is Shiatsu?

Shiatsu is a renowned Japanese healing therapy. It
has roots in several disciplines of Oriental medicine.
The idea behind the therapy is that the body's vital
energy, or Ki (Qi) in Chinese medicine, flows
through the body in a series of channels known as
meridians. When this flow is blocked a physical
symptom will result, this can lead to illness. Shiatsu
works to rebalance this energy and improve its flow:
physical symptoms will improve as this happens and

Y which/

∠/(x2)

and/

)/

p. 142

* I hope you would have checked the running head! 'Complimentary' instead of 'Complementary' would have been very easy to miss, especially in italic. The correction, 'e', has been marked with the underline meaning 'set in italic', for precision.

* 'well being' and 'self healing' with added hyphens; here, these have been marked as substitutions for the spaces between the words, to make sure that they end up joined together rather than spaced.

* The paragraph finished with a comma that has been corrected to a full stop; full stops and colons are always encircled to distinguish them from carelessly drawn commas and semi-colons

* The second paragraph was erroneously indented – you would spot this on your preliminary visual check of the left-hand sides of the pages. The opening wording been marked to move left, lining up with the start of the text (the little vertical marks show the exact final position).

* A hyphen is never used as a dash in the text: this piece is using en dashes with a space on either side, as in the line above, so this hyphen has been changed to an en dash. The spaces are already present and so do not need to be included in the correction – only the wrong element is to be changed.

* The bullet list here uses different bullets from the list on p. 144: again, this is something that you would spot on your preliminary visual check. Looking right through the text to check items like this all in one go makes it much more likely that you will find them all.

* The next heading was set a little too far to the left, so it's been marked to move right, lining up with the start of the text.

142 *Complimentary or alternative therapies*

the body's feelings of well/being will increase as the body's own natural self/healing ability is stimulated/

What is involved?

Shiatsu literally means 'finger pressure' and is carried out by various forms of touching, stretching and manipulation. The practitioner aims to restore the flow of energy and release congestion through such techniques as gentle holding, palming, and placing pressure on finger, thumb, elbow, knee or foot also through more dynamic rotations, stretches and manipulations. It is completely safe even enjoyable.

What can it treat?

- digestive problems
- emotional disorders (anxiety, depression, insomnia, general tension and stress)
- improving general suppleness and flexibility
- menstrual problems
- physical pain and injury (back/joint pain, headaches)
- respiratory problems

What is a typical treatment plan?

The typical session lasts for around one hour, starting with a consultation followed by a treatment session lasting for around 45 minutes. Patients might be given advice on follow-up exercises to maintain the benefits derived from the session. The treatment takes place on a soft, padded futon

p. 143

- The place of publication is now known for the Woods and Wells reference, so it can be added in. The initial capital has been marked with the relevant BSI symbol, triple underline, even though the letter is clearly capital: there are some letters for which this is not clear (e.g. S, C, P, O) so marking all capitals is a good habit to get into.

- Websites: it is helpful to the reader to stipulate when websites were accessed. Here, adding the date to each one will cause problems by adding one, maybe two, further lines of text to the page, so the problem has been bypassed by adding the information to the heading (underlined for italic so that it matches). Doing it this way might not please everybody, but it does the job without causing problems! If all websites were accessed on the same day, perhaps when the copy-editor checked that they were all current, a better solution would be to have a separate note at the start of the book giving the date there.

Complimentary or alternative therapies 143   e/

mattress and the patient remains fully clothed
throughout (light, loose-fitting clothing is advised)   ᵕᵀ/

Where can I find out more?

Books and articles

Hands-on Guides Ltd, 2003. *Shiatsu: A Hands-on
Guide* (Oxford)
Herron, Liam, 1987. 'Which Therapy is Right For
You?' *Journal of Natural Medicine* 14: 34–46
Woods, Philippa and Wells, Christy, 2001. *From East
to West: Complementary Therapies and Cultural
Difference*

(Henley)

Websites   (accessed 3 May 2010)

General information on complementary medicine:
Council for Complementary Medicine,
<ccm.org.uk>
For shiatsu in particular, <shiatsu-practice.com>

HOMOEOPATHY

What is Homoeopathy?

Homoeopathy, which was developed in the ~~fifth~~ eighteen
century and gained popularity ~~in this country~~ in the
twentieth, is a treatment that is holistic: that is, it
treats the whole person and not just a particular
physical symptom. Physical symptoms are believed
to be expressions of an underlying general imbala-

p. 144

* p. 143 ends with a horrible word break: for a start, it's bad to break a word over the turn of a page, but the word should not have been broken in mid-syllable anyway! The final letters plus the following comma have been marked to go back to the previous page; the typesetter will be able to tweak the spacing between the preceding words in order to accommodate these extra letters. Notice that you don't need to worry about marking the hyphen: it is a 'soft' hyphen, created by the typesetting machinery as it arranged the words, and it will disappear automatically when 'nce,' is brought back and the word ends up all together on one line. 'Hard' hyphens, those typed as part of the word (as in 'self-publish'), are a different matter: they will be there no matter what, just as if they were a letter in that word.

* 'suffering' was missing its opening quote mark – notice that the symbol is drawn distinctly as an opening quote mark, different from a closing quote mark. Many people write the two identically, but that is not helpful to a typesetter who might end up inserting it in the wrong place, next to the wrong words: you should write exactly what you want, then that is what you'll get.

* 'trea-tment' is a terrible word break – follow the pronunciation and break it as 'treat-ment' (the soft hyphen will stay in the right place when the 't' is taken back). Even if the wording shuffles around when 'nce,' is taken back to the previous page, leaving 'treatment' joined back together again, it's still helpful to show the typesetter that they must not break this word in this place.

* At the end of the first paragraph the wording has been tightened up by means of deletions. This was done for two reasons: (1) it improves the text considerably; (2) we need to save space on the page to bring back the last line of the bullet list, which has ended up on the next page (thereby becoming a type of widow). See more on this below.

* After 'related' there is an extra space. With practice, an over-large patch of white between words becomes easier to spot.

* Your preliminary visual check will have alerted you to the fact that the next heading looks different from its fellows – the type size is too small. Just in case there are other issues as well, the correction points to an example of a correct heading: the typesetter can then check the other aspects of a heading's design,

144 *Complementary or alternative therapies*

nce, and it is that underlying imbalance that is to be treated. The name 'homeopathy' comes from the Greek words for 'the same' and suffering': the treatment is based on the principle of 'like cures like' in a similar way to vaccination. The body is exposed to a minute trace of a substance that would produce certain effects if given in larger quantities, and this is what stimulates the immune system to get to work to heal and those symptoms.

What is involved?

The patient will first have a consultation with the practitioner who will ask questions related | to the patient's medical history, present and past ailments and illnesses, even about their likes and dislikes and what affects them emotionally. This builds up a picture of the patient's general personality and functioning, which the homeopath will then match with appropriate remedies (as pills, powder or liquid) for that person's unique character and needs.

What can it treat?

- allergies, asthma and eczema
- chronic fatigue and feeling run down
- digestive disorders, e.g. IBS
- emotional disorders such as anxiety, depression, insomnia, phobias, grief
- fertility issues, help in pregnancy and labour, menstrual and menopause problems
- physical pain

from p.145

(A) Irritable Bowel Syndrome

203

such font (typeface) and the amount of space that follows. It might be that the size is the only thing wrong, but marking it in this way allows the typesetter to check fully.

- You already noted on p. 142 that the bullet lists are not consistent in the style of bullet used. You will need to mark every instance throughout the book so that they can all be found quickly and amended if necessary, once the answer to the query is decided. Don't leave it to the typesetter to hunt around to find them all – it's much better to mark each one quickly as you encounter it (see the abbreviated mark beside the final bullet point at the top of p. 145, indicating that this is another instance of something already queried) and then you know the job will be done properly.

- The first item in the bullet list has a closing full stop that must be removed. This came about because this item was the last on the original, non-alphabetically ordered list, and the copy-editor forgot to check the punctuation when they re-ordered the list. Easy to do!

- 'IBS': abbreviations should always be spelled out for the reader. As writing 'Irritable Bowel Syndrome' in the margin would clutter it up, and lack of room might lead you to squash your writing so that legibility would become a problem, it's better to code your correction with 'A' in a diamond (followed by 'B', 'C' and so on if you have more than one on a page) and then write the correction clearly where there's room: here, at the foot of the page. Notice that the initial capitals have been confirmed with the triple underline.

- Finally, the bullet list should ideally all be on the one page, so the wandering last line has been marked to be brought back to this page from the next one. As that would make the page a line too long, we can use the 'tightening up' of the wording in the first paragraph to save a line and make room for this addition to the page.

144 *Complementary or alternative therapies*

nce, and it is that underlying imbalance that is to be treated. The name 'homoeopathy' comes from the Greek words for 'the same' and suffering': the treatment is based on the principle of 'like cures like' in a similar way to vaccination. The body is exposed to a minute trace of a substance that would produce certain effects if given in larger quantities, and this is what stimulates the immune system to get to work in healing those symptoms.

What is involved?

The patient will first have a consultation with the practitioner who will ask questions related to the patient's medical history, present and past ailments and illnesses, even about their likes and dislikes and what affects them emotionally. This builds up a picture of the patient's general personality and functioning, which the homeopath will then match with appropriate remedies (as pills, powder or liquid) for that person's unique character and needs.

What can it treat?

- allergies, asthma and eczema
- chronic fatigue and feeling run down
- digestive disorders, e.g. IBS
- emotional disorders such as anxiety, depression, insomnia, phobias, grief
- fertility issues, help in pregnancy and labour, menstrual and menopause problems
- physical pain

(A) Irritable Bowel Syndrome

p. 145

- Of course you will have checked the sequence of page numbers: whenever you meet a sequence of any kind, stop and check it! It's unlikely that a page number will be wrong, but it's a good exercise.

- The second heading on this page has once again been wrongly set, this time in the style of the 'C'-level headings that follow it.

- The 'C'-level headings have problems with the space around them: the first one has too much space beneath it, the second one needs space inserted above it.

- Still looking at the layout of this section, you can quickly see that some of the lines should be indented to match the other entries. If more than one line is involved, as at the end of the page, you can mark the whole block rather than each individual line.

- In the first reference, there is no space between the sentences. This can be as easy to miss as the extra space on the previous page, so your proofreading eye will become trained to looking closely at the ends of sentences!

- The place of publication for the second reference is now confirmed as Oxford, so it has been written in with the capital 'O' confirmed.

- The wording and page numbers of the third reference have also been checked and need to be corrected. If you re-wrote 'Which is the Right Therapy' as 'Which Therapy is Right', what a mess it would make of the margins – compare the beautiful simplicity and clarity of the two BSI symbols that do the whole job!

- The final correction is the page numbers for that article: '46–59' must be changed to '34–46'. As '46' is already there it does not need to be deleted and written in again: simply add the new numbers before it and delete the unneeded ones that follow it. Notice that '34–' has been marked to 'close up', or join on, to what follows it; this confirms for the typesetter that it is not a separate item but part of a sequence.

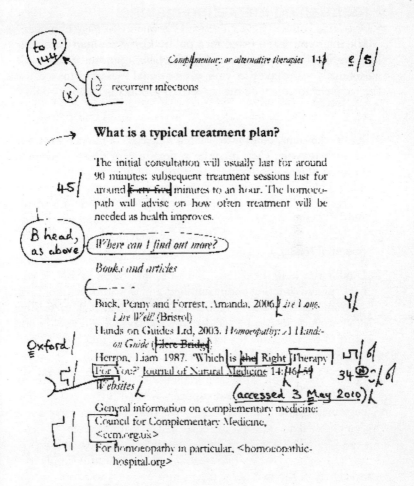

to p. 144

Complementary or alternative therapies 14♭ e / s /

(x) recurrent infections

What is a typical treatment plan?

The initial consultation will usually last for around
90 minutes: subsequent treatment sessions last for
around ~~forty-five~~ 45 minutes to an hour. The homoeopath will advise on how often treatment will be
needed as health improves.

B head, as above

Where can I find out more?

Books and articles

Buck, Penny and Forrest, Amanda, 2006 *Live Long, Live Well* (Bristol)

Hands on Guides Ltd, 2003. *Homoeopathy: A Hands-on Guide* (~~Here Bridg~~) Oxford

Herron, Liam 1987. 'Which is ~~the~~ Right Therapy For You?' *Journal of Natural Medicine* 14: 46–54 34

Websites

General information on complementary medicine:
Council for Complementary Medicine,
<ccm.org.uk>
For homoeopathy in particular, <homoeopathic-hospital.org>

Proofreading marketing material

Marketing material to promote a publication will almost certainly last less time than the associated product, but needs to be taken just as seriously – mistakes in your promotional messages may cause the recipient to conclude the associated product is of poor quality. A few tips:

1 If mistakes have crept into printed materials, and they were not of your making, there may be a pressure for you to accept a printer's judgement that what you are examining is 'commercially acceptable' which means they do not want to bear the expense of reprinting and may consider offering you a discount instead. While saving money may appeal, be aware that circulating substandard material will affect how your book is seen by the potential reader.

2 Double check all the details. The title, subtitle and ISBN. If you have quoted ordering phone numbers and web information, ring/ send an email to each number/address quoted. It is surprising how often digits can be accidentally transposed and you do not want to require your readers to have to investigate how to buy from you – most will not bother.

3 Ensure you are on your own mailing list (postal and email) so you can see how information appears when it is received as your customers see it.

14

Book production

with Katharine Allenby

Production is the part of the publishing process that turns your words and spaces, thoughts and ideas, into a real book. It becomes a physical object that encapsulates everything that you have put into the project and becomes something that will last, if not for ever, at least for a very long time. However, production is also the technical, expensive part of publishing, and something that even some professional publishers can find daunting. Make a serious mistake in the production process and it is hard or costly to undo. And it is a world full of its own colourful jargon that can seem impenetrable.

This chapter will demystify book production for you and break it down into a series of choices to be made about paper, inks and binding. Many of these decisions are interlinked, so you will need to read right through this chapter before making your mind up about the best way to produce your book.

Self-publishers, and for that matter professional publishers with inexpert staff, can often fall into the trap of making a book that looks and feels all wrong when you pick it up and open it. There should be a 'rightness' to the feel of a well-made book. A wonderful designer I once worked with described it as the 'heft' of a book – the combination of the size, weight, paper and binding together producing something that feels right in your hand, and is fit for purpose.

Paper

Paper makes up about a third of the cost of producing a book, so your choice will make a difference to the overall cost of manufacturing your book, and thence to the selling price. The quality of the paper you choose will make all the difference to how your book looks and feels; but bear in mind that too expensive can feel as wrong as too cheap.

Paper for books falls into three distinct categories, although it comes in any number of weights, colours and finishes. A standard novel will probably be printed on a **book wove**, which is a slightly rough textured paper with a good **bulk**; that is each sheet is quite thick for its weight. This type of paper maximises the width of the spine for the number of pages, making your book look substantial. It also has good **opacity**, which means that the print won't show through very easily from one side of the page to the other, and it is reasonably economical.

However, any book containing photographs, printed in black and white or in colour, will need a much smoother paper surface, and you should consider using an **art paper**. This is much more expensive, but will give that luxurious feel you get in lovely art books. Art papers are usually bright white, and come in gloss, matt, or silk finishes, silk being a halfway house between gloss and matt. Gloss is rather reflective and not ideal for books – the glare off the page makes it harder to read text; matt or silk are probably safer choices. Art paper has a surface added to the paper (this is kaolinite; often referred to as **size**) which gives that smoothness, but also makes the paper much heavier, so a book printed on this type of paper will weigh considerably more than one printed on other sorts of paper. This is a consideration if you want to post lots of copies of your book, or need to think about transportation or storage.

A mid choice is **offset paper**, which is not dissimilar to photo-copying paper, and is often used for educational books and travel guides. It is smooth enough for a nice crisp image, and some papers in this category can even be suitable for printing a few black and white photos, or coloured shaded areas, though it isn't recommended if you have many pictures or want to include lots of colour. The sheet is not as thick as a book wove paper, so if you have a lot of pages and don't want your book to be too fat, it would be a good choice.

We are all familiar with paper that goes brown around the edges in time. The cheaper papers are made from the wood of the whole tree and, on exposure to light, the wood from the part nearest the bark contains chemicals that will cause the paper to discolour.

However, so-called **wood-free** paper is made from wood pulp from which this section of the tree has been removed, so it should not discolour in the same way. Wood-free paper is slightly more expensive, but you may think it is worth the extra cost if your book is likely to be kept and read for a long time. Most types of paper are available in wood-free versions.

The weight of paper you need will vary depending on the type you choose. Paper weight is measured in grams per square metre (shortened to gsm) in the UK but in the US it is measured in pounds per 500 sheets and also depends on the type of paper selected. For a book wove, something between 60 and 80 gsm (US 40 to 55 pounds offset stock) is common. With offset paper you would probably choose 80 to 90 gsm (US 55 to 60 pounds), and with art paper probably 115 to 135 gsm (US 80 to 90 pounds). Be wary of choosing a paper that is too heavy: it will cost you a lot more and make the book feel stiff and awkward. However, one that is too light will increase the show through (when you can see the image from the reverse side through the paper) and make the book thinner and floppier. Try to find a good balance.

Spare a thought for the colour of the paper. Like wedding dresses, if you compare lots of apparently white papers you will find the shade can vary enormously from bright white to cream. Bright white sets off any illustrations and photos well, but it does tend to glare so it is not ideal for a book you will sit down and read for long periods. Cream papers are much easier on the eye because there is less contrast between the colour of the paper and the black ink (and it has been proven that readers with dyslexia find books printed on cream paper easier to read). Black on cream also has a more traditional look to it. You will also find that there are numerous off-white shades, which offer a happy medium.

Your printer will be able to give you samples of the paper stocks they have, and will be able to source other types of paper too if you want something special, although that will usually cost more. Ask them for advice on which type of paper will best suit the content of your book. Copy the style of another book you like, which is similar to the one you are publishing. You could also ask the printer to produce a **dummy**, which is a book of blank pages made up with the right number of pages and in the right size, usually with a cover attached too; this is the best way of ensuring your book will end up with the feel you want. However, the printer will probably charge you for doing this as they have to be produced by hand. Alternatively they may be able to show you other books they have produced that are similar to what you are planning which will help you to decide.[119]

Inks and colours

Books printed in 'black only' are straightforward. However, for some books such as educational books or guide books, it can be really useful to add another colour for diagrams, headings, or shaded areas. Choose any colour or colours you like, but make sure it isn't too pale or it won't show up well on white paper, and bear in mind that using colour will add to the cost of the printing quite significantly, so don't venture into this unless you are sure it is contributing something important. Printers use the **Pantone colour matching system**, and have books of colours to choose from, a bit like paint charts in DIY stores. The colours are coded, such as PMS 485, which identifies exactly which colour you want, and tells the printer how to mix it. If you are using design software such as InDesign or Quark Xpress you can select a Pantone colour on screen. If you do decide on a second colour, take care when choosing. Strong colours tend to date quite quickly and a muted, 'muddy' colour may turn out to be both longer-lasting and softer on the eye.

If you are including colour photographs or illustrations your book will need to be printed in **full colour**. Actually only four colours are used, called the four process colours, or CMYK which stands for cyan (blue), magenta (pink), yellow, and black (denoted by the K). Many computer printers now use this system for their toners, so it may well be familiar to you. Your design software (see chapter 12 for more detail) will convert your photographs into a series of tiny dots which can only be seen under a magnifying glass, and combinations of the four process colours and the size

[119] Along similar lines, if you are preparing to produce leaflets, depending on what paper you are thinking of using, a printer can estimate the weight of the finished item; very useful if you are planning a mailing and do not wish to exceed a certain postage band.

of the dots will create all the colours you need. You can also use the process colours for coloured headings or graphics, but it is not advisable to have colour for ordinary text as the tiny dots make the letters harder to read than a crisp black outline.

Binding

The most common styles are paperback and hardback, but your book could also be stapled, or wire-o (spiral) bound.

Paperbacks (also called limp or softback) are economical to produce and suit most kinds of book. There are two sorts of paperback – sewn and unsewn. Unsewn are by far the more common, where the spine is simply glued. Unsewn paperbacks are fairly durable, although don't like being forced open too hard and don't open completely flat. Sewn paperbacks have their pages sewn together with thread before the glue is applied. This is a stronger (and slightly more expensive) binding, but will last longer and tend to open slightly flatter. Books that are going to be used a lot, such as reference books, tend to be sewn. We are all familiar with old paperbacks where the glue has cracked and the pages start to fall out, but modern glues are much more flexible so this should not be a problem in future. However, printers who specialise in producing books are much more expert at this than smaller companies who only bind books occasionally. Look at other books your printer has manufactured, and check that the glue isn't coming out at the ends and clogging the pages, or that enough glue has been used to fix the cover on securely. Also check that the spine is nice and square.

Hardbacks (or cased books) are much grander, and should be longer lasting, but do cost quite a lot more to manufacture. As with paperbacks the pages can be just glued together, or sewn and glued. The case (the cardboard part surrounding the pages) can be covered in bookbinding cloth or paper, or paper printed with a design (known as a **printed paper case**). You will need to choose **endpapers** – the pages that fix the text pages into the case, which can be either coloured paper to tone in with the case or jacket colours, or just match the paper the pages are printed on. The book title and author's name can be **blocked** (embossed) in gold or silver or another colour onto the spine and perhaps the front of the case, and you may want to have a printed **dust jacket** wrapped around the book carrying the book design. Hardbacks require specialist manufacturing, so you will need to choose a printing firm that undertakes that kind of work, and they will be able to guide you about the choice of all these materials. You will also need their advice on the size and type of artwork you will need to give them for a jacket or blocking.

Saddle-stitching (or stapling) is the cheapest way of binding smaller books up to a maximum of about 64–80 pages, depending on what sort of paper you choose. A saddle-stitched book is durable, will open flat, but doesn't have a spine, so it is not so easy to find on a bookshelf. Almost all printers are able to do saddle-stitching, so you won't need a specialist book manufacturer for this.

Wire-o (or spiral binding with wire) is wonderful for books that must open flat, such as music scores, cookery or some educational books. It is quite expensive, and you will need to look around for a printer who has this facility. You also need to be careful that the wire doesn't get crushed if you are sending books by post, or doesn't damage other books next to it on a bookshelf, so don't choose this option unless your book will really benefit from this style of binding.

Covers and finishing

Your book, if it is paperback, stapled or wire-o bound, will need a cover, which is usually printed in colour on the outside only, but can be printed inside too if you wanted to. As with the text pages, you can opt for printing it in one or two colours chosen from the Pantone range, but it is more usual to print in the four process colours so that photographs or illustrations can be included. Book covers are usually printed on one-sided art board, which gives a nice smooth outside to print on, and a more rigid inside so that it isn't too floppy; 240 gsm board (US 90 pound cover stock) is about the average for a paperback, but 200 gsm (US 75 or 80 pounds) would be fine for a smaller book, and 300 gsm (US 114 pounds) would better suit a chunkier reference type of book that will get harder use.

After it has been printed the coverboard will need a finish on it, to help protect it from finger marks, scuffing and general wear and tear. The cheapest form is **UV varnishing**, which is a sprayed on gloss coating, and often used for novels. More expensive books, or ones which will have harder wear, are usually **laminated**, where a thin plastic film is applied over the printed surface. Laminate reinforces the board, helps to stop tearing and creasing, and it comes in gloss finish or matt; the latter giving that silky feel you sometimes find on books.

If you are publishing a hardback, you might want to produce a **dust jacket**, to help promote the book in the same way as a paperback cover. All the same principles apply as for covers above; except that jackets are printed on art paper of approximately 135 gsm (US 90 pound offset stock).

There are other finishes that you could add to your book, but bear in mind that each will add to the cost, so think carefully before committing to these, and certainly resist the temptation to over-indulge; ironically spending more on additional finishes may make your product look amateurish. Bear in mind that just because a book costs more to manufacture that doesn't always mean you will be able to charge more for it. Think about how other competing books are presented and priced, so that yours fits into that market. However if you are producing a special volume, perhaps for an occasion, you could think about adding **ribbon markers** (only possible on hardbacks), or **head and tail bands** (again, hardbacks only) which are those stripy silk parts that cover the glue on smart books, **coloured edges** (possible on hardbacks or paperbacks), or **spot varnishing** on a paperback cover, where part of the cover or jacket design is highlighted in gloss over the top of a matt laminated background.

Choosing a printer

This is one of the most important decisions of all, but you will need to decide how you want your book to look before you can select a printer, as their equipment varies and you need to find someone who can cater for your needs at a reasonable price. Price should not be the only consideration though: you will want to find a company that can offer a good quality product, and can manufacture your books when you need them. Larger book printers are sometimes committed to contracts with commercial publishers, so may not be willing to take on smaller projects, but you may be willing to wait in the interests of the romantic appeal of having your book on the same presses as those whose work you admire. Smaller printers can be easier to approach and more eager to please, but be sure they have the right skills and equipment. Ask around for recommendations of reliable printers, or look in the front of books similar to your own and see who has printed them. A local printer might be a good resource, and you may save money on delivery, but ask to look at similar work they have done and see whether it looks good. Most printers now print to a very high standard, but if you want to be sure of professional standards when it comes to binding – and hardback binding in particular – you might be well advised to go to a specialist book printer, as smaller companies do not always have this equipment and may not be able to produce such a professional product. The BPIF (British Printing Industries Federation) lists members of its Book Production Section at www. britishprint.com/sigs.asp?s=bps which you might find helpful as a starting place. In the US you can find book printers listed at www. printaccess.com; search in your area and then look for books in the products and capability search (books are sometimes listed as a speciality).

The size of your print run is likely to determine whether you should choose a digital printer or a litho printer. If you are printing 500 copies or fewer, **digital printing** is probably the most economic choice. Digital printing is just a high quality photocopying process, and is quick and easy to set up, so it is cheaper for smaller numbers of books. It also enables you to try producing a small number of books, and then go back for reprints as and when you need them if successful, this is often referred to as **print on demand** or POD. Print on demand is a business process whereby copies of a book (or other document) are only produced once an order has been received. Using old printing technology, such as letterpress or offset printing, it was not economic to produce a single copy, but with the development of digital printing, which is a similar process to photocopying, producing a single copy became possible. Smaller publishing companies, or those trying to meet demand for highly specialised titles (e.g. academic houses) find print on demand a very useful technology as it avoids printing and then paying for the distribution and storage of material for which there is not yet a potential sale. Larger publishers may use print on demand to keep titles permanently available or as a marketing gambit, to test the appeal of new work. Print on demand is very useful to the self-publishing author as they can gain a small number of titles at a cost-effective price. The quality of print on demand products is usually distinguishable from those produced by conventional methods (and of a slightly lower quality), but is getting better all the time (see also pages 218–219). You may not want lots of boxes of books filling your spare room until you have sold them, so be careful not to order too enthusiastically until you are sure how many you can sell or distribute. Bear in mind that you will need somewhere clean and dry to keep the books, so storage might be a critical factor in your decision, and books do take up a lot of space. Small print runs are also lower risk – you don't want to pay out for lots of books you might not be able to sell, or might take years to cover their cost. Keep a copy of the files you send to the printer, so that you can update or make changes to the text should you want to produce a new edition, or need to change printers in the future for any reason. Commercial publishers are turning to digital printing more and more, so that they don't have warehouses full of unsold stock; following their lead may be sensible for you too.

However, if you know you will be able to sell lots of copies, or perhaps have guaranteed orders already for your book, offset litho printing is likely to be cheaper for print runs of more than about 500 copies.

Litho is the traditional method of printing, where printing plates are inked, and the image transferred to the paper via rollers. Although not new, it is still amazing technology, where the surface of the printing plate is treated so that the ink (usually made from vegetable oils) is attracted to the image area and repelled from the background. It is time-consuming and expensive to set up the printing machines correctly, but once ready they produce copies very quickly and economically. Certainly for colour printing, and for books with lots of pictures, litho printing tends to be better quality, although it has to be said that digitally printed books are improving all the time, and it is increasingly hard to tell the difference. Some printing companies offer both methods of production, and it is always worth asking for a price for each type and seeing how they compare.

Get written quotes from several different companies, as you may find they differ enormously. It is a good idea to ask the price for several different quantities, say 100, 200 or 500 books, as it may help you decide what would be a sensible number to print. Any printer will need to know the following so that they can give you an accurate quotation:

* Number of copies (or a range of numbers)
* Trimmed size/format
* Number of pages
* What sort of file or artwork are you going to give them to print from?
* Do you want to see proofs? This may add to the cost but will ensure the finished product is exactly as you want it
* Text pages printed just black, black and other colours, or four process colours?
* Cover printed just black, black and other colours, or four process colours?
* Text paper – what sort of paper and what weight? Let the printer know if the images or background colours print right to the edge of the pages (called 'bleeds'), as they will need to buy a different size of paper to accommodate that
* Cover board – what sort and what weight?
* What sort of finishing you want on the cover?
* What binding style?
* Where do you want the books delivered?

Talk it all through with your printer and make sure they understand what you are looking for. You may also need to discuss how quickly you need the books, when the work can be fitted into their schedules, and payment terms. A successful relationship with a printer often comes down to good communication between you, so do ask for explanation if they use technical language that you don't understand. Don't be afraid to ask for advice and guidance from the experts!

This chapter has covered much technical information, which may be hard to absorb at first reading. You may subsequently decide to avoid having to learn about the technical side of book production, and use a publishing solutions company to manage the process. But some understanding of the range of choices involved in book production will help you understand the options available, appreciate when decisions have to be made, and spot when an effective solution has been reached.

15

Using an author solutions company

'An SFA is a self-financing author, and Manutius is a vanity press. Earnings high, overhead miniscule ... Normal publishers ship to booksellers, (we) ship only to authors ... The main thing, Signor Garamond says, is to make sure the authors remain loyal to us. We can get along fine without readers...

Finally, the moment of truth. A year and a half later, Garamond writes: Dear friend, as I feared, you are fifty years ahead of your time. Rave reviews in the dozens, awards, critical acclaim, ça va sans dire. But few copies sold. The public is not ready. We are forced to make space in the warehouse, as stipulated in the contract (copy enclosed). Unless you exercise your right to buy the unsold copies at half the list price, we must pulp them.

About fifty authors a year, and Manutius always ends up well in the black. And without remorse: Manutius is dispensing happiness.'[120]

Using a one stop self-publishing firm

Long before the age of the iPod, people had stereo systems in their living rooms, while their children often had much simpler devices. Our family was no exception. I left for university with a simple Philips tape recorder, to which a friend had kindly attached a single loud speaker. My twenty-first birthday was looming and I decided I would ask for a stereo system. I wanted the then highly fashionable music centre – a record deck, tape recorder and radio all in one neat box, with two speakers to plug into easily identifiable holes.

[120] Umberto Eco, *Foucault's Pendulum*, London: Vintage (2001)

I was, however, blessed with a vociferous group of friends studying astronomy who were heavily into hifi. They were convinced that what I really needed was a sound system; a compilation of different component parts delivering a high quality musical experience. I was taken to a warehouse in Dundee where four enormous boxes were purchased, watched while the whole was assembled and told to appreciate the results. Quite frankly their evident delight eluded me, and I never learned to put the thing together on my own.

The same decision awaits those seeking a self-publishing solution. Should you go for one completely packaged service, available from a single point of contact with one human interface, or try to track down the various component parts you need? Off the peg or bespoke? The answer will depend on several factors:

1 **How much time do you have?**
There will be some who want a book very quickly (due to illness or an impending anniversary), others who can take their time and will relish taking it slowly.

2 **How much control do you want over the process?**
Do you want to manage each component part of the process or leave it to someone else to do that for you?

3 **Are you ever likely to do this again?**
Do you want to learn about the processes of publishing, to enjoy every stage and even consider doing it again, or do you just want a book?

4 **How much experience do you have of making choices in this area?**
Are the aesthetics important to you? Do you have a preferred typeface, type of paper, cover look? If you have never noticed these things at all, you may like to grow your awareness, or you may prefer the choices to be made for you. If you have looked at other self-published books and appreciated that production values could have been higher, and felt embarrassed for the author, then think about employing expert assistance where needed. Most self-publishers would have a very steep learning curve to manage all the stages involved to a high standard, unless

they already have some knowledge or experience of design and publishing. You can learn along the way, but it takes time and mistakes can be expensive. Publishing is much harder than it looks.

Case study: Barbara Abbs, author of gardening titles

'I had a book contract with a publishing firm to write a guide to French gardens. Unfortunately the firm was taken over and my book, already at copy-editing stage, was abandoned, along with several others. It sat sadly in a cupboard for a few years until I met someone who self-published a lot of local books, and this spurred me on to do something with mine.

I set the book to edit on screen and wept tears of frustration, as every time I corrected an error, the pages went doo-lally. I printed two hundred copies and then tried to sell it. I tramped round bookshops in Brighton, Lancing, London and so on. I was lucky enough to get a mention in *The Garden* (magazine of the Royal Horticultural Society) and after that I sold the rest through mail order.

I discovered that the cover on the book was too thin, and when put in a shop window in the sunlight, tended to curl up. I reprinted, using a thicker card, and replaced a few copies without being asked. Then Quiller Press in England and Saga Press in America bought it and Ngaere Macray at Saga Press (a fantastic business woman) managed to place the guide as a 'reward' for Air France frequent flyers – and sold 20,000 copies.

While I did not make any money from my self-publishing venture, since then I have managed to get publishers for my garden books (although sadly not for my fiction). That first book does however give me particular pleasure. Years later I wrote a piece for the *Garden Writers Guild Newsletter* saying it was the most satisfactory book I had ever published. It had all the things I thought were necessary in a guide book, and it was indexed properly by me in a way I thought gardeners would like. And it got my writing career started.'

There is a range of companies offer self-publishing services (often called 'author solutions') which in general offer a method of achieving a product in finalised form. These range from large organisations, many of which are based in the US (e.g. Lulu, Blurb and Createspace) offering the author the opportunity to produce an (often illustrated) book through printing what is uploaded onto a website without further amendation and at a high per copy cost (ideal for books of photographs with an intentionally limited circulation); to smaller organisations offering a service that is more geared to individuals who want to sell the resulting product to a wider audience through booksellers, Amazon, Kindle etc. There are many overlaps of ownership (Authorhouse, iUniverse, Xlibris and Trafford Publishing are all owned by Author Solutions Inc). A wide range of these organisations is helpfully reviewed in *To Self-publish or Not to Self-publish* by Mick Rooney in which the author comments on the services and standards of around 40 such firms, and gives each an overall score out of ten based on the information they make available about themselves, and feedback from those who have used them.[121]

Particular issues when looking for the services of an author solutions company

1 What do you want from an author solutions company?
Are you seeking a book to sell, or a one-off to be completed in time for a particular occasion? Your needs may vary over time; some authors want management of the entire process, others use publishing solutions companies to get a single reading copy of their book, just to get a 'feel' for how it will look in book form, how it will 'bulk up', and as a basis for further editing and proofreading. Clarity before commencement is helpful.

2 Publisher brand
One of the key advantages of being published rather than self-published is that you gain *external* validation and authentication

---

[121] Leicester: Troubador Publishing (2010) www.troubador.co.uk which owns Matador, a self-publishing imprint

of your writing project from the brand of the sponsoring publisher. The potential reader is encouraged to build on a package of physical and subliminal values associated with the publisher's name, demonstrated in their products and services; their confidence in your publication augmented because it comes from the same stable. In a world where there is a vast number of options of different things to read, this *mediated choice* is very valuable.

But for an organisation offering author solutions, whose business model depends on selling publishing services to paying clients, this is difficult to achieve. Most self-publishing firms offer a range of different publishing services, of varying levels of quality, but it is the client who decides which ones they need, and they select the eventual publishing package. The overall quality of the final object depends on how much the client has been willing to spend on the component parts of the publishing process (e.g. editorial advice, copy-editing, proofreading and the physical and design component) not on the demonstrable brand, and associated physical qualities of the publishing house. Large organisations offering self-publishing, who have expensive buildings, teams and advertising plans to support, can find that the physical standard of their output ranges widely in quality, and that as a result the potential self-publishing author may not wish to be part of the same stable.

Looking to the future, if a self-publishing services company can convince the market that their products are well produced and that their brand signifies a level of appropriate quality to the consumer, they will be in a very strong position within the publishing market – not just the self-publishing market; they might become a first port of call for authors seeking a trouble-free route to publication.

3 How much support you need in preparing a product for publication

As discussed in chapter one, 'to publish' is a multi-layered verb, and what you present will be compared, whether consciously or unconsciously, by the market with what else exists for the same market sector. This may not matter to you if your aim is to produce a unique product, perhaps a book that will grace a special anniversary or make a bespoke present, and have a very limited print run.

If on the other hand you seek to produce something with a market fit, which will be recognised by retailers as the sort of book they want to sell, and customers as the kind of book they usually choose to buy and read, you may need more guidance on the options available. Ironically, spending more money on advice, and less on the production values for your titles, may actually augment the impression your product is able to make. Publishing solutions companies offer additional services, which may appeal to the self-published author, but which may diminish the chance of the book's being taken seriously by the market. For example, the self-publishing author may decide they would like the best quality paper (heavier than is usual for the category of book being produced) or to have book's edges sprayed with a coloured ink (which is not usual except for very highly priced or special edition publishing e.g. leather bound bibles with gold edges). Both are examples of services that may cost the commissioning author more, but end up impacting negatively on the retailer's willingness to stock, or the customer's willingness to choose the title.

If you are trying to break into a market and sell your work, paying an organisation for detailed advice on the product characteristics that the reader expects to find may be more helpful than just a list of what is technically possible (as offered on most self-publishing websites).

4 Marketing

Marketing is often the area that self-publishing authors are least prepared for. Lacking prior experience they can feel ill equipped to inform the wider world of the availability of their new title.

Author solutions companies often offer assistance with marketing, but it is vital for the prospective author to be clear about what it is they are securing. Are they giving you what amounts to a self-help book and a message of good luck, or is there more substance to what they intend to provide? Be clear now to avoid disappointment later. A good way of spotting a marketing orientation in an organisation you are thinking of working with is to consult their website. Is it bulging with the books they have produced (as are those of the traditional publishers) or is it just selling *their* services? If the latter, you have a clearer understanding of their priorities.

5 Distribution

Persuading bookshops to stock titles, managing the despatch, ensuring a prominent position in store and then a constant supply is difficult. Some author solutions companies advertise that any title they publish will be stocked by relevant retailers, but this may be in return for an augmented fee, or higher band of service level. This may sound impressive, but be sure to check on the practicalities of this offer and the level of service in return. There is a difference between being technically *available* (the title can be ordered in if requested by a customer) and being physically *present* in the shops. And in any case, without a marketing 'push' to potential customers, to encourage them into shops in search of a title that is available there, and getting a bookshop to agree to stock, it may be wasted effort.

Also with the requirements of the retailer in mind, if self-publishing authors want to get their titles into retailers' outlets, you have to work to their deadlines. The key chains and wholesalers work six months in advance, and if you want to take advantage of their marketing and sales mechanisms (e.g. regular catalogues and being included in their list of available titles) you have to work within this framework. It is technically possible to produce a book more quickly, and if it is for private dissemination rather than retail sale that may not be a problem, but if you circumvent the normal selling processes there is little chance of selling books into[122] retail outlets pre-publication. Impatience on the part of the author is inevitable, but this cycle of selling into stores to ensure stock is available on publication to meet orchestrated demand is part of the established selling cycle for books.

6 Ownership and ease of extraction from your contractual arrangements

If you decide to work with an author solutions organisation, you will have to sign a contract for production of your book. You will pay them for management and production of the text, but you need to pay close attention to the future ownership of the layout used to print (usually referred to as the PDFs,[123] which provide the

---

[122] Note the vocabulary; you sell books *into* a retail chain, in the hope they will *range them across* their stores (i.e. stock them in all of them)

[123] See pages 177, 183

image to be printed for each page). Do the rights belong to you or the publishing company? And if you are locked into remaining with the publishing company, how long is this for (this varies, but companies have been known to require two or even five years). A digital print edition of a book is a great bargain if you are buying a small number, but if the title is a success, and more are needed, it would almost certainly be cheaper to switch to a conventional litho printer (see chapter 14 on production). You need to be clear about who has ownership of the material, and if possible to agree only to non-exclusive rights, so that you are free to publish another edition or move to another publisher too.

Within a traditional publishing house, the income from high-selling titles offsets the development costs of new products, and the lower profile of those that sell less well but add prestige to the overall list. It can be very difficult to predict which titles will do best; some books may have strong literary merit and take longer to write, but have a narrower appeal (unless they are brought to public attention through winning a prize). As all authors belong to the brand, there is an overall adjustment and mutuality; bestselling authors were once starters too. But within a self-publishing structure, where each unit belongs, and has been paid for by an individual author, there will necessarily be less interest in the common good of the organisation as a whole. *Caveat emptor*,[124] or in this particular case, pay close attention to the contract.

7 How easy to communicate with is the self-publishing company you are considering?

Many advertisements for self-publishing solutions concentrate on the low cost of the finished item. Low costs tend to imply low profit margins, and if individual customers are on the phone, occupying the time and attention of staff members, they cannot be getting on with their main roles. Traditional publishing houses have long complained that authors tend to appreciate only the needs of their own publication rather than the house's overall priorities, can become over-frequent communicators – and have tried to encourage them to consolidate their suggestions rather than sending in a few every day, as they think of them.

[124] Buyer beware

Consumers meanwhile have got used to obtaining a wide range of products and services online, from flights to car insurance, and understand that while this speeds the process, and reduces the associated costs – you get penalised for changing your mind. The same principle works in publishing. To keep costs low, many self-publishing firms insist on email contact only, which has the added advantages of encouraging the customer to be precise about what they want, and ensuring a permanent record of what they have asked for – both useful if things start to get sticky. If you want to be able to talk more to your self-publishing company, be prepared to pay for a commensurately higher level of service.

8 Editorial services

All books need editing. Is your planned publication going to get enough?

We have already discussed in chapter 10 that there are different levels of editing available. A 'structural edit' involves consideration of the shape of the book; whether it is well organised and whether key parts of the story/the text the reader would expect to find are missing (both fiction and non-fiction can benefit from this process). A 'copy-edit' works towards the creation of a perfect text; concentrating on grammar, punctuation, spelling and clarity. If you are being offered a package, look to see how many hours of editing are included, and think whether this is likely to be enough. Spell checkers are notoriously unreliable, and 'find and replace' may not be appropriate for an entire manuscript (your instructions need to be particularly specific or you end up deleting real words by accident). Could you read your book in the number of hours they have quoted, let alone edit it at the same time?

9 Minimum ordering quantities

Does the self-publishing package you have been offered mean you are paying for more copies than you really want?

What self-publishing firms offer

Most self-publishing firms specify the various services they can offer you. These will probably include:

- Some form of initial discussion, online or on the telephone

- Limited copy-editing, usually a certain amount's worth

- The creation of cover artwork

- The design of the interior of the book – selection of typeface, width of margins, position of page numbers, a decision on the 'headers' and 'footers' for the page and how footnotes will be managed. The application of the combination selected to your work (often referred to overall as 'typesetting' – see chapter 12)

- The allocation of an ISBN

- A proof for you to check, probably electronic (you will have to print it out yourself if you want to check it on paper, which will almost certainly result in a higher standard of proofreading)

- Printing (usually through digital printing – see chapter on production)

- An imprint (or brand mark e.g. Penguin) on the spine – theirs

- Binding, according to a series of options from paperback to hardback with various additional sophistications available at additional cost

- Digital formatting as an ebook, allowing readers to download your book through various portable ereading devices

- Distribution through outlets with which they have an agreement – several self-publishing houses have an arrangement with Amazon and Waterstone's, that titles will be held in stock for a certain number of weeks. On Amazon all books are technically in stock as they can be ordered from the publisher for despatch to customers

- An account with a wholesaler (e.g. Bertrams, Gardners, The American Book Company). This means booksellers can order your books and stock them. If they do not have an account, your book will not be available through bookshops which will greatly reduce its availability

- A first printed copy for you

- Other copies available to order at a discount off the published price

- Limited marketing consultancy (although this may be at an additional cost)

What is generally not included

- Sufficient copy-editing to ensure an error-free, fully readable text

- Your own imprint for the spine. If you decide to publish under your own organisational (or imprint) name, you will have to pay for the creation of an associated design and logo

- Textual advice and manuscript consultancy

- Proofreading

- The writing of a blurb for the back cover and its effective layout

- The preparation of author information for the inside front cover or back cover

- Empathetic and objective advice on how the book should look in order to be an effective part of the market for which it is intended

- Cover laminating, if you want this, and other specialised techniques such as the colouring of the edges of the paper, insertion of marker ribbons, spot embossing and varnishing of the cover, you will pay more

- The provision of a bar code if you are seeking retail sales

- Shipping and handling of your books back to you; complimentary copies included

- Advice on whether what you are offering is publishable

How to spot (quickly) a poorly published book

1 The back cover blurb is difficult to read – contains mistakes, is set over too wide a measure, is reversed out from a solid colour (white text on a solid background, or even worse, a photograph), is printed in capital letters or italics. The back jacket is to me the most significant – and speedy – indicator of a poorly published book.

2 Unappealing or unattractive cover design; in particular difficulty in reading the title and other key details.

3 Unattractive colour of the book, strong single Pantone colours look more amateur than muted colours.

4 Unattractive typeface inside: e.g. Comic Sans or *handwriting* fonts.

5 Text measure inside is too wide, with narrow gutters (the space between the text and the binding) which means the book has to be peeled back in an uncomfortable manner in order to access all the words (usually done in order to put more words on each page and hence reduce the number of pages needed). Similarly, a wide text measure means the reader's eyes have to scan over a lot of material and hence their head has to move (like watching a tennis match). A well laid out book enables the viewer to scan down the middle of the text and speed read.

6 Lots of pages left over at the end. Book production using lithographic printing is printed in whole sections, usually of 16 or 32 pages; the layout managed with this in mind. Lots of pages left at the end can look odd; and this effect is exacerbated if you have 'Notes' written at the top of the empty pages. Material that is digitally printed is produced on single sheets so you can have the number of pages you need, but the quality of print may not be as high. For information on the different types of printing chapter 14 on production.

7 Jacket does not wrap around the pages effectively; spine is misaligned (too narrow or wide for the book).

8 Poor glue/sticking which seeps out at the ends of the spine.

Final general advice to consider before making a decision on which self-publishing firm to instruct

1 What is your deadline?

The marketing information of many self-publishing firms tends to be based on two core messages: firstly cheapness and secondly speed of delivery of the final product. Is this their rush or yours?

Remember that most self-publishing firms make their money from providing you with a service that results in a delivery, not from guiding you through the process of deciding whether or not your manuscript is worth publishing. To put it bluntly, it is in their interests to get you onto the printing presses sooner rather than later.

How soon do you want your product? Has being turned down by traditional publishers dented your spirit? Do you want to make choices and progress the project quickly, both of which can feel empowering and exciting, and move on with creating something else? Or do you want to pay a little more and wait a little longer to ensure you consider all the relevant options? If you want to take it all much more slowly, look for a firm that depends on repeat business and recommendation from other self-publishing authors for client acquisition. And if you want to get it into bookshops, you definitely need to pay attention to their key selling cycles, and work a good six months ahead.

2 Gut feeling

Do the people you are dealing with sound empathetic; are they likely to be a pleasure to deal with? Do they sound as if they are listeners or are they too busy selling their service? Have they seemed interested in your project or just expressed general enthusiasm? Do they understand the particular criteria that matter to you e.g. time/ quality/weight?

At literary festivals you will usually find at least a few self-publishing firms pitching their services. This can be an odd experience. Whereas most of the book business proceeds in a calm, dignified, if not slightly disdainful manner towards the author, the representatives for some self-publishing firms tend to be unashamedly outward-facing and extremely eager to communicate. Does this keenness to sell block their ability to guide you towards a product you would want to own? Do you think you will be proud or apologetic to have been published by them?

3 Location

Where are they calling from? Does this matter to you? How local do you want them to be? Will their precise communication channels encourage you to be more professional in your requirements?

4 Samples

Have they provided you with a sample of their previous output? It's not enough to look at their material on the web; you want to hold it in your hands. Reading books is a physical experience, and you often only appreciate the careful decisions behind a product when you are confronted with something that has not involved the same attention to detail.

Their job in general is to manage what you send, not delay its arrival on the machine by further manipulation of the text. How rigorous do you suspect they will be in ensuring you submit appropriate material for wider dissemination? What is the editorial standard of their own communications?

5 Stages of production

Is their breakdown of stages achievable; do you feel as if they are making the whole process sound simpler than it really is? Can you see the various amounts they have allocated to the stages involved? Do they seem realistic?

6 How many copies do you want?

Even though an attractively reduced price per copy can be obtained by ordering in bulk, it will only be on receipt of the first copy that you spot all the errors. A quick reprint will save your blushes and this is easier to accommodate if your first order has been slim.

Case study: Jeremy Thompson, MD of Troubador Publishing Ltd, a self-publishing solutions company

'My background is in academic publishing, and after mainstream publishing jobs in scientific, technical and medical publishing (usually called STM) with Elsevier and Butterworths, when the company was relocating from Guildford to Oxford I took voluntary redundancy and decided to set up on my own, editing academic journals and publishing books for a range of STM publishers. Troubador[125] was launched in 1990 and we still publish around 70–80 academic titles a year.

In the late 1990s we started to get approaches from individual authors seeking a publisher for manuscripts that had been turned down by the traditional industry, and in each case helped out on a one-off basis. But demand grew; others recommended us, and we continued to be presented with valid manuscripts that were not finding a professional publisher which we felt deserved publication, and with our support in editorial, production, marketing and sales could grow into effective contributions to the market. We experimented further and continued to find a heavy demand; in 1999 we set up a bespoke self-publishing imprint, Matador, but with the aim of publishing quality books to a high standard and getting them marketed and sold. From the start we wanted to concentrate on publishing good books, but unlike most self-publishing companies we actually wanted to get them into shops and selling well. We thus concentrated considerable efforts on getting a strong distribution and sales offering, comparable to that which many commercial publishers have.

There continue to be two sides to our business; publishing on our own behalf (Troubador) and self-publishing (Matador) but of course they are mutually reinforcing and the expertise built up as publishers now supports a much wider client base. The demand is certainly there; as an informal metric of interest our staff has grown from four to eleven just in the last three years, and each year we find we need to take a stronger presence at the London Book Fair. Clients can either be published as part of our imprint

---

[125] www.troubador.co.uk

(Matador) or through their own, and we guide them through the relative advantages and disadvantages of either route (e.g. do you really want your home address listed as a contact point in your book?); helping them create their own organisational imprint, and associated logo and styling, if they so wish.

Our self-publishing customers keep all the rights to their materials, and have ownership of the PDFs and typesetting files that made up their book; we generally store them on their behalf, but they have immediate access. Once the initial contract has been fulfilled, the requested number of copies printed and delivered, they are entirely free to move to another fulfilment or printing house should they so wish. We also offer a range of supplementary services to our authors, all entirely optional but all at a very low cost to enable our authors to promote themselves as authors and their books. We publish ebooks, create and host author websites, produce podcasts and our website hosts video, audio and print media coverage of our authors and their books.

As clients, we find most authors hungry for the service we provide and eager to be involved – an associated issue however can be the effective management of their expectations, and encouraging them to assist in an appropriate way. We are always honest with them, and guide them if we feel they need advice. The cover is particularly important and we will tell them if we feel the author's cover suggestions are inappropriate for the genre within which they are writing. In fact, it's so important that we reserve the right to turn down a cover if we feel it is simply unusable. Ultimately it is their book, and there may be reasons for its publication other than its optimum selling through retail outlets, but we always give straightforward advice to give a book the best chance.

We do question the claims made by some of our competitors – "available in Waterstone's and through retail outlets worldwide" may mean it is technically possible to obtain a book, but not that it is physically present anywhere. And paying a company to put a book into a retailer is appalling; most of our sales go through high street retailers... taking money from authors to do this is not right, it's a basic function of a publisher to get books into shops! Our sales and marketing team, and our team of retail trade sales reps, aim to give titles a physical presence in retail outlets, and we have considerable success in placing books into retailers. In fact most of our sales still go through the likes of Waterstone's and other high street stores, though online is of course a large market too. We also sell thousands of books through our webshop, which is great for our authors as they get a far better return on sales this way.

As regards production, we produce books using print on demand, short run digital printing or longer run litho. Most of our authors want to get their books into retailers, which POD can't do, so they tend to print between 300 and 2,000 copies at a time. But we use print on demand as well if it's appropriate for a book or author.

Because of our long track record and the results we consistently achieve with our authors' books, we're now recommended by a wide range of organisations, from *The Writers' and Artists' Yearbook* to writers' services companies like the Writers' Workshop and Bubblecow, from PR companies like Midas PR and Smith Publicity to printers like Biddles and Martins, and literary consultancies like Cornerstones and The Writers Bureau. In fact most of our authors come to us through recommendation of one form or another, whether that be existing authors or those in the industry who know that we do the best we can for our authors.

It's an exciting time to be in what is after all a relatively young industry. Self-publishing has for a long time been seen by many as a last chance to get into print, but that's just not the case anymore. We have been increasingly seeing excellent books that can't get a mainstream publisher either because their target market is relatively small (under 1,000 copies) or because the commercial publishers are tightening their belts and publishing fewer and fewer first-time authors. We're seeing mainstream published authors switching to self-publishing, and authors not even considering mainstream publishing at all. The market is maturing, and at Matador we're pleased to be at the forefront.'

Case study: publishing *Cells* by Harriet Grace

'It's every novelist's dream to be accepted by a large, mainstream publisher and sell lots of copies, and it is certainly mine, but in the autumn of 2007 I signed up for an assisted publishing deal, independently of my agent, and agreed to contribute some money towards the publishing of my novel.

Background to the decision to self-publish

I have been honing my skill at writing novels for the last thirty years, completing five novels, three of which have done the rounds of the publishers: I found an agent in 1989 and in the mid-nineties my second novel was nearly taken by two publishers. I was accepted on to an MA in creative writing at Sheffield Hallam University and received an MA Distinction for my novel *Cells*. I found a new agent and again the novel was circulated until Simon & Schuster, a large American publisher, expressed a strong interest and asked me to develop it further. Six months later, the editor very much liked the new version. She said I'd done a 'stellar job' – 'it was a joy to read' – but unfortunately another editor in the publishing house had just commissioned another novel on the same theme so she much regretted they could not take it. Having been encouraged to improve the book and then be turned down was very upsetting but I had to try and move on. About a year later I entered *Cells* for an online competition with a publisher who was looking for undiscovered authors. My novel was highly commended and the publisher approached me saying they would like to publish it if I was willing to contribute towards the costs. I felt I had nothing to lose and decided to do it.

Reasons for going ahead

The publishing house was founded by its managing director to do two things: give existing authors the opportunity to reproduce their books that were out of print; and allow authors who had failed to find a mainstream publisher to publish their book with financial support. There was, thus, a mainstream sector of the business as well as an assisted-publishing side.

The offices were at a smart, literary address in Mayfair, giving it kudos and status; their publicity material was professional and there was a team of people running what seemed like an efficient business. The firm was recommended to me by one of their authors who had chosen to leave her mainstream publisher to join them and was successfully selling her historical novels, and I had access to a good editor (freelance but paid by the house). They had an account with the wholesalers Gardners and Bertrams, which meant bookshops would be able to order my books, and an account with Amazon, so books would be available here too.

Production of the book

My experience of the production of the book was, on the whole, good, but I think some of this was luck. The editor recommended by the publisher had very little experience, but I was recommended a good editor by one of the other authors. My other piece of luck was that a very efficient and effective author manager was appointed and ran the business during the whole period of the production and publication of my novel. During this period, the office moved from Mayfair to above a print shop in Acton.

I probably had more control over the production than I would have done with a mainstream publisher, but when it came to the production, marketing and selling copies of the book the people concerned had much less experience and influence. There was no one who really cared what I had written or minded particularly about the quality of writing, apart from the editor, and she had no influence on the marketing side.

In the autumn of 2007 I signed a non-exclusive world-wide, assisted-publishing contract with the publishers. This gave me:

- Copy-edit
- Bespoke typeset and cover design
- UK & American sales & distribution
- Access to my novel through Amazon in the UK and USA
- Local/specialist press release service including the despatch of ten review copies
- A publicity kit including a listing in their catalogue
- 20 copies including 15 hardcover copies
- ISBN number

This package was billed as £1,999 and this included a 'substantive' edit. Having gone through an MA and many re-writes for my agent and Simon & Schuster, I felt the novel didn't need a full edit, so I negotiated to pay £1,650. I paid half the amount on signing the contract and second half on receipt of a printed copy of the book.

I sent my manuscript to the editor and realised immediately that she had a feel for the story and was a very good editor, with the result that she did more than copy-edit. She was being paid late and very little, so I paid some money direct to her, and together we ended up with a better novel.

I then had to consider the cover, which was new territory for me. The novel is about infertility and what happens when what is technically possible is not successful, and those who have expected to be able to become parents have to give up the idea of parenthood and try to move on: cells in the body that refuse to fuse together, but also cells that each character is trapped inside. The characters in the story live in London and work in Canary Wharf. I was asked by the managing director to come up with some images for the story, and was put in touch electronically with a graphic designer. With the help of my son and his partner we sent him various versions, images of cells circulating over the cover often containing iconic pictures of the Canary Wharf tower and the river Thames. The work was done remotely through emails, jpegs and on the phone. The designer was good at manipulating images that we had supplied him, but not good at providing new images or ideas. The more we tried different approaches, the less satisfactory the situation seemed to become. In the end, my husband took a photograph of the footbridge over the Thames at Putney, which is in the story, and the designer manipulated the picture to include cell shapes in the river and the outline of Canary Wharf in the distance.

On the back cover, I wrote the blurb, with no help at all from the publishers. I also obtained supportive quotes from two well-known novelists, Jane Rogers and Jenny Newman. These were printed as white 'reversed-out' text, which showed up better than in black or another colour.

I had a choice of the kind of typesetting and the layout of the text. I was sent proofs which I had to proofread and return with corrections, detailing the pages and lines where the corrections were needed. I was working with the author manager mentioned above, and I could trust her to carry out the alterations accurately. The one mistake that got through was the wrong name of an artist, which I didn't notice until an artist friend had read a published copy.

The novel is digitally printed which means that copies are printed only as they are needed – in theory this makes it easier to correct mistakes although in practice it took some time for the artist's name to be corrected.

My novel was launched at a bookshop in Kew, where I live, on 10th July 2008. Getting enough copies for the launch was nerve-racking. In theory the books should have been available from the wholesalers, but the Kew Bookshop found it easier to order the books direct from the print shop. Some copies arrived, but the author manager arrived from the office just in time on the launch evening with a very heavy bag of extra copies. They were needed, as all eighty copies were sold in the first half hour.

Marketing

It was a very successful launch but I quickly realised that I would have to do all the marketing myself, in spite of what was officially promised in the package I had signed up for.

The publishers provided a publicist whom I never met, but to whom I had to email my biography and other information. We talked on the phone several times and she was very pleasant, but her press release gave the wrong tone to the story, making it sound like an airport novel. I re-wrote quite a lot of it. In theory she emailed it to all her contacts, but the only response was an invitation to talk at an event which turned out to be completely inappropriate. It was a 'book swap' event held in the rather cavernous glass space of the Winter Garden in Sheffield. My books were displayed on the corner of a stand containing children's books, and the attendees were not expecting a reading from a *new* novel that they might want to *buy*!

The novel is about a very modern dilemma, and it is set near where I live and I tried to use these factors to achieve local cover-age. I contacted all the newspapers and magazines in Richmond,

Kew, Kingston, Putney, Wimbledon and received good publicity. I visited all the local bookshops, including Waterstone's. Most of them agreed to order copies, and the Putney Waterstone's agreed to display the book. I contacted the *Newbury News* which is near Inkpen where part of the story is set, and visited bookshops in Newbury, Hungerford and Marlborough. I asked everyone I knew to spread the word, including my daughter in America, thus managing to sell a few copies in the USA. I gave talks in libraries and at a couple of Festivals, and I have had a very nice local review. All that worked well. It was when I tried to gain a wider audience that I came up against an impenetrable barrier.

I found the names of the editors of the review pages of national newspapers and sent them each a copy. I approached *Woman's Hour* because I thought the subject of infertility and IVF was relevant, but heard nothing. A well-known novelist read it, liked it and promised to try and get it reviewed but didn't manage to. I submitted an article to a regular 'firsthand experience' column in the *Guardian* about my 30 year struggle to publish and they politely turned it down. I contacted the writers' magazine, *Mslexia*, which had published one of my poems, but also heard nothing. I approached *Richard & Judy* through another contact I had.

The result is I have sold just under 300 copies but I have not managed to break into a wider audience: being known, winning a prize, or getting a review in a national newspaper is probably essential to reach this audience.

Looking objectively at my situation, I am not known and my publisher does not have an established imprint. National reviewers will not consider reading a book with an unknown publisher, and may be prejudiced against the idea of self-publishing. These two factors are very difficult to overcome. But I do not regret self-publishing my novel and would love to reach a wider audience. I have had a very positive response, and have learned a lot about the publishing process and the realities of marketing and selling copies.

The postscript to this account is that my publisher has very recently stopped producing books, due to the recession. I have signed up with a new publisher, SilverWood Books, very much the wiser from my experience. They will be producing a new edition of *Cells* available July 2011 and are showing themselves to be a thoroughly professional organisation, offering excellent support in the production and the marketing of the book.'

Case study: Helen Hart of SilverWood Books
www.silverwoodbooks.co.uk

'In order to understand how SilverWood works, it's probably useful to know something about me and my background as a professional writer, because I believe this is key to the way I've set the company up, and to how it functions.

I've been a published author since the late 1990s. Writing under a variety of pseudonyms, I've been published by Scholastic, HarperCollins, OUP and several non-UK publishing houses. My books have been translated into many different languages including Swedish, Danish, Greek and Japanese. The books are detailed on my author site (www.authorhelenhart.wordpress.com). I've also worked as a commercial copywriter for SilverWood's sister company Redwing.

My writing background means that I have a deep and intimate understanding of the writing process and how important each book is to an author. I know from my own experience how much heart and soul has gone into the creation of a book, and how important is the relationship between a writer and their publisher/editor.

When I founded SilverWood Books in 2007, it was with the aim of providing writers with an alternative to what I perceived as the unscrupulous business practices, expensive publishing packages, and poor quality books offered by many other publishing services companies. I place the writer and their needs (and their aims for their book) at the heart of what SilverWood Books offers. My aim is to offer a close, supportive working relationship and therefore a similar experience to that which the writer might have if they were signed to a mainstream publishing house.

I genuinely believe that if a self-publisher wishes to sell their book beyond family and friends, then they need a book that matches as closely as possible the output of mainstream publishers. It's not enough that the content be outstanding – *all* elements of the book must be outstanding if that title is to compete in an already crowded marketplace.

The key feature of a book produced by SilverWood is that it aims to match the production values of mainstream publishing houses – and this means our authors stand a better chance of convincing bookshops to stock their book (often self-published titles are refused due to their amateur nature).

SilverWood offers friendly one-to-one support throughout the publishing process. Services include professional editing, proofreading, page layout, book jacket design, print on demand and book publicity. Authors can choose from a comprehensive range of paperback and hardback book sizes, with or without dustjackets and foil stamping. We don't use templates, so each book is individually designed specifically for its target market, just as it would be in a mainstream publishing house. We offer a selection of publishing packages which cost-effectively bundle services together. And if an author's work isn't quite ready for publication, SilverWood can assist with manuscript appraisal and editorial support.

We do turn down fiction that we feel isn't commercially viable, unless the author has clearly stated that they are producing a short run for friends and family. Conversely we also encourage selected writers not to self-publish but to seek mainstream literary agent representation if we feel the work deserves that. This is because we acknowledge that self-publishing, however good, can't yet match the mainstream in terms of distribution, marketing and credibility. We offer appraisal and guidance on covering letter/ synopsis/sample chapters to ensure that a writer sends the best possible book proposal to literary agencies.

I believe SilverWood Books is offering something different in today's rapidly expanding self-publishing market. We provide high quality professional services. Our authors work in partnership with a small, friendly, supportive team who care about the book and the writer, and who have the skills and expertise to offer impartial guidance. Most of our authors come to us through word-of-mouth recommendation, or they are repeat customers who were pleased with the experience of publishing their previous book with us.'

A quick Google of the words 'publish a book' and you will find many more solutions for managing print and online production than you may have thought possible. And very quickly you will come to appreciate just how speedily and cheaply it can be done – but neither adverb necessarily implies *well done*.

The best advice is to take your time. Consider the overall quality and standards you want to achieve; your wider objectives for the project (e.g. time and number sought), and the particular blend of skills and experience that you either have now, or would like to acquire in future. Or, as comedian Hugh Dennis responded to the question:

'What is the most important lesson that life has taught you?'

'That everything is much longer than you think and you don't really have to hurry.'[126]

[126] Interviewed in *The Guardian Weekend*, 12 February 2011

16

Self-publishing ebooks

with Kay Sayce and Darin Brockman, Firsty Group
www.firstygroup.com

The act of publishing your own work because you couldn't find a literary agent or publisher prepared to take it on was, until recently, seen as a sign of desperation. And there were many agencies out there to feed upon that desperation, going under the heading of 'vanity publishers' who offered grand promises in return for large down-payments. As word got round that this was not the way to go, and as mainstream publishers became more risk averse and closed their doors to unsolicited manuscripts, and agents, in turn, became more difficult to elicit a response from, other than the standard rejection letter, it seemed that there was no place to go.

Until recently. With the advent of ebooks and the ease of online book promotion and selling, the door not only to getting published, but also to promoting and selling books has been blown wide open. Authors – from those venturing out for the first time to seasoned authors with considerable backlists – have been quick to realise that now there is some place to go. Self-publishing has become respectable, and there is a sense of empowerment in the air, coupled with excitement about the opportunities for innovation that is inherent in ebook publishing and marketing.

To maximise these opportunities, though, authors need to know the answers to these questions:

* What is an ebook?

* What are the advantages of self-publishing ebooks?

* How are ebooks are created?

* How are ebooks distributed, marketed and sold?

* What do authors need to do to publish, promote and sell ebooks?

This chapter will address all these issues from the vantage point of the self-publishing author, but it comes with a very large caveat. The world of ebook publishing is evolving rapidly, with ongoing changes in formats, software, retailing, reading devices, etc. So, although much of what we say here will broadly apply over the next few years, some of the detail (e.g., on software, format, devices) could change before this book comes off the press! If you're venturing into self-publishing ebooks, it's very important is to keep yourself up to date with the changes – or keep in close touch with someone who does.

What is an ebook?

The word 'ebook' is short for 'electronic book'. *The Oxford Dictionary of English* defines an ebook as 'an electronic version of a printed book', but while some ebooks do start out as print books that are then converted to ebooks to reach a larger audience, many ebooks exist without any print equivalent.

An ebook is a computer file with text and/or images that has been programmed to look and read like a printed book. The different types of computer files are generally referred to as 'formats'. ebooks can be read on ereaders (e.g., Barnes & Noble Nook, Kindle, Kobo eReader, Sony Reader) as well as on other devices such as computers (PCs, Macs, laptops), tablets (e.g., Acer, Galaxy, iPad) and smartphones (e.g., iPhone, LG, Nokia, Samsung).

Currently, the most common device that book buyers are using for reading ebooks is a computer, followed by smartphones, then ereaders and then tablets. This might seem surprising, given the apparent ubiquity of the Kindle. Over the next year, many new devices will appear in the market place, with tablets possibly taking centre stage.

'The arrival of dedicated reading devices can be seen as a massive boon for book-lovers, who now have the flexibility and immediacy of digital book delivery combined with a portable and eye-friendly way to consume content. You can travel with a choice of hundreds of books now, and you can adjust text size to suit your eyesight. You can even have your book read out to you if your eyes are not up to it. Far from reducing the status of the book, the dedicated ebook reader is the ultimate compliment to the form: it turbo-charges your reading.'

Dr Julian Smart, software designer and creator of Writer's Café and Jutoh

ebook formats

Back in about 2006, when we started thinking about moving into ebook conversion, there were dozens of different ebook formats. This meant, in effect, that for each ebook we would have had to convert the source file into dozens of different formats! There are still many formats around for creating ebooks, but they tend to be limited in terms of which devices they can be read on. The formats that you, as a self-publisher, need to be aware of are:

* ePub: this is the standard format that can be read on most devices apart from the Kindle

* Mobi: this is the format that is output by Amazon's proprietary .azw software (it's not clear what 'azw' stands for; possibly 'Amazon Whispernet'); the Mobi format is suitable only for the Kindle device and other devices running the Kindle app (i.e., the app you need to read Kindle files)

ePub was created by the International Digital Publishing Forum (IDPF; http://idpf.org). It has become the most widely supported ebook format; that is, it can be read on more devices that any other format. It's likely that ePub ebooks will soon be readable on Kindle devices as well. The use of other ebook formats has diminished considerably, one exception being PDF (portable document format); this is widely used in a variety of contexts, but whereas a few years ago people were still calling a PDF an ebook, this is incorrect now. A PDF page cannot always be viewed, as a whole, on a device (especially ones with small screens) and still be readable, and PDFs lack an essential characteristic of a standard ebook.

What is that characteristic? Reflowability. If an ebook is downloaded onto an ereader, the text and images will automatically reflow so that every word and image is clearly displayed within the screen area, however small the screen is. A standard ebook retains this 'reflowability' when downloaded onto PCs, Macs and laptops.

The different types of devices used for reading ebooks work in different ways:

- **Computers** (PCs, Macs, laptops): use Adobe Digital Editions and App software
- **eReaders:** use ePub and Mobi files
- **Smartphones:** use operating systems (OS) – Android (LG), Apple iOS (iPhone), RIM (Blackberry) and Windows (Nokia)
- **Tablets:** use operating systems (OS) – Android, Apple iOS, RIM and Windows

ebook layouts

So far we've talked about standard ebooks. But there are more advanced treatments that you need to be aware of, even if you don't think your work warrants these treatments or the costs they involve.

With the advent of touch-screen devices, particularly the iPad, it is becoming more common to produce ebooks not only in reflowable layout (for ereaders and computers), but also in fixed layout (non-reflowable: for smartphones and tablets). 'Fixed' means that the layout of the text and images does not move, but a page can be expanded or reduced by touch, depending on what the reader wants to see; a fixed ebook looks like a book on a screen, and page turning is simulated to look as though you're turning the pages of a print book. The experience, therefore, is far closer to reading a printed book than the experience of reading reflowable ebooks on an ereader. For books with a lot of illustration, fixed ePub layouts for tablet reading are becoming very popular.

The advanced ebook treatments lend themselves particularly well to fixed layout. They fall into two categories:

- enhanced
- app (short for 'application')

An enhanced ebook is an ePub file with additional functionality (e.g., audio and video features). Adding functionality to a standard ePub file helps meet readers' expectations that ebooks should be more than simply an electronic version of the printed book. The current version of ePub is quite restrictive in terms of layout and functionality. For example, it doesn't support text-to-speech (text synchronisation), text can be displayed in only one column, and images have to sit in their own space, not wrapped around by text. So, although this version is suitable in most cases for novels, which tend to have text-only one-column layouts, it is less suitable for non-fiction titles where images and two- or three-column layouts are common. The IDPF is due to release ePub3 in late 2011. This will have far greater functionality than the current version (e.g., text synchronisation, animation, dynamic layout, and the ability to handle two- and three-column formats and to wrap text around images).

Whereas standard and enhanced ebooks remain familiar book-like products and can be read on most devices, book apps are for touch-screen devices only and they take the reader into a different world where animation and interactivity are the dominant features. Book apps truly came into their own with the arrival of the iPad. Given the huge increase in tablet and smartphone devices due to reach the market in 2011–12, the popularity of apps seems guaranteed. If you think you have a book that merits app treatment, the best advice is to find a book app development company and talk through your ideas. It may be that what you want to do would be more appropriate as an enhanced ebook – and a great deal less expensive!

ebook costs

With standard and enhanced ebooks we tend to talk of 'conversion costs'. With book apps, it's 'development costs'. As these terms imply, it is a relatively straightforward procedure to convert source material into a standard ebook – it's simply a case of making what is available in print form (text with/without images) available in electronic form and readable on ereaders and other digital devices. With an enhanced ebook there is the extra work of adding functionality.

Book apps require a lot more than this. Decisions need to be made not only on visual and audio features, but also the level, nature and intricacy of animation and interactivity. To get this right often involves roundtable discussions involving publishers, authors and app developers, the creation of samples for review and storyboards for guidance, and so on. All of which explains why creating apps is a considerably more expensive process than creating standard and enhanced ebooks.

As with everything else in the digital world, the costs of conversion and development are coming down and will no doubt continue to do so. The costs vary from one country to another, as does the quality of conversion and development. And they also vary according to the source files provided, as described later in this chapter (see pages 254–255).

With all the variables involved, it's not possible to be specific about the costs of ebook conversion and book app development. Generally, though, we're talking tens of pounds for ebooks (c. £50–100), hundreds of pounds for enhanced books (c. £800) and thousands of pounds for book apps (£3,000 upwards).

What are the advantages of self-publishing ebooks?

The overriding advantage of self-publishing ebooks is perhaps author empowerment, as noted in the opening paragraphs of this chapter. Other advantages include:

* **Customer access**: ebook self-publishing has given you, the author, the means to take your work directly to your customers, quickly and inexpensively; you don't need 'permission' to do so from the various people on the long and winding conventional publishing road (readers, literary agents, publishers, retailers).

* **Customer convenience**: An ereader can carry a whole library of books. There is no longer any need for readers to lug heavy books around. The advantage of this hit the headlines in summer 2010 as people set off on their holidays and realised that decisions about how many and which books to take were a thing of the past. ereaders also offer the opportunity for discretion; what someone is reading on their ereader is difficult to see, which can be quite liberating.

- **Customer experience**: You can decide what you want your customers to experience when reading your ebook. Do you want them to read it in the traditional way, from page 1 to the end, with no deviation? Do you want to give them a more linear experience, where they can deviate from the text into interesting supporting content you have created? With ebooks, there are endless opportunities for authors to create – if they want to – something that moves away from the experience of reading a traditional book.

- **Cost**: The costs of producing and distributing ebooks are very small compared with print books, where the costs of printing (the process as well as the materials – paper, cover, wrapping, etc.), storage, delivery and disposing of unsold stock add considerably to unit costs.

- **Distribution**: Print book distribution can be a long and complicated process, involving many steps along the way between authors and customers; with ebooks, distribution is a far easier process, not least because you no longer have to think about physically moving print books from A to B, storing them, protecting them, and getting them into bookshops.

- **Marketing**: You don't have to rely on publishers and retailers to market you book, or suffer the frustration of seeing less effort expended on this than you expected, and being kept at arm's length in marketing decisions; you can make your own decisions, for example, about what the cover should look like, what reviews to seek, what social media to use to create awareness about your ebook, what promotional events to organise around it; this is an area where you can be particularly innovative and where, because it is your book, you are likely spend more time and effort than a conventional publisher.

- **Selling**: You are free to experiment with an array of approaches to selling their work. You could consider such options as selling a first ebook at very low prices to attract customers in large numbers, to build a following in advance of the publication of your second ebook. Or selling in stages whereby you offer, for example, the first two chapters of a novel for free, then charge for the remainder of the ebook. Or selling a book episode by episode (did someone mention Charles Dickens and *Blackwood's Magazine*?) Watching how other self-publishing authors sell their work can be very worthwhile, as this is where most innovation in selling is currently coming from.

* **Updating**: A print book is, essentially, out of date as soon as it is published. With some books (e.g., novels), this is not an issue; with others (e.g., reference books), it can be. To update a print book (i.e., publish a new edition) involves going through the costly conventional publishing process again. With an ebook, there is one file and the content in it can be updated quickly and easily when necessary. There is the added sales advantage here that customers know, with ebooks, they are buying something that is up-to-date; this is particularly attractive in the case of reference books, which can become outdated quite quickly

* **Backlists**: ebook self-publishing offers you a great opportunity to resurrect your backlist titles when these rights have reverted to you. Conventional publishers usually allow a book a very short shelf life; if it doesn't sell well within this period (often, only about six months), then they will often stop any further promotion and let it go out of print, with rights eventually reverting to the author. With dedicated marketing by the author, as ebooks these titles can be brought back to life.

* **Environmental considerations**: Unlike print publishing, ebook production does not involve the use of print and packing materials (paper, cardboard, wrapping), the need for physical transportation (fuel consumption) or the waste produced by disposing of unsold stock (dumping, pulping). Although print on demand is becoming more widely used to address the problem of unsold stock, it remains an expensive option.

* **Control**: We're back to empowerment. The greatest advantage of self-publishing ebooks is that it gives authors control of every stage of the process, and none of those stages is difficult to manage. It also gives authors the freedom to experiment with producing their work in different formats, using different ways of marketing their work, building a digital audience,

interacting directly with customers, and planning what to do with their work further down the line (updates, repackaging, etc.).

There is a final but very important point to make here. Everything points towards a world where ebooks will dominate the market. Amazon is already selling more ebooks than hardback books. Publishers are reporting huge increases in ebooks sales (e.g., Pan Macmillan's ebook sales increased fifteenfold between the first quarter of 2010 and first quarter of 2011). Everything is also pointing towards there being a new publishing model. What shape this model will take, and whether it will see self-publishing becoming the norm, is not clear. There are frequent reports now of highly successful self-publishing ventures (in June 2011, it was reported that the self-publishing author John Locke had sold one million ebooks via Amazon in five months, and was now inviting customers to buy his latest book entitled – yes, you guessed it: *How I Sold 1 Million ebooks in 5 Months!*).

What is clear is that ebooks are the future and getting into self-publishing ebooks now makes sense.

Novelist J.A. Konrath announced in 2010 on his blog that he was abandoning his traditional publishers and would be self-publishing future books in ebook format.

'I love print publishers. But the traditional publishing industry is flawed, and I don't see any signs it will be fixed anytime soon. It used to be the only game in town. If you wanted to make a living as an author, you had to accept small royalties, no control, and a system dependent on others who may not have your best interests in mind. With ebooks… I set my prices. I pick my titles. I choose the cover. I don't worry about returns. Going out of print is no longer a worry. I'm not tied in to any contract. I get paid once a month, not twice a year. And I don't have to answer to anybody. ebooks truly are the greatest thing to happen to writers since Gutenberg.'

Joe Konrath, author, jakonrath.blogspot.com

How are ebooks created?

Although some self-publishing authors might want to venture down the book app route, currently most of them are concerned with standard ebooks, with a growing number showing interest in enhanced ebooks. The discussion from here onwards, therefore, focuses on standard and enhanced ebooks, and not on book apps. (For more on creating apps, and going through the process of submitting them to Apple's App Store for review and then marketing them, see developer.apple.com/resources.)

The process of creating an ebook starts with the source file. You need to supply an ebook conversion company with a digital file that is ready for conversion (see below). The following digital files are suitable: Adobe InDesign, MSWord, QuarkXPress and PDF. The nature of the source file will affect the conversion cost, depending on what you use and what the conversion company prefers working from.

If your source material is only in print format, you'll need to get it scanned and to ask the scanner to produce a digital file. Most scanners offer a choice of digital files, the most common being MSWord and PDF. Remember that scanning is not 100% accurate, and you will need to proofread the document. If you know the text by heart and could easily spot a missing sentence or paragraph, then proofread the document yourself, alone. Otherwise, ask a kind friend to help, with you reading the original and your friend simultaneously checking the scanned document, or vice versa, and you then making the necessary corrections.

Conversion process

The conversion process involves using software to convert source files into ePub and/or Mobi files. Although you could use software that is available on the net and try to convert source files yourself, we wouldn't recommend this course of action at the moment. Considering how fast and inexpensive ebook conversion is, it's far more cost-effective to have this work done by an experienced conversion company. However, if you do want to have a go yourself, then we'd recommend that you take a look at Jutoh's ePub ebook creation and conversion software (www.jutoh.com). There is some background about its creation in the second case study at the end of this chapter.

Among the many things that need to be considered in the conversion process are:

- **Fonts:** The fonts in a source file might not work for an ebook file. That's not to say you can't embed any font you want in an ebook – you can. But unless 'safe' web fonts (e.g., standard fonts such as Times, Arial and Helvetica) are used in the ebook, there could be problems uploading it to ebookstores. So, if there's an unusual font in the source file, a substitute web font as close as possible to the original should be used.

- **Headings and the use of italic, bold, etc.:** Source files that have been created using stylesheets, and using them correctly, will make the conversion process far easier. Where this is lacking, the converter will need go through the whole original text to ensure that the use of italic and bold, and the way headings and sub-headings work (the heading hierarchy), is matched in the ebook.

- **Images:** Text-only source files are the easiest to convert. If your source file includes images, the converter might ask you to consider reducing the number of them. Including and placing images correctly can be time-consuming.

- **Tables and charts:** These items tend to format badly in a standard ebook; a converter might encourage you to change tables and charts into lists where possible.

- **Footnotes and endnotes:** These items also tend to format badly in a standard ebook; the converter might ask you to include these in the main text in some way (e.g., in brackets).

- **Page numbers and references:** Page numbers are irrelevant in reflowable text, and hence references to them will not work. So a converter might remove page numbers and advise you to replace references to page numbers with references to, for example, chapters or chapter sections (e.g., replace 'see page 16' with 'see Chapter 2, under subheading New Horizons').

Digital rights management

A major concern in the publishing industry is to protect print books against copyright infringement; that is, to protect them from being printed and sold without the publisher knowing about it or receiving any revenue from sales. With ebooks, unless access to them is controlled, a similar thing could happen. Applying DRM means your ebook can be read only by those whom you have authorised to download it. It cannot be shared with another person using different reading software, although can be used on multiple reading devices, providing the reading software (usually Adobe Digital Editions, ADE) is registered to the same user. The technologies that have been created to restrict the use of digital content come under the umbrella term of 'digital rights management' (DRM; also referred to as 'encrypting', but DRM is the term more commonly used). The industry standard DRM technology is Adobe Content Server (see www.adobe.com/products/contentserver).

DRM is applied by eretailers when ebooks are uploaded to their sites, although with most eretailers you can opt not to have DRM. Why would you choose not to have DRM? Well, the topic has become quite controversial. Whereas some people see it as a necessary precaution against copyright infringement, others say that there is no evidence that DRM does this and that it is too restrictive in terms of competition, innovation and ownership. Here are some arguments for and against DRM.

For DRM:

* You retain some control over how your ebook is read and by whom.

* You remind the market that someone created the ebook they are choosing to access (i.e., you encourage them to respect the basics of copyright and intellectual property).

* You retain some control over the reading experience, so if there are delivery formats you consider substandard, you do not compromise your ebook through association.

* You build exclusivity into your ebook.

Against DRM:

* A book has no relevance unless it is read; the more media through which you encourage people to read your material, the more likely they are to spread the word about it.

- Recent research has shown[127] that rather than recommend services and products on which they have long relied, people are more likely to recommend recently acquired enthusiasms. So if your ebook excites them, it is a pity to put barriers in the way of it being shared immediately.

- There is a growing dislike for DRM and the restrictions it imposes. You could choose not to apply DRM and use this as a selling point for your ebook.

- Some piracy could actually increase your ebook sales through the associated publicity.

Validation and testing

In talking earlier about problems with uploading an ebook, what we were touching on was the issue of validation. A good conversion company will use software tools to validate and test every ebook it creates. Validation is done in order to ensure the ebook's acceptance by ebookstores. For ePub files, for example, the validation tool 'epubcheck' is used to identify any errors, which the converter then eliminates to ensure that the ebook will upload successfully. Testing is done in order to ensure that the ebook can be read on as many devices as possible.

Validation and testing constitute the final stage in creating an ebook. If these processes are done properly, your ebook has the ingredients to reach the widest audience possible.

Conversion companies

There are many companies that can manage the whole conversion, validation and testing process for you. Some of them are, to some extent, DIY operations, such as Barnes & Noble (pubit. barnesandnoble.com), Kindle Direct Publishing (kdp.amazon.

---

[127] Professor Robert East *et al.*, 'Fact and Fallacy in Retention Marketing', *Journal of Marketing Management*, 2006, 22, 5–23. More recent research, not yet published, looks at the decay in word of mouth in the six months after the service was used or the product was bought. In most cases there is a fairly rapid decline in advice-giving in the first week or two. Sometimes, half the total word of mouth reported happens then. When as product are continually used (e.g., mobile phone) the decay is much slower. On the basis of this work, he would expect that much of the comment on a book happens when it is being read and for a brief period afterwards.

com), Lulu (www.lulu.com) and Smashwords (www.smashwords. com). Smashwords publish a very helpful guide to the process: (www.smashwords.com/extreader/read/52/12/smashwords-style-guide. Some companies, such as ours, offer a more hands-on service that can sometimes, but not always, involve face-to-face meetings with authors. There are also companies that, although they do offer an ebook conversion service, are more geared towards large publishing operations than individual self-publishers; these include Ingram Digital, LibreDigital and Overdrive.

How are ebooks distributed, marketed and sold?

Compared with print book distribution, ebook distribution is relatively simple and inexpensive. It involves uploading an ebook onto ebookstores. You have several options for doing this, including handing it over to someone else to do it for you!

Marketing ebooks can also be inexpensive, but here you're unlikely to succeed in getting the sales you want if you hand this task over to someone else. It requires the right tools, and they aren't difficult to master. And it requires dedication and innovation – you, as the author, are the best person to provide these ingredients.

eretailers

The eretailer stores onto which ebooks are uploaded include the well-known Amazon and Apple (iBookstore) outlets, other major ebookstores such as Barnes & Noble, Kobo, Sony, Waterstone's and W.H. Smith and a host of smaller ones, the more prominent ones including Blackwell, Book Depository, eHarlequin, Foyles, HarperCollins and Powell's. By the time this book is published there will be another very important player in the market – the Google ebookstore.

To upload an ebook, you have three main options:

* set up your own accounts with eretailers you favour and who accept individual accounts

- ask your ebook conversion company to set up and handle your accounts

- go through an ebook distributer or aggregator to set up and handle your accounts

In the case of (a), creating accounts with some eretailers is fairly straightforward, but with others (including a few major ones) it is not, and it's likely you would end up seeking professional help anyway. Our advice is to choose (b) or (c). They will do all that's necessary for you – set up accounts, negotiate commissions/discounts, upload ebooks, provide sales reports and track payments. Many companies, including ours, work with large ebook disributers, such as ePub Direct, which links to more than 70 eretailers on five continents.

You should, of course, also link directly to your customers by being your own eretailer through your own ecommerce website. We would advise you to do this in addition to (not instead of) using the normal eDistribution channels described above. For more on this, see 'Marketing and selling ebooks', page 260.

Pricing ebooks

A crucial aspect of ebook publishing is to get the price right. With print books, there is a fairly standard spectrum of prices that customers are used to; they know more or less what they'll pay, for example, for a 200-page paperback novel, or for its hardback equivalent, or for a full colour heavily illustrated hardback.

With ebooks it's not so clear; the market place has not yet settled down, and there is much debate on how to price ebooks. Currently, they tend to priced low, selling at an average of about 30% less than the print paperback equivalent. This won't necessarily be the case in the long term. It could change, for example, when there is a predominance of ebooks created from scratch in the market, as opposed to current situation where most ebooks are electronic versions of existing print books that have borne all the development costs (e.g., author advance, editing, design, typesetting, proofreading). The price of ebooks created from scratch will need, at some point, to reflect the development costs.

'Drop the prices of ebooks. [It is] painfully clear how cheaper ebooks make more money than expensive ones, with reams of data and dozens of examples to support this.'

Author Bob Mayer blogging on http://jakonrath.blogspot.com

As a self-publisher, you set the retail price of your ebook, but eretailers aren't obliged to sell it at this price. The best way to determine the retail price is to:

* consult the conversion/distribution companies you work with; they will be able to advise you not only on pricing, but also when and why to sometimes offer ebooks at discount prices or for free

* conduct your own market research; look at the prices of comparable ebooks to yours (e.g., same genre, similar length, similar illustration content) being sold through major eretailers, to get an idea of what customers might pay and to avoid overpricing your ebook

In determining a price you also need to take account, of course, of the commission (discount) that eretailers charge. This can range from 10 to 65%. Again, we would advise that you get more information about this from conversion or distribution companies.

Marketing and selling ebooks

With the huge rise in the number of ebooks now being produced, all vying for ebookstore shelf space and visibility, the most important goal in marketing an ebook is discoverability. Your ebook could sink without trace on the eretailer sites. You need create awareness about your ebook and make sure that potential customers are able find it easily.

There are many ways to achieve this goal, some requiring hard work and lots of time on your part, others involving the companies you (might) have used to convert and distribute your ebook. These include:

* ensuring the ebook is well-produced and that it is readable on as many devices as possible

- creating a website with the facilities to promote your ebook (e.g., book promotion pages, blog space), and keeping it updated

- using your website to build an interactive 'community' (digital audience) around you and your ebook

- promoting your ebook through all the social media available (e.g., Twitter, Facebook; people who use social media tend to be frequent returners and information sharers) and getting it reviewed (e.g., on Amazon)

- organising events to promote your ebook, and creating marketing materials (e.g., leaflets, postcards) that you can hand out at these and other events

If you do create a website – and we'd strongly advise all self-publishing authors to do this, preferably using the free web software WordPress – you should also consider using a website development company to help you add sales (ecommerce) facilities to your website. A key factor here is ensure that, for your customers, the purchasing process is fast, simple and clear.

There are some ebook companies now helping authors to create websites with the facilities to market and sell ebooks. In April 2011 we launched the Firsty Author Package (www.firstyauthors.com), based on our experience in ebook conversion, in building ecommerce websites and, last but not least, in working with authors. The package gives authors all the tools they need to create, promote, distribute and sell their ebooks: that is, it provides facilities for uploading source material for conversion and it creates a customised website with book promotion pages, a blog space, social media links, ecommerce facilities, DRM, and support in sales reporting and payments. The package also contains links to organisations providing services that authors might need but we do not offer (e.g., manuscript assessment, editorial services, book scanning, erights advice). Given that many self-publishing authors want to promote and sell books in print format as well as ebook format, we work in partnership with a range of author service providers to add a print dimension (printing and distribution) to the Author Package, and also to offer editorial, design and proofreading services and, where requested, marketing services.

Examples of our Author Package websites include www.jamierix.com, www.shelleyweiner.com and www.star789.authorpack.com.

It is essential that self-publishing authors become self-promoters. For an example of how to do this well, see www.catherineryanhoward.com. This is an attractive website with a lively upbeat tone. There is a regular blog and the chance to sample and then buy the books. She shares information on the self-publishing process, and puts new material up often enough for there to be something to return to. The tone throughout is confessional and sharing, typified in the recent posting: 'I'm going to try to think of ten things you maybe don't already know about me. This is hard because I've already smeared the entrails of my life all over this blog and I may have to include one or two non-surprises, but let's see....'

What do authors need to do to publish, promote and sell ebooks?

Now that we've discussed what an ebook is, how it's created, what's involved in distributing, marketing and selling it, and what advantages ebooks have over print books – in other words, why self-publishing authors should consider producing their work as ebooks – it's time to get down to basics. What do you, as a self-publishing author, need to do to publish, promote and sell ebooks?

We describe here the series of stages you should go through when you have decided that you want to self-publish your work as an ebook. Some of this is, of course, a recasting of the foregoing discussion, some of it is new.

Stage 1
Check your rights. Ensure you have full rights to the book you want to self-publish as an ebook, if it has previously been published in print form by a publisher. For books published since the mid-1990s, most authors will have signed a contract defining their ebook publishing rights; before that, the issue is little hazy. We strongly advise you that, however long ago the book was published, and however you interpret the contract you had with the publisher, you should talk to your publisher and/or literary agent. If in doubt, seek professional advice from, for example, the Society of Authors.

Some authors have chosen to work with their publishers to build an audience by making access to the ebook version free at the same time as the publication of their physical book. A good example here is Cory Doctorow (www.craphound.com), novelist, blogger and journalist. He is published by conventional print publishers (Tor Books and Harper Collins UK), but has always released the ebook versions free on the web under Creative Commons licenses that encourage their re-use and sharing. This has encouraged his readers to promote his work and has increased sales of the print versions of his books.

Stage 2
Obtain copyright permissions. Copyright relates to the use of text written by other people and images created by other people. For example, if you want to quote a poem in your book, or feature someone's painting on your cover you will need, in both cases, signed documents authorising you to reproduce the poem and feature the painting.

Stage 3
Get your book assessed, edited and proofread. You don't have to do any of these, but we strongly advise that you do all of them – for the simple reason that ebooks that have been through these traditional pre-press stages stand a much greater chance of selling. No author can really assess his/her own work or be his/her own editor; you do need an impartial outside opinion. Editing ranges from simple copy-editing (checking it for narrative consistency and factual and grammatical errors, etc., as well as checking the preliminary pages – title page, imprint page, contents list, acknowledgements, foreword, etc.) to structural editing (rearranging, removing, adding content, etc.).

Stage 4
Obtain an ISBN. An International Standard Book Number (ISBN) is a 13-digit number that uniquely identifies a book. Every book intended for sale should carry an ISBN. ISBN numbers are allocated in batches of ten. Your ebook conversion company might have ISBN batches, in which case it will ask to complete an ISBN form giving data about your ebook and then send you a number

to include in your book. Or you can apply directly yourself for a batch of ISBN numbers (see www.isbn.nielsenbookdata.co.uk). If you're converting a book that exists in print format and therefore has an ISBN, you will still need a new ISBN for your ebook. Most eretailers will not accept a book without an ISBN.

Stage 5

Prepare your document for conversion. Your document needs to be in digital format before you submit it for ebook conversion. If you are self-publishing a book that exists only in print (i.e., no 2375 files), you will need to get it scanned to produce a digital document. The most suitable digital formats for ebook conversion are Adobe InDesign, QuarkXpress, MS Word and PDF.

Stage 6

Prepare your cover. The cover of a book is the first thing that customers see, so it needs to be attractive and to deliver a message that makes them want to find out more about the book. It's very important to get the cover right. If you already have a cover, submit it in JPG, PDF or TIFF format (72 dpi is fine, and the larger the image you provide, the better – don't compress it). If you want to create a cover yourself, remember to obtain copyright permissions where necessary. We would advise going to a professional designer, who will produce a cover that suits your specifications as well as the requirements of the ebook conversion company you're using. Some ebook companies offer design services; alternatively, there are many design services you could approach.

Stage 7

Prepare your website. Whether or not you intend selling your ebook through your website, ensure that you have all the facilities there to promote it. These include a blog and links to social media such as Twitter and Facebook. Ensure that your site is as visible as it can be to search engines (good SEO). If you do want to sell through the site (i.e., turn it into an ecommerce site), you will need a website development company to add the necessary facilities to your site, or build a new one incorporating all the book promotion and selling facilities required. This can be created very quickly.

Stage 8
Check the conversion. Assuming you've made all the right preparations, from the time you submit your source file for conversion to the time you receive it in ebook format could take from a few hours to a few days. If you don't have an ereader or iPad, the easiest way to check ePub conversions is to view them on your computer using Adobe Digital Editions.

Stage 9
Prepare the metadata for uploading. The metadata refers to information about the book (e.g., book description, contents list, author background, ISBN). Ensure that this information includes keywords that potential customers are likely to use in searches and could lead them to your ebook

Stage 10
Market your ebook. Use all the tools we've mentioned – and any more you can think of – to market, market, market!

Eight top tips for producing ebooks

1 **Write a great book:** Your reader's time is more valuable than their wallet, so respect this by publishing the highest quality book possible.

2 **Write another great book:** Once the reader trusts you'll respect their time with a great read, they'll be more inclined to sample and purchase your other titles.

3 **Maximise distribution:** Availability is the precursor to discoverability. The more bookstores that carry your book, the more chances you have to connect with a reader.

4 **Give (some of) your books away for FREE:** Free works best if you have a deep backlist. If you have only written only one full-length book, consider issuing some of your unpublished short-form writing as free ebooks.

5 **Trust your readers:** Some authors don't publish ebooks due to fear of piracy. Piracy cannot be prevented, and often when an author or publisher takes steps to prevent piracy, they only encourage it.

6 **Have patience:** Unlike traditionally published print books that hit store shelves and usually go out of print soon after, ebooks are immortal. With time and proper nourishment, ebooks have the chance to build deep roots (customer reviews, sales rank, SEO).

7 **Marketing starts yesterday:** Start building your marketing platform before you finish your book. Participate in social networks, and more importantly, contribute to social networks. If you view your Facebook and Twitter followers as people to be sold to, you'll hurt yourself.

8 **Architect for virality:** Since readers will determine the ultimate success of your book, you, as the author/publisher, can facilitate the virality (word-of-mouth) by making it easy for readers to access, enjoy and talk about your books. Eliminate friction that impedes discoverability, accessibility, purchasing and sample sharing.

Mark Coker, Smashwords

Case studies

1 Why I share, by Catherine Ryan Howard (www.catherineryanhoward.com)

'I very much lucked into this self-publishing ebooks, in that when I set out I did not have a master plan. Back when I started thinking about this whole self-publishing process, I did some research online and found that while there was plenty of information on the internet, it all came served with a generous helping of what I call self-publishing evangelism, i.e. it was written by people who have nothing but contempt for the traditional publishing model, referred to agents and editors as "gatekeepers" and seemed to think that by self-publishing, they were sticking it to The Man. I can't stand this kind of attitude, and longed for some realistic, straightforward and non-contemptuous information on the subject – so I started blogging about it myself. I decided early on to blog about everything: if something went well, I'd tell my blog readers, but if something went terribly wrong (for instance, if I didn't sell any copies), I'd tell them that too. As well as this, I involved them in the process, asking for their opinions on things like cover design, blurb wording, etc. For the first six months (from release date, so March–September 2010) I had a good readership, but it wasn't until the 1st September 2010, when I revealed in detail how many copies I'd sold, my royalties, etc. that I really won a following. I think this is because there is so much information about self-publishing online that is anything BUT straightforward, realistic and conveyed with some common sense. People don't want to topple 'Big Publishing' – they just want to get their book out there. And before they do that, they want to see how people have done it, and whether or not it's worked for them. In terms of sales, I think many of mine have been from people who just wanted to see for themselves how the book had turned out, and/or support me.

I do share a lot on my blog, but only about self-publishing. None of my personal life is online, and I keep my personal activities separate (my personal Facebook profile, for instance, is locked down and only for 'real life' friends; I have a separate page and profile for my writing activities). But then I have written a memoir, so there's very little point in trying to be mysterious on my blog!'

2 Me and the ebook, by Harriet Smart (www.harrietsmart.com)

'I don't think I could have become a novelist without the associated technology. It is the recurring theme – ironic when my love is historical fiction – but this is a story about making the apparently impossible very possible.

For years I had been trying to write on a typewriter and then I met a fellow student at St Andrews who had a BBC micro with a word-processing chip in it. This machine sat in great state on a Singer sewing machine table that he had bought from the Gilbert and Sullivan Society. With this machine I started to get results I liked, and I banged out the first third of a novel while said student revised for his finals.

Reader, I married him.

It does seem a long way from there to the elegant simplicity of a Kindle ebook, where you can just write, edit, upload and sell your work throughout the world, and do so from a writing location that may or may not be home.

It was the early Amstrad word processor that allowed me to continue to write and get my first five novels published (through Headline, now part of Hachette). With such a promising start, I thought I would continue to write and publish using the traditional method of submitting to my agent, who would then pass the novel onto the publisher, who would give it the nod and send it off to the printer. On reflection I realise I was both very lucky and a little naive.

In the mid 1990s, I hit an impasse with my writing. My novels began to be turned down. I took the rejection personally, as a reflection on the quality of my work, and since a great deal of my self-esteem was bound up in this, it was very painful indeed. I did not understand at the time that the economics of publishing were undergoing a violent contraction; that the mid-list in which my work can be squarely placed was slowly dying. Fortunately, I had just had a baby, so was happy to have a few years off. But my confidence took a further knock when my books went out of print, and my income from public lending right fell as the books, much loved and much lent, fell to pieces and were not replaced by the library system. It was hard to think about writing more.

I did not give up, but my novels kept just failing to pique the interest of the publishing industry. Given that my published work, once a great asset when talking to publishers and agents was now hard for anyone to get hold of, let alone read; past achievements seemed to be somewhat irrelevant. What was the point trumpeting about your past publications if there was nothing in the bookshop to prove that you were a writer?

I had sufficient confidence to remain convinced in my heart that I could write well and that my fiction was something that people wanted to read. Sometimes encouragement came from unlikely sources. I sent my accountant some figures for my tax return printed out on the back of a spare manuscript of *The Wild Garden* and the office staff reported back that they had got sucked into reading the fragments.

So I continued to write and submit to various publishers and agents, keeping my eyes on the commercial realities. I was not writing experimental fiction, but what I hoped was entertaining, mainstream fiction. I wrote and rewrote. I accepted editorial suggestion and direction. I was welcomed and encouraged to a point and then the verdict would follow with monotonous regularity – "well written and crafted, but not sufficient commercial appeal".

It was painful to keep hoping and then seeing hope die. At the same time, I began to perceive how the figures would not add up. Even if I made the sale to a publisher, I began to see that even if I was wildly successful, I would not make a living. And there was still a huge risk – that the book would not even get published let alone distributed and marketed successfully. The traditional publishing model began to feel all wrong for me and my writing.

We had begun to publish and distribute our own software – firstly my husband (now a software engineer) was developing tools for other software engineers, and then a little piece of software called StoryLines, which we had come up with to help me with my plotting. Simple and easy to use, it proved wonderfully effective – a way of speeding up the process of story development using index cards laid out in horizontal lines. Sales of StoryLines were healthy and we expanded the product into a suite of tools for fiction writers called Writer's Café, which we sold both as a boxed product and also as a download (www.writerscafe.co.uk). Writer's Café has continued to be popular. From each copy we sell, we make a reasonable profit. How many copies we sell is due to how much work we put into selling them, and how good our product is. We have complete control. And no-one ever told us that our software was not a good idea or of limited commercial possibility. We did not have to apply for permission to do what we wanted to do. We applied our common sense and our instincts to our product, added our passion and skills, and saw the results.

My first venture in what I prefer to call indie-publishing was in fact Writer's Café – in which we included an ebook called *Fiction the Facts*, a basic primer on creating successful stories, and we also included the full text of my Regency romantic comedy *Reckless Griselda* as an example of story structure. But those previously published and unpublished novels remained a problem, an under-used asset. How should we get them out to their market? We thought about reprinting them but this was still prohibitively expensive – people were beginning to self-publish but the quality was always dreadful. My husband, convinced that ebooks were coming sooner rather than later, was keen to get them into some sort of digital format. He had lots of ideas about distributing ebooks on CDs. I paid for one of them to be scanned into this format, early on, but the results soon were unusable as formats changed.

But then scanners and optical character recognition (OCR) got cheaper and better. I bought a cheap but speedy scanner, broke the spines of my paperbacks and found that I could pour the text straight into word files and edit them. I had my novels as proto-ebooks. I got a graphics tablet and designed some simple covers using Illustrator.

Ebook readers began to appear as mainstream consumer gadgets, but still at the top end of the market. The question of distribution and formats began to be one that needed to be answered. We pondered setting up our own website for people like me, who had been traditionally published and wanted to republish their back lists and also market their own new work. It turned out we were in tune with the Zeitgeist because soon we discovered Smashwords and then Kindle ebooks. Suddenly the opportunities to sell the work were there.

And I had discovered Twitter and through this it was soon clear to me that what I had to do was to build an 'online platform'. I already had a personal website and a blog, but it was a bit rudimentary and hard to keep updated. So I began to investigate better blogging platforms, and discovered that WordPress was practically idiot proof. Using WordPress I set up a better website that was also my blog (www.harrietsmart.com) and discovered that my more frequent blogging and tweeting (@fictionwitch) seemed to actually support sales of Writer's Café and, more importantly, our other new product, Jutoh (www.jutoh.com).

Jutoh was a happy accident. The first time we went to upload one of the novels on the Smashwords site, we saw that there were special format requirements to be included in the premium catalogue. My husband came up with a neat little tool to help the conversion of manuscript files into suitable and acceptable ebook formats, such as ePubs. It seemed worth trying to sell such a useful bit of kit, and it has done extremely well, showing that there is a great demand for a simple-to-use but comprehensive ebook conversion tool.

So with the help of Jutoh I began to put up my previous novels on Kindle and Smashwords, as well as some new work, *Reckless Griselda* and the first volume of a historical crime series, *The Butchered Man*. This I puffed through the website and through Twitter, and when Christmas 2010 arrived, and with it many Kindles under the tree, people began to buy and review the novel. They also began to recommend it to other people without my prompting them. Now, I have to be honest, the numbers are not startling, but it is a start, and I feel great pleasure in every sale. And already readers are telling me they are waiting for the next title in the series.

I also started another experiment in epublishing. It is an acknowledged fact that a well-written blog is the key to an online presence, but fiction writers often find non-fiction blog writing a drain on their creative resources. I decided I would write a blog in the form of a serial, inspired by Alexander McCall Smith's serials in *The Scotsman* and *The Daily Telegraph* that had proved there was a taste for serial fiction. I had in my head a group of characters and various situations that I had tried to work into a novel plot, but I could not find the climax or the resolution to any of their stories. They were too big, too real for a conventional narrative. This open-endedness seemed the perfect jumping off point for a serial, and so I began *Naked Angels*, in the summer of 2010 (www.fictionwitch.wordpress.com).

I have written the first 50 episodes, and will soon be issuing them in the form of a free ebook, before resuming the blog again. Writing serial fiction with an uncertain outcome is an intensely liberating and exciting experience for a writer. It turns fiction into a form of performance, and from the feedback I have had it is certainly an approach that readers like.

Of course there will be many people who still feel that traditional publishing is the only way to go, that gatekeepers are necessary and that the ebook can never replace the pleasure of a real book. For my part, as someone who defines herself as a storyteller, I think that it is not how great fiction is delivered that matters, just that we continue to strive to tell the best stories that we can, to entertain our audience to the best of our ability.'

17

Distribution

For those producing ebooks, most of the distribution networks are established by the mechanisms through which the title is created. Distribution of a physical product needs additional and extensive careful attention. It is worth noting that the issues to be discussed in this chapter are not avoided by larger publishing houses, for which stock management is an ongoing problem.

Often the main surprise for self-publishers is just how much physical space is taken up by books. Choices for book production through publishing solutions companies tend to be made from a catalogue of options: how many words per page, how many pages per book, what kind of format, binding, cover, and there can be attractive financial incentives for ordering more than you originally intended.

When it is the author who is making arrangements there are decisions to be made all the time. Ray Compton of printers CPI Bookmarque Ltd in Croydon commented:

'When books come off the production lines we stack them to parcel height, in multiples of eight. So depending on the width of the spine there can be anything from 48 to 120 books shrink-wrapped together in plastic. The requisite number of parcels are then put on pallets and delivered to the customer. If the customer wants them put into boxes as well, this can be arranged, but would obviously cost extra, as would additional storage materials such as an additional layer of protection between the plastic of the wrapping and the boxes, such as polystyrene chippings. And both protective cases for individual copies (which can be overprinted) and outer boxes can be sourced in all sorts of shapes and sizes.'

It can be a real surprise to find out just how many boxes a relatively small number of books actually produces – and how heavy they are. Careful packing matters. Although robust and likely to last for a long time, most purchasers and recipients want a pristine copy; customers may examine a title on top of the display in a shop, but the edition they take to the payment point tends to be one from further down the pile.

As with every aspect of self-publishing, you need to assess your overall aims and match them with appropriate solutions. Are you producing a few copies for your grandchildren, or seeking to sell through retail outlets nationwide?

Producing a small number for distribution among family and friends

The supply of 48 copies of a book may result in one box of books; wider distribution however will need planning. Those you can give away now can be dispatched in padded bags. But for those you have in mind for generations to come you might want to think about longer-term storage issues. Printers can source packaging of archival standard (to ensure minimum deterioration) and some self-publishers deposit copies of their titles in bank vaults, along with valuable paintings and jewellery, to ensure they get passed on to the next generation. Further proof of just how much such a project can matter.

Producing a larger number for wider distribution and sale

If your printer is producing your item on a litho machine, you may find yourself under pressure to buy more copies than you are able either to sell or house, seduced by the thought of a lower price per item. Once the printer's set up costs have been paid for, your only costs are machine time, ink and paper, and so producing more copies than you estimate you need right now may be an attractive option. In general, if you are going to be selling your title, it is still probably a good idea to keep the initial print run low because:

- Regrettably it is only when you are presented with a first printed copy of a book that you tend to see the mistakes; difficult if your first print run gives you 2–3 years' stock (disposing of even a less-than-satisfactory book of your own can be hard, and the loft fills up...). A short first print run allows you to make the changes, and announce a second edition.

- Storage is tricky. What may sound like convenient locations can have surprising disadvantages – your garden shed is almost certainly subject to damp, your garage may smell of petrol or barbecue fuel, your family may resent large boxes being piled up in their bedrooms. Parents and friends can often be persuaded to take stock, but then you become subject to their own short-term need for additional space or to move house. An empty bedroom may be a solution, but if you turn the heating off again you may find the paper curls. It's not long before a hastily agreed to solution and pride at your proactivity becomes resentment of 'that bloody book of yours'. In any case, storing in a variety of locations makes it difficult to assess overall stock levels.

- Short print runs allow you to manage transportation more easily. Your printer may deliver to you, but if you are required to take stock on to third party sellers, you may end up having to hire a van. On a regular basis, this is expensive.

- A short print run may support the long-term value of your publication. One of the reasons that first editions of poetry books are often valuable is that the print runs tend to be low – perhaps no more than 200.

Case study: *The Silence at Song's End*, Nicholas Heiney, edited by Libby Purves and Duncan Wu

I spoke to *The Times* columnist and the presenter of BBC Radio 4's *Midweek*, Libby Purves. Having battled depression for many years, her son Nicholas took his own life in the summer of 2006. There was no suicide note, but they did find a bundle of papers, poems, writings which his former Oxford Tutor, Professor Wu, insisted should be published. They did talk to a couple of publishing houses about publication but found publishers immediately parked it in the 'poor me' category; dwelling on the bereavement rather than celebrating the life and the writing. She and her family were also very particular about the format they wanted. Nicholas was a bibliophile; he had worked in an antiquarian bookshop for books rather than payment, so the format of the book – how it would look, feel and what would be on the cover – was very important. They also wanted to put any monies raised from its sale towards projects their son would have encouraged rather than supporting a publisher's general overheads. They decided to self-publish.

The process of publishing was complicated – it involved far more than they had anticipated. They had to handle all the obvious things – editing what they had, writing linking passages to explain context – but they also learnt about a lot of things they had not expected: discount levels (really high, how does one make any money?); delivery (move the lawnmower out of the garage right now to make room for 16 boxes arriving tomorrow); transportation (deliver to the wholesaler Gardners in a Skoda whilst surrounded by pantechnicons on their forecourt); just how much books weigh (not having a handy forklift truck they had to be lifted by them – back-breaking); packaging for posting (wrap-around with sticky patches is cheaper than envelopes); matching supply and demand ('If we delay the reprint, and order 150 more, can we still meet the Christmas requirements?').

The book raised money for charitable purposes, but rather than linking with a specific charity (there was none that was completely relevant and they did not want to set up one of their own) they declared the proceeds as income, put it in a ring-fenced account and gift-aided the total – and from this account they have been able to make a series of grants to relevant projects and individuals, offering both assistance and motivation.

This is an interesting story, and a valuable demonstration of just how much is involved in the process of self-publishing. She and her family had a particular and specific situation, and of course a media connectedness which enabled them to get the book featured in the press. *The Times* serialised it and this led to the sale of virtually the whole first print run of 1,000 copies. Subsequent orders have benefitted from this initial momentum and come through word of mouth.

Some may like to take up the challenge and go for it – and indeed the process of nursing your book through all the above may make you feel energised and ambitious. The clear implication from Purves and family is that you should not conclude is that self-publishing is an easy option.

Distribution to retail outlets

If you are planning to sell your title through retail outlets, then one of your responsibilities will be to ensure they get the stock they need. I mention retail outlets rather than just bookshops, because there may be shops other than the book variety that may take your work: garden centres; charity shops; supermarkets; mail order operations.

This is not straightforward, because those unfamiliar with stocking books may need display materials (shelving etc) on which to present stock – and manufacturers who have already provided such facilities for their own merchandise may not be willing to have their goods moved up to make room for yours. A few years ago in the UK there was a public spat over small shops selling ice creams – there was only room for one deep freeze within most such facilities and this had been provided by their major supplier, who was unwilling to then accommodate other producers' merchandise.

Many retailers find it more convenient to order from a few wholesalers rather than lots of different independent producers, each of which sends in separate parcels in idiosyncratic packaging.[128] So bear in mind that while you can see your title would fit perfectly within a particular outlet, and appeal to their itinerant visitors, the prospect of dealing with a single-supplier may not tempt, particularly if it encourages other similar suppliers to get in touch too. The easiest and quickest option may be to say no.

Selling to larger retail chains
Retail chains with multiple outlets usually prefer to buy centrally and keep things simple; buying for all their shops at the same

---

[128] There is a particular resistance towards heavy duty staples from many retailers

time, with one point of delivery, they gain negotiating muscle. Stock is delivered to their central warehouse, and from there they organise distribution of titles to individual outlets, according to an appreciation of local demographics, customer base and previous sales patterns.

In the UK, the buying team at Waterstone's is interested in stocking a broad range of titles to meet customers' likely purchasing needs, and they regularly see presentations from publishers at their headquarters. Stock may be ordered on several different levels, in various quantities, but in general will become either campaign titles or part of the firm's long-term range.

Campaign titles are generally new ones, and those forming the backbone of 'category promotions'[129] that are mainly displayed at the front of the store. Range titles are everything else; backlist and core stock. Core stock is a very long list of titles in each category that have proven sales history, and within this general grouping there will be different levels of stocking, the highest being 'super tier', meaning that every store will have copies in the relevant section. There is a rolling review of the composition of core stock to ensure there is still demand for what is on the shelves. So classics such as *To Kill a Mockingbird* will probably always be part of the range, whereas a celebrity autobiography or a women's commercial fiction title, both of which gain a lot of temporary publicity and sell well for a while, may not be permanent fixtures.

Managers also have the freedom to choose stock from any book in print for which they either perceive a demand, or receive orders from customers. Stores are grouped into regions and managers meet regularly at both regional and national get-togethers, where additional ideas for stocking are discussed.

'Technically all these opportunities are open to self-published titles, although in practice not all self-published titles would be appropriate for all stores. Traditional publishers (both the large and independents; the latter sometimes working in consortia) present their wares to us throughout the year, but even they have to pick from their lists and offer the selection they think best suited to our needs. We would not

---

[129] Titles within a certain identifiable type, e.g. books which might help promote new year's resolutions in January or offer 'beach reads' in July

have time to be briefed by all individual author-publishers, but would certainly look at information on anything sent to us for a potential stocking decision.'

Jon Howells, Waterstone's

If you are asking for your title to be considered within this process, they would expect you to behave like any other potential supplier: offer professionally produced material that makes sense in today's market; inform 3–4 months ahead of publication that the title will be available; provide the information about it that is needed in order to understand what is proposed (they would need to see an AI, or advance information sheet[130] and the proposed cover).

Titles should also be consistent within their genre, so the buying public – which is inclined to make impulse/quick buying decisions – knows what they are purchasing. This requires close attention to detail; if you want to know what a crime novel looks like, have a look at all the others for the same market.[131] Whereas bookshop browsers rely on the look of the book, as well as the author name and its supporting brand to attract their attention, every title submitted for consideration for stocking must also have its own unique ISBN and barcode; these are non-negotiable as without them retailers cannot monitor sales.

In the long run, it may not be in the self-publishing author's best interests to become too widely stocked too quickly. Bear in mind that titles featured in campaigns are needed in huge quantities, with equally huge quantities available in quick reserve should there be sufficient demand, and are often given financial support from the publisher, and this may be too much commitment (financial or emotional). There is however the 'staff recommends' slot, usually near the front door, where members of the staff team choose their favourites, and cards display their hand-written comments. Gaining a recommendation here can be an excellent way of securing national attention. At head office staff examine both national and regional trends, and if they see local 'spikes' they often call in a copy of the title in question to consider it for wider stocking.

---

[130] See chapter 19
[131] These are often referred to as 'category clues' e.g. women's commercial fiction having candy floss coloured covers, and crime fiction often covers in red, black and white

'We do appreciate that a self-publishing author has to be writer/ publisher/marketer/publicist/production expert/networker – and in addition find some time to develop ideas for their next book. We understand that fulfilling so many roles at the same time is highly demanding, particularly if they have no previous experience of book production. But we have high standards because our customers demand them. And if what is presented to us feels right for our market, and proves popular with our customers, then we will stock it – whoever published it.' Jon Howells, Waterstone's

In the long run, the best way of getting a national stocking decision from a chain may be to start with a local branch, and then be recommended on, as possible core stock.

Case study: Lisa Piselli, Manager of a local branch of Waterstone's

'I manage a Waterstone's store in Milton Keynes, but my previous role was manager of the smaller store in Berkhamsted (Hertfordshire). It was the town's only bookshop and a strong asset/meeting place for the bookish local community (birthplace of Graham Greene and today home to several well-known writers including Sophie Kinsella).

In Berkhamsted we regularly offered local authors the opportunity to launch their new books within our store, and we extended the privilege to both the published and the self-published. We wanted our store to become a hub, and offering events enabled us to engage and build relationships. Although this was something that Waterstone's encouraged throughout the company, it was very much left up to the individual store to plan their own events programme. We were lucky that Berkhamsted is a close-knit community in which people love to encourage culture and creativity and so we chose to make local author events our real strength. We were very much appreciated for it, both by company and local community.

But given that we always had more authors wanting events than we had time available in the schedule, what influenced my decision on whom to accept? The most important thing was always an awareness that the author understood they would have to do some work to support a bookshop launch. Probably unsurprisingly, many authors have little real idea of how book retailing works, and think that simply by putting a title on a shelf in a bookshop it will sell. The reality is much more complicated. We need to promote awareness, bring in associated traffic, and persuade them to want to own or buy, preferably both, the title in question. Simply shelving a title means it will probably still be there when we do our next stock check.

I would always favour a genuinely local author who had a large body of supporters likely to want to attend an event, and who had already been in touch with the local media to try to create some coverage. "Local" to me means that you are living reasonably near, can be relied upon to bring in friends to promote purchase at the event, and spread the word to others in the locality, through local media.[132]

We have no budget specifically allocated for such events but there are associated costs: staff time, light, heating and security as well as incidentals such as photocopying for leaflets. We would expect the authors to provide the refreshments for their guests, and to be conscious of the fact that some visitors to the store will not want to get involved with their launch, and be respectful of that. Remember too that store managers talk to each other, so be as helpful and easy to deal with as possible.

I would also want to see a copy of the book before making a decision about an event as obviously the standard of production for self-published titles varies enormously. We would not want to host an event for a title that we would not normally stock, and the Berkhamsted store sold very little within the categories of Body, Mind and Spirit and Fantasy. If on the other hand an author could convince me that they were a representative member of a wider community of similarly minded local individuals, who really needed a place to buy and exchange news about titles that attracted them all, then of course I would take notice.

---

[132] Notable that there is a tendency for the term 'local author' to be used as a euphemism for 'self-publishing author'

Authors should also have a rational view on how generally interesting the subject matter of their book really is. Obviously if you have just spent years writing about a subject it probably engrosses you, but the interest may be much less widespread than you think. I regularly had highly specialised titles offered to me for possible events, presented on the basis that interest was almost universal. These may be the kind of titles where blogging on a relevant website, or feeding information to members of a particular society, and then encouraging online ordering, might be a much better use of everyone's time.

A good example of an author who managed the process well is crime and spy novel writer Adrian Magson,[133] who I believe now has a contract to be published. He was self-published for many years and would come and do events for us, delivering posters and leaflets to the shop beforehand, arranging local publicity and liaising with the media. And on the day he would walk around the store talking to customers – but without making them feel awkward if they did not want to buy. He came back to us repeatedly.'

Selling to independent bookshops

Independents are often very important to self-published authors. As they are usually run by owners/local managers they can stock what they like, and given that they cannot match the deep discounting of the chains, they will attract customers by anticipating the kind of purchases they want to make, and offering them the chance to meet like minds in a congenial environment.

The key staff of independents are frequently to be found on the shop floor, and often behind the till. They like to do this as it helps them maintain contact with their customers. So it's not the best start to arrive and ask the first contact you see if you can speak to the manager, thereby implying that you assume they must be busy doing managerial things in an office.[134]

Jane Cholmeley, founder of the independent Silver Moon Women's Bookshop commented:

[133] www.adrianmagson.com
[134] Along the same lines, don't assume that the manager of a chain store is bookish – many now employ retailers who have experience of retailing rather than bookselling

'A love of books, and a strong desire to assist the individual author in our world of increasing conglomerates may be noble intentions, but these have to live alongside a stern business brain – and I must admit my heart would sink every time a self-published person came into Silver Moon to sell me something. Often they were desperately unprofessional and I would sit there thinking, "I've been guilt tripped by better people than you".

Bookshops may vary in this, but I always hated the drop-in. I always liked people to make an appointment (and of course to be punctual). Dropping in to sell a title has the underlying subtext that your time is more important than the time of the person you are trying to see and sell to. Why should the bookseller interrupt what they are doing to see you at your convenience?

Bear in mind too that the finances may not be great for the bookseller. Here is an example:

10 copies of a book priced @ £6.99 of which you sell 5:

Turnover = £34.95 @ margin 35%, gross profit = £12.23.

But from this must be deducted:

  The cost of taking payment by cheque (£1)
  The cost of returning unsold copies: (£3)

Giving a net profit of £8.23, or a net margin of 23.5%, which takes no account of time or labour (including the setting up of an account with the supplier) and the additional costs of keeping the outlet open (heat, light, business rates).'

Eight top tips for selling a self-published book to your local bookstore

Chain bookstores will usually have one book buyer per category (women's fiction; literary fiction; picture books etc). In the case of an independent bookstore, depending on the number of staff, you may be selling to the manager/owner or to a member of staff with much broader responsibilities.

1 **Know the store, preferably as a customer.** Know the kind of thing they sell and what appeals to the local market. Appreciate

that different stores in the same region, or even the same town, may have very different clientele, stock and hence associated promotions/events. Acquire this knowledge on prior visits, not ten minutes before you start trying to persuade them. Asking a shop to sell your books in a location where you are known as a regular customer is a good basis for a relationship. If you don't support your local bookshop why should they support you?

2 **Understand the market for your book**; the main; the peripheral; what else they buy and what section of the shop it might be housed in (bearing in mind that not everything can sit on the table by the door).

3 **Go prepared.** You will almost certainly have less time than you need, and may have to share their attention with the customers they are serving, so be prepared to think quickly and listen for key buying signs from them ('Oh yes I spotted this in the press/ heard about it on local radio'). Go armed with a sales kit so there is something to look at while you talk – an AI, a picture of the cover, a marketing summary sheet giving key points, information on you the author, a press release. At the end of your sales pitch, always leave the AI with the buyer. They may wish to refer to it or pass it round their staff to generate enthusiasm.

You will not have time to cover all of the following, but you do need to know the answer, should they ask you:

* What is the product? You could try describing it as a book with parents (James Patterson meets Tom Clancy; Joanna Trollope meets Ruth Rendell) or part of a genre (e.g. romantic novel/romance noire; detective/crime fiction/true crimes – the differences may sound slight, but you need to appreciate the subtleties).
* Where it would sit in their shop, within which particular subsection, and what is doing well within that section at the moment?
* The likely level of interest in the title, i.e. what marketing you are doing and with what success in terms of local publicity? These are the drivers that will push people into their shop.
* An interesting anecdote about the book/author/project's origins with which to open ('I have lived in this town all

my life. This shop used to be Waitrose, which is where my parents did their grocery shopping – so I have already spent lots of time in here!')

4 **Always remember that they have a choice.** If they were not stocking your titles, there would not be a hole on the shelf – someone else's stock would be there instead. Individual titles ordered from individual sellers create more administration, as you still have to have invoicing and credit control facilities set up, however much business you do together. If you are difficult to deal with, they may decide it is too much effort (and difficult includes over-intense engagement with the shop's staff; asking how your book is doing too often and regular visits to rearrange the stock – they will notice). As proof of your business-like stance they will need to be reassured that you are reliable (and hence able to sustain stocking levels) and informed about business relationships (e.g. that you have thought about the arrangements for return if the titles do not sell, and the levels of discount you will give them). Go on your own, not with a buggy or small children in tow; return with them to buy!

5 **Have a book that is worth the interest of a professional book retailer.** They will not want to put their brand behind something they would not ordinarily stock, however close to the shop you live.

6 **Be truly local,** and offer proof of local interest in your work – friends, relations, work associates, parents from the local schools your children attend, all of whom are longing to come to an event in the store and buy then. Support your book through engaging the interest of local media – get in touch with the local paper/radio station and get them on side before you try to set up an event.

7 **Don't cream off the local market by selling to your friends and relations,** however much greater the associated margin will be for you. Stocking or at best an event in a bookshop is a privilege, not a right, and to cover the retailer's costs for displaying your titles, sales will go through their tills not directly into your pocket. If they offer you an event it means they are offering you a home within which to present your material for appreciation

and possible sale, not a market stall within their premises. In any case, a successful bookshop stocking/event may mean that your work ends up being stocked on a regular basis (core stock), and hence will be available to those in the locality who *don't* already know you.

8 **Be polite**. If they say no, and you have made your best case, don't throw a tantrum. Try to exit leaving the door ajar for the relationship to be maintained (without sounding as if you will stalk them). If they offer you an event, remember to write and thank them afterwards (take trouble over this and do it quickly).

Some self-publishing firms offer packages that include stocking in a chain bookstore as part of the deal, but the depth of their commitment needs exploring in more detail. Having the title stored spine on for two weeks in the depths of the organisation may not fulfil what you thought 'stocking' really means. But if this window of opportunity is part of your deal, put some energy around it. Persuade your friends to go in and buy it rather than obtaining their copy from you, go in and buy a copy yourself if need be. All will register that the title generated interest and may lead to a reorder at the till point.

Working with other large retailers

Large retailers talk about 'ranging titles across stores' – which means they are stocked in various locations. They may be willing however to work only with the larger UK publishers and then deal via external wholesalers or representatives for smaller suppliers or individual author submissions. For example, the general stationers W.H. Smith have set up a system with the wholesaler Bertrams whereby they acquire titles from small publishers and self-published authors via recommendations from their buying team, but a certain degree of latitude is maintained for purchasing of particularly local interest. Their website informs:

'We do not, unfortunately, have the resources here to review the massive volume of submissions in appropriate detail and so work together with Bertrams to get the best titles into W.H. Smith. Please accept our apologies that we are unable to review all items individually and place orders directly. If your book is about places of local interest or refers to local history, and is not a children's book, you may approach the manager of your local store. He, or she, may agree to sell your book in their store. Please note that they are in no way bound to buy it. Their decision is final and will largely depend on their local book budget and whether they believe the title to be in demand in their area. Please be aware that all local titles are bought on a sale or return basis.'

Having a recognised distributor

For retailers to be interested in stocking your title it is important that you have the book listed with a recognised distributor who can manage the process of distribution quickly (hold stock, take orders, package up and despatch). Most large chains will only stock books from distributors with which they have an established trading relationship. In the UK this includes TBS (The Book Service), Littlehampton Book Services, Grantham, Marston, Turnaround etc, as well as the two major wholesalers, Gardners and Bertrams.

Working with wholesalers

It is also vital to have your title listed with wholesalers. Wholesalers take a range of titles and supply specialist book chain stores, independents as well as other retailers and sales locations who do not primarily stock books (e.g. garden centres and historic houses). Some retailers delegate to wholesalers the selection policy on titles, and you have to be listed by them before they will consider your work.

Summary of what information is needed before trying to get your title stocked by a national chain or wholesaler

* Author and title

* An International Standard Book Number (ISBN)

* A Bookland European Article Number (EAN) barcode

- Your title information already available on Nielsen BookData

- Your title already stocked by a recognised distributor

- Pre-printed stock available for despatch (not still to be printed on demand once an order is received)

- A synopsis of the book, and an indication of whom it is likely to appeal to

- Information on any specific geographical regions where this book could sell well

- Information on planned marketing/PR to promote the book

- Sales data of any previous publications, either your own or related titles that have been popular

- Jacket image

And all this needs to be succinctly and professionally presented, preferably in no more than a page, and sent with an accompanying letter introducing yourself/the author, and offering your return address and email address. If it is already available, send a copy of the book too.

What happens next?

Most retailers or wholesalers do not acknowledge receipt of information on titles submitted for stocking consideration. If, after a specified period of time, you have not heard back from the organisation (usually four to six weeks) then it may be permissible to email to check the title information was received. Feedback on negative decisions is generally not available. Do not expect the bookseller to mail back your title. You should allow for the expense of submission copies in your costings.

If the retailer or wholesaler decides to stock your title(s) then you will be contacted to discuss commercial terms (i.e. the levels of discount they require off the published price, the payment terms etc). Almost without exception, books from new publisher relationships will be taken into stock on a consignment basis (i.e. the stockholder holds the titles and pays monthly on sales achieved). As a general rule of thumb, all books that are held as stock lines are 'sold' to the retail customer on a sale or return basis (they can be returned if not sold), whereas listed/non-stock lines (special orders) and books provided as print on demand are sold on a firm sale basis (the retailer assumes the risk and must keep and pay for what has been ordered).

Even if you are unsuccessful in your submission to the central buying team, and no stocking decision is made, books may be listed by the wholesaler, which means they are available to fulfil requests from individual stores or special customer orders through a 'special order service'.

Once titles have been confirmed for stocking or listing, then full details need to be submitted. A spreadsheet is usually available from the organisation requiring all criteria and bibliographic information; the above supported by:

- ISBN and barcode

- Title

- Dimensions (length x width in UK; vice versa in US)

- Extent (how many pages)

- Binding

- Price

- Publication date

- Illustrations (how many, colour or black and white, and what sort – e.g. photographic or line drawings)

- Series

- Author

- VAT element if applicable (books with space for the owner to write in count as workbooks and attract VAT, so be aware that diary-style travel guides with a strong element of reader participation may be subject)

- Single line synopsis (perhaps no more than 70 characters)

- Territorial rights (where the book can be sold)

- UK publication date

- UK distributor

- It is also a good idea to upload a jacket image, as this will help both buyers, booksellers and customers

In general, cover images need to be provided as:

- PC format (or PC formatted file if using an Apple Mac)

- 24bit RGB colour .jpg

- Full frontal view of the cover, with no border

- Minimum of 100 dpi 640 pixels

- Saved as its ISBN13.jpg (i.e. 9780713679328.jpg)

- Images can generally be supplied over the internet, or mailed on a CD/DVD ROM

Obtaining an ISBN

You will need to obtain an International Standard Book Number (ISBN) from your organisation with national responsibility for this. In the UK the UK ISBN Agency is organised by Nielsen BookData isbn.agency@nielsen.com, and in the US by www.isbn.org

Do not expect ISBN allocation to be instant; it may take up to six weeks. You have the option to buy a series of numbers, the minimum being ten.

Systems in support of distribution

You will need:

- A price

- A policy on discounts

- Terms and conditions for your business, including a policy on returns

- Arrangements with a carrier
- A system for accepting orders (and capturing appropriate information about your customers)
- A system of chasing payment
- Monitoring procedures for all the above
- Samples to show people
- A source of further information on the service/products you offer

A price

How do you price a book? On the positive side you have a range of market research available to you in every bookshop, showing you what a book of the kind you have in mind officially costs and for how much it is selling (the two are not the same thing as there is much discounting within the book trade).

Some self-published authors price a book on the basis of what it cost them to produce, and what profit they may make on each copy sold. While it is easy to understand the emotional logic behind this, and it may establish a product's value to those you wish to give it to, if you are seeking to sell copies and create a market, this method ignores the consumer, and their likely perception of the associated value.

> 'House sellers often base the price they want to charge on how much they need to make from a sale in order to finance their next purchase. This is not a particularly good way of establishing a price, as it ignores market perceptions, and small differences in price can make a house look good value or overpriced. And if a house sticks, it can be really difficult to reawaken the market'
>
> Allan Fuller, estate agent

Of course a house costs vastly more than a book, but the principle stands – plus in the case of the book, it's difficult to take it off the market and then put it back on again six months later; you really have only one chance to make it work (retailers will seldom be interested in restocking something they have already failed to shift).

A common tactic is to use the .99 ending to a price to make a title *look* cheaper; the theory being that $9.99 sounds cheaper than $10 (although of late I have detected a tendency among some retailers to move towards rounded prices; which perhaps sounds more straightforward). More significant perhaps are the *pricing points* we perceive. So an £11.99 price might be pushed to £12.99 or £13.99 – whereas £15.99 sounds significantly more expensive.

Bear in mind too that the price on the cover is not what you get (unless you are selling them yourself) as any retail outlet will require a discount and if the book is included within any wider discounting or special production (e.g. putting in the window of a shop) you will probably be asked to contribute to that too. If you add in all the production costs for your title you may find the unit cost is even more expensive – e.g. the cost of review copies; those that get damaged, are returned and cannot be resold; the marketing costs. And of course the cost of sale is based on the number you print, not on the number you sell.

Other tactics for charging a bit more

Is your book going to be on sale where there are no other books competing? Art publisher Prestel[135] regularly sells titles through art galleries and at art events, where there are no other titles on sale and hence the price of a book compares very favourably with the price of the art available. Self-publishing authors have also experimented with selling door-to-door, through local school fairs, or farmers' markets.

* A book as a present, with associated wrapping, can support a higher price. Could you offer free gift packaging (some manufacturers of china include wrapping paper in the box, and in the case of a book it can be slipped inside the pages).

* Can you add any value? A slip case, an associated book plate, a signature in the front, a free accompanying postcard of the cover, a limited edition, a numbered edition, a special edition bound in leather? All of these, if effectively produced and lovingly described, can make a higher price seem justifiable. In the UK

---

[135] www.randomhouse.de/prestel_eng/

today, virtually the only bookshops selling all their titles full price are those at literary festivals, where the addition of a signature justifies customers paying the full price.

* Non-fiction may be less price sensitive than fiction if you can make a particularly strong argument for author expertise.

* Mail order sales may be less price sensitive still, if the message is focussed on value for money, meeting needs, convenience and direct delivery.

* Really effective copy, making the title sound different, interesting and invaluable – see the next chapter on how to do this.

Money saving gambits to avoid
* Within the planned book, reducing the text size, increasing the text measure and/or reducing the margins, all of which may allow more words on the page – and hence require fewer pages. Similarly, printing on thinner (and cheaper paper) which permits 'show-through' of ink. All may result in making the title look both obviously self-published, and unreadable.

* Promotional gambits not used by the book trade e.g. buy one get one free, which may look a little too desperate.

* If your book is slim, perhaps poetry, make sure it has a proper spine with title and author on it. Stapling or spiral bound will not do.

* Printing too many to get a cheaper overall price. Print enough to cover anticipated sales in the first year, and to provide stock for those you wish to give away.

* Selling too many too quickly can be a real difficulty for a first time publisher. It is difficult to finance the printing of a second edition before the money has come in from the first, and you never know whether it is all sold, or just pending a stock return.

* Having a minimum order quantity; insisting on providing larger stock orders than bookshops are wiling to take on, to save on postage. They may end up ordering none.

Should you put the price on the cover?

Most paperbacks have it on the back and most hardbacks on the inside corner of the book jacket, from where it can be cut if the title is to be given as a present. If you can't make up your mind about whether it should be there or not, consider stickering stock post-delivery. But if you are planning sale through bookshops, ISBN, barcode and price need to be there.

A policy on discounts

You may be surprised at the discount off the cover price required by retailers in return for the stocking of your book; probably at least 35–40%. This is the business model you are entering, so it may be best not to begin by resenting it, and instead understanding why it is there – to cover the overheads of running a retail outlet such as staffing, lighting, recording sales in order to generate reorders, selling and promoting. Space at the front of the store, in the window, or by the till point may require further discount. The other mechanism with which the retailer can negotiate is the commitment of the business arrangement: are titles being ordered as firm sale or as sale or return. In return for firm sale an even higher discount will be required. To console you, the mark-ups in the clothing business are at least 100% and in the catering business the cost charged to the customer will routinely be 400–600% of the cost of the ingredients.

You may be successful in persuading a retailer to accept a sliding scale, so more discount in return for a larger order. Another effective gambit is to get your product adopted as an incentive by a firm keen to make a positive relationship with its customers,[136] so perhaps in return for a larger order of their goods, or with a first purchase. If you are to pitch your product for this kind of arrangement you will have to have a very clear understanding of their customer base and why your product would be just the incentive for them. The advantage is that you shift the stock for firm sale, and the book is promoted as being worth owning (and so may result in more sales to people who found it attractive, but did not want to commit to the organisation offering it – these are known as halo sales).

---

[136] See story of Barbara Abbs, page 222

Terms and conditions for your business, including a policy on returns

You will need to establish your payment terms and the conditions of business. Are you asking for payment of invoice on receipt of goods, on their sale or 30/60/90 days after delivery? You may have to agree to more disadvantageous (to you) terms than initially desirable in order to promote wide stock-holding. Ideally at launch time you want the book on the retailer's shelves to encourage those who have heard the associated publicity to pick it up and buy it. If you are servicing the educational market you may want to offer slightly longer as schools can be slow, but reliable, payers. To avoid the cost and time of credit-checking an institution such as a state-funded school (which is unlikely to disappear), you might consider accepting an order on their official letterhead.

You could put an invoice in an envelope on top of the parcel to avoid it getting lost when the parcel is unpacked, or even post separately. Traditionally the publisher pays the cost of postage to the retail outlet, but the customer pays postage on mail order goods (or it could sometimes be given free as an incentive for a bigger order).

Arrangements with a carrier

You will need a system for despatching what is ordered; maybe a parcel firm who will collect from your home address if there is sufficient quantity. Otherwise either know precisely how much your book costs to post, and buy packaging and stamps to fit, or consider a subscription to Smartstamp.[137]

Systems for taking orders, capturing appropriate information, chasing for payment, passing bad debts for collection

You don't necessarily need different members of staff to do all this; you can create the illusion of a team of willing helpers by giving each function a different email address. This may also help you, the writer, get into 'servicing mode' for what comes in on each. When it comes to chasing bad debts, you can appoint a collection agency, an individual, or make the phone calls yourself. As an individual author, sometimes just making the call and reminding

---

[137] www2.royalmail.com/discounts-payment/smartstamp

an organisation that you need to be paid can enhance the moral obligation and produce the desired result, although bear in mind that there are individuals who see avoiding payment as an art form.

Samples

Offering a potential stockist a free sample is a good idea; it permits them the opportunity to try out your material and a small profit if they decide to put it straight on the shelves. Returned stock, perhaps slightly damaged and that cannot otherwise be sold, can be useful for samples.

Mail order

Setting up a mail order distribution service may seem the obvious solution to not being able to secure stocking of your title in bookshops or other retail outlets. I will confine my comments to two particular areas of the operation, the marketing material you make available to encourage orders, whether website copy or door-to-door distribution of leaflets, and the manner in which you manage the resulting parcels.

Marketing materials trying to encourage an order need to be:

* Strong on product benefits and reasons to buy. Ask yourself, would I buy from me?

* Correct – the ordering details and associated mechanisms (have you called the book by the same title each time?)

* Stimulating. Using the book title too often is boring.

* Interesting. 'This book…' lacks impact as an opening.

* Clear. Is it obvious what the price is and how much should be added for postage and packing etc? How does the customer order and by when? Is there an incentive for ordering swiftly (an 'early-bird' discount)? Are the publisher's name, address, telephone, email and website on all the elements in the package? If they are only on the order form, this may get separated. Have you checked each one? Check the website, ring the telephone number, send an email to the address quoted. A single transposition of a digit can make it unusable. If you are so familiar with the information

that it is impossible to be objective, then get someone else to check it.

- Easy to read. Are the contact details large enough to find and read in a rush?

- Helpful. What does the customer do if he or she is unclear about some aspect of your product; are you offering a telephone number for enquiries? Don't offer more than you can deliver, as this will only cause frustration.

- Grammatically correct. Triple check the wording for consistency and to avoid errors. As a publisher you are expected to get these things right!

- Strategic. Have you included an option for capturing non-buying prospects? How is your marketing piece to be followed up: by re-mailing; with telemarketing etc? Have you sought permission to remain in touch so you comply with data protection legislation? Marketing communications are now based on the customer choosing to opt in rather than opt out. If you offer an option for those who do not want to order now saying 'Please send me further information on...' have you sorted out what you are going to send? Have you told everyone who needs to know, including family members who may answer your phone?

- Returnable. If you are mailing, is your address on the outer envelope so that undelivered materials can be returned – and you can update your contact list?

How to create a relationship through sending a parcel

Most people love getting a parcel, but if there is no one at home to receive it, they tend to love going along to the sorting office on a Saturday morning to retrieve it much less. If your titles are being posted there are several ways in which you can make the experience a pleasant one, in the hope that they will remember the experience, your name, and order from you again.

For the packing of individual copies of your book there are padded bags and wrap-around packaging available. Investigate all options and see what comes out lightest and hence cheapest to post – and ensures the contents arrive in best condition. You can make the parcel extra-special by wrapping the book in bubble-wrap or tissue paper, perhaps with attractive stickers holding the covering securely. Think what else you can include within the same postage band to encourage them order again; maybe a list of forthcoming events for readers or a postcard offering a second copy.

Case study: Lynne Quirk

'My mother, Lizzie Barton, was born in 1909 in Haughton Green, a small village in Lancashire. She was a clever girl, but as the eldest of ten children had to leave formal education at the age of 14 and begin work in the local mill. When we were children, she would constantly tell my two brothers and I stories of her childhood, and always wanted to write them down. Much later on in her life, hearing about a woman in London who published the story of her of her childhood made her think that she could do it too, and in her late 80s and early 90s she wrote it all down, ending in 1923 when she entered the mill. This was a continuous narrative (without sections or chapter headings), written longhand in lovely copperplate writing; but although her memory of events and people was as sharp as ever, her grasp of punctuation had completely gone. She had never written before, and was not a great reader (although she was an avid radio listener and loved plays and poetry) but the stories had been polished in her mind for years and just seemed to flow out of her.

In the last years of her life I was her carer, and just would not have had the time to think about publication of her manuscript. Although by then it was finished, she would remember additional snippets and I would write these down – and I did always think I would try to get it published for her one day. She died when she was 99.

About a year after she died I turned back to what she had left, and my notes. First of all I typed it all out, inserting the punctuation. I was wondering how I would divide it up into sections, but in the event found there were natural breaks. I looked up some popular songs from the period and used lines from these to give a title to each chapter.

She had wanted to call the book *Our Lizzie* and so was disappointed when someone else had used that title for a historical novel. She came up with *A Collier's Lass* instead, but this never felt quite right. But as I was reading the book I realised that a common theme was a shout of 'Where's our Lizzie?' – usually from her mother who was always finding her paid odd-jobs to help the family finances. This became the title, although I added the subtitle *A memoir of a collier's lass* to give a bit more background information.

Having typed it, I started trying to interest local publishers, but the things they asked me (Can you summarise it in 100 words? Where is the market for this title?) made me realise that I could probably manage the process myself; I am a retired teacher and we have often produced publications for school. I had various photographs for the front cover, but was struggling to fit the those into the format offered by Lulu and asked a teaching friend to help me. On finding out what I was doing she volunteered to help me further, managing the text into pages through InDesign and helping me get the whole thing ready for production. She put the text in two columns, added decorative letters for the opening of each chapter, and suggested a typeface. For production, she recommended using a local printer in Oldham who manages their school year books; the cost was greater than could be found for the same service online, but she had found them very easy to deal with and the quality high, so I went ahead with them. They had no minimum order and as my friend had done the formatting, all I had to pay for was the printing (through print on demand). I ordered 30 copies initially, and they cost me £10 each. The book has three line drawings by my mother and three photographs. I priced it at £12.99.

I did not order an ISBN as I was not planning to sell it through the big retailers; initial copies went to family and friends. I made the book available through *Get British Business Online* which showed me how to set up a website. The Google search engine will not pick up this site immediately – people need to know my website address – so I have now put a sticker with my website address on the back of each book sold. I applied for an account with PayPal to handle the money. They take 75p from every transaction, but this is a small price to pay for them managing the differences in currency (three of my orders have so far come from overseas) and easing the formalities. I also make a bit on the postage, so this helps me offset the costs of printing. I am not locked in to using the original printers, and could take my file elsewhere if I want more copies, but the quality was so good I have so far stayed with them.

I decided to hold a launch party at home – more of a celebration of publication than a bid to gain publicity. I put up a display of my mother's manuscript, press cuttings she had kept relating to the times she was talking about, an interview about her life done by a local journalist just before her death and printed in the local paper (and of which she was very proud) and other items of interest.

I thought about refreshments, and decided that food was very important to my mother – so many of her stories centred on how hungry she and her siblings had been in their childhood, and how poor they were (her mother had just one skirt and two blouses). So I cooked the food she talked about – potato hash ("Taterash"; potato, onion and meat scraps fried together), potato pie, boiled pudding and Yorkshire pudding (served with syrup or sugar as a desert, which is common in the area). "Taterash" was particularly important to her story as the local Methodist church would cook this on Ash Wednesday to give to the poor families of the region, and having benefitted from this my mother kept the memory of this alive every Ash Wednesday of her life.

Information on the book is creeping out. Tameside Historical Society has been interested and news has spread through websites for those involved in genealogical research. I called my website by the name of the area,[138] hoping I would attract others searching for related information, and in the process have found long-lost relatives who have been keen to learn what is included in the book. My mother would have been thrilled by this, her reasons for writing were to share the stories and remind people of happy times – and show her descendants just how much life has changed.

---

[138] www.haughtongreendentonhistory.co.uk

Overall, I am just delighted by how the project has worked out – and can't quite believe I have managed to do this. Each stage of the process meant learning how to do something new, and having navigated my way through feels very satisfying. Just this morning I found someone had found their way to my site and ordered a copy from Canada. It fills me with delight to look at the book, and I know there is nothing my mother would have been more proud. And if I can do it, anyone can.'

MARKETING

18

Marketing

The big issue with a self-published book is how do you persuade others that it is worth reading?

> 'People simply don't buy novels or poetry by authors they have never heard of, especially from imprints they have never heard of. Getting reviews is the only way to go, and that too is not easy for self-published work. In general I think to self-publish you have to do it more professionally than the publishers.'   Jill Paton Walsh[139]

If you are a self-publishing author, and want to make your work sell, marketing is likely to be the biggest, and most unexpected, journey of discovery. Whether you are planning the preparation of a printed book, an ebook or a blog, most of the stages of layout, finalisation and production will seem logical, and can be learnt. Marketing, on the other hand, can seem a completely alien field.

The other complication about involvement in marketing is that it requires a competition for your creative attention. Obtaining quotations from printers and deciding on page layouts can offer your writing brain a break; stretch you by involving you in areas that relate to your book and require an intense, short-term concentration. But once the associated decisions have been made, the whole project can move on.

As a process, marketing is much more open-ended. It needs to begin early in the project's life, and continue late (there is always a little bit more to be done), and it requires the same energy and concentration that you put into your writing, just differently focussed. Yet if you spend too much time on it, there will be no writing to promote. Dividing your attention between the two will almost certainly give you difficulties.

[139] See also quotation, page 2

What is marketing?

There is a lot of discussion about what marketing is and is not. It is certainly a word that has negative connotations and there is often an assumption that anything that has merit does not need marketing; rather it attracts customers and advocates through its own intrinsic value. But potential customers cannot make value-based judgements (like 'should I read it or not?') about a product with which they are unfamiliar; marketing helps them become aware of the range of their options (note, borrow, buy, read, recommend, lend, give, dismiss, ignore).

Marketing is often thought of as the media through which it is effected; so perhaps as a checklist of advertising, leaflets, public relations and publicity. While this may be your practical experience of marketing, in theory marketing is rather an *approach* to presenting a product or service to those who might want or need to know about it; its positioning so that the constituency of designated consumers (and anyone else likely to be interested) are both aware of it and want to buy/own/give it to someone else. Effective marketing requires a complicated juggling of possibilities, everything from the words used to describe, the colours in which the message is presented, to the selection of people charged with handling the sale.

There have been many attempts to summarise the nature and practice of marketing through snappy summaries, and one of the most useful is the theory of Ps: product, price, promotion, place. Thus marketing involves considering the nature of the **product** or service to be offered to the public; the **price** at which it will be most attractive and sustainable within the market; the type of **promotion** through which information will be circulated (radio or television advertising, door-to-door leaflets) and the **place** through which it should be offered (e.g. online, retail outlets from small shops to supermarkets). To these, other Ps can be added such as **period of time** over which the product will be made available (limited short term offer or sustained campaign?); **personnel** (who will do the selling as this will have an impact on how it is perceived) and **profit**, without which a business cannot continue to offer a product or service (unless it is receiving external funding, but in which case there will be other criteria to deliver such as closeness to funder's mission and efficiency).

Getting used to the terminology of marketing, and thinking of your book as a product may be difficult, but is essential. In the case of an author, the product is what you have to make available – almost certainly your manuscript, but bear in mind that you too are part of the offering; most readers are interested in the package of book plus author, not just book, and will want to know more about the person who wrote it.

The other ongoing key issue of marketing is who is the customer? The customer is the person to whom you are making your product available – the reader, purchaser or recommender, via a variety of information and purchasing mechanisms (bookshop, other retailer, supermarket, stall at literary festival, local fete).

Whereas these questions are constants, how marketing is effected changes all the time. Twenty years ago the communication channels for telling people about new books were well established – and the range of broadcast and printed media through which messages could be broadcast was relatively limited. It was possible to predict who would be watching a particular station or reading a specific interest magazine at any given time – and hence place associated advertising or promote public relations to reach that market. Today the consumer is much harder to predict, and hence to target. This creates both difficulties and opportunities for the self-publishing author.

Whereas previously most titles were sold through bookshops, today the ability to order anything at the click of a button has undermined the traditional model of high street retail sales. Confused by this wealth of connectedness and possible activity, the potential recipient of information on what to read increasingly looks for a trusted mediator to advise – to identify the sorts of things they like and save them the trouble of searching. This may be an online forum or a physical club they belong to, a commentator whose opinion they respect or a network which mirrors their own taste (e.g. Oprah Winfrey, Richard & Judy, Mariella Frostrup). Given the wealth of new publications that come out each year, and that other forms of media (magazines, television and radio stations, online entertainment) are also competing for their attention, many readers welcome help in navigating a path through all that is on offer.

If you are planning a long-term career as a self-publishing

writer, effective marketing will rely on meeting your customer needs profitably, and finding ongoing marketing means both to inform and sell your wares, without breaking the bank. Matching resources to desired outcomes will be part of the juggling required.

Particular difficulties in applying marketing to the promotion of books

1 **People generally only buy a book once** – because they usually only want to read it once. They may buy a second copy for a friend, but in general the writer's task is to persuade them to want to return for their next book, and to enthuse about it to other potential purchasers. And bookshops will want to stock on the same basis; materials that create satisfaction for customers who return

2 **The number of books** on the market is enormous and so getting a product noticed is difficult. In the UK in 2010 there were 151,969 new books and new editions published,[140] the comparable figure for the US in 2010 was 316, 480.[141]

3 When there is lots of choice and not all the parameters for a new product are known (e.g. the author or subject is unfamiliar), it is reassuring for the buying public to spot a brand they trust and try on that basis. **But it's difficult to convey brand in publishing;** the reading public is often more influenced by the name/look/ reputation of the author than that of the publisher (although interest may be piqued by making a book *look* like a particular type of read).

4 **Book selection takes time**. A book is seldom an instant purchase, given that it has to appeal to the would-be purchaser and they have to be willing to invest time and attention in getting to know it, before a decision to purchase is generally made.

5 **Book purchase stores up future effort** – the commitment to read what has been bought. And there are also a range of entirely

[140] www.publishers.org.uk
[141] www.bowker.com which also revealed 'explosive' growth in the non-traditional sector, of a further 2,776,260 books in 2010 i.e. nearly nine times the size of the conventional industry

human issues to be considered: the deferred gratification of book purchase ('I will treat myself to that once I have got through this pile of stuff I have to read for work'); storage and clutter acquisition (minimalism is fashionable), and the desire to avoid the guilt complex gained by acquiring more books than you have time to read. Every now and again I am forced to weed the pile of yet-to-be-read-books beside my bed and put some back, unread, on the shelves downstairs. The experience always makes me feel guilty; perhaps it is just easier just to avoid it by buying fewer books.

6 **Book purchase attracts high levels of meanness.** Given that books represent such very good value for money (a paperback costs much less than a round of drinks for four; about the same as an organic chicken to feed the same number) one might have hoped potential customers would be willing to try out a writer they don't know by buying a copy of their book. Regrettably not. It people seem to apply different standards to assessing the money:satisfaction ratio when books are concerned.

7 **Literacy is demonstrably good for you, and books are on the curriculum at school** – and so risk attracting negative attention or being seen as boring.

8 There is a growing assumption within society that **information is free** and downloading at no cost is a basic human right. This spills over into an attitude to all reading material.

9 **Bookshops are intimidating places to the uninitiated;** you need a degree of confidence to go in and browse; an appreciation of the systems by which stock is stored and additional information can be found. To those unfamiliar, this can feel daunting.

10 **Books are loaned to shops rather than bought as stock** – so if they do not sell they can be returned to the publisher (who cannot send them back to the printer). This practice was established to ensure that booksellers could take a wide range of stock in order to represent the variety of material available. This has however become a means through which the responsibility for merchandise stays with the producer rather than the retailer.

Particular difficulties in applying marketing to the promotion of self-published books

1 You have no brand to fall back on; reassurance for the retailer you hope will stock that titles under your imprint are likely to sell.

2 There is no objective measure or external reinforcement from someone else's belief (and accompanying financial investment) in you, your writing or your book. It is difficult to assess whether or not it is any good, and worth the investment of the reader or retailer's time.

3 Potential partners (e.g. the associated media, likely retailers and wholesalers) may be wary of working with you, simply because you are self-publishing.

On the positive side however, this is your baby, and you are working on it without the inevitable misunderstandings that creep in through using intermediaries. Having decided to self-publish you have presumably decided your work has sufficient merit, that there is enough latent demand within the market, and you have enough energy to work toward linking the two. You can learn as you go along. None of the associated difficulties are insurmountable – or avoided by professional publishing houses. Nor is lack of experience in publishing necessarily a handicap – looking at marketing in general, rather than specifically how books are promoted, can be a more effective way of starting. There has been a tendency within the publishing industry to assume that readers buy one kind of book in preference to another, whereas in reality they are being assailed by a whole range of different marketing stimuli, and may choose to spend their money on something completely different. Experimenting with different marketing techniques and testing which ones work best can be a very effective way of learning more.

Understanding your product and to whom it appeals

All authors are likely to have a basic understanding of those to whom their work will be of interest, but before developing marketing plans it is a good idea to think about the key concepts of product and customer in more detail. Two standard thinking tools used in marketing may be helpful: SWOT and PEST

SWOT refers to strengths, weaknesses, opportunities and threats, and is a useful formula for remaining objective about your work. Strengths and weaknesses refer to the (internal) qualities of the product itself, opportunities and threats to the (external) wider environment. Thus for a new book for children aged 8–12, the following might apply:

Strengths:
Empathetic characters who really appeal; writing that excites this particular age group

Weaknesses:
Not a lot happens; suspicion that there may not be enough plot to maintain the reader's interest

Opportunities:
Children's reading has received higher attention of late due to the Harry Potter influence; *World Book Day* and local schools' associated *Children's Book Week* are coming up

Threats:
Entertainment on screens is more popular with the designated age-group; competition from digital consoles and associated games may use up all the budget parents might have spent on books

PEST is a useful acronym for thinking about the environment into which you will launch your particular product, and stands for political, economic, social and technological. It is a helpful reminder of forces in wider society which you can either harness, or just refer to, in support of your product and its availability. Thus accessing the paper for printing from a manufacturer who purchases from renewable sources can be used to demonstrate your responsible attitude towards the environment and resources, or using a political story to spread awareness of your new book ('despite library cuts, a local author shows children do still read!') can both be effective routes towards gaining an increased energy for your marketing.

What is it like?

Similarly, it is a good idea to understand how your work relates to what else is on offer. Most authors tend to see their work in splendid isolation. It is the product of a single mind (theirs) and hence different from everything else in existence. Potential purchasers, whether individual or retail outlets, are more likely to see it in the context of what else is available (and hence in print), what is currently selling (and hence for which there is demand) and what they have just read and enjoyed. You could demonstrate this by announcing your book as having parents (e.g. 'Jacqueline Wilson meets Stephanie Meyer') or referring to a section heading in retail outlets ('young adult fiction') or a recognisable genre of title, which is in high demand (e.g. 'paranormal teenage romance').

Both retailers and purchasers are more likely to be convinced by the merit of something that other investors have shown is a good prospect than something completely different. If there are no other competing titles it may show that there is no competition – but it could also reveal that there is no market. Try to keep up-to-date on what else is being published and read; keep track of the literary press/watch and listen to related programmes in the media, and be a regular visitor to bookshops so that you can spot trends and make a link to your title.

Finding endorsements and backers

Another useful boost for your book is to find a relevant endorsement, so start thinking about who could be a credible witness on behalf of your product and promote purchase. See chapter 8 for more information.

Along the same lines, are there any local/national joint ventures with which you might collaborate; setting up a link with other websites or businesses in return for promoting your work to their customers or wider audience? Such arrangements can be paid for (a commission on sales; a charge for displaying your leaflets or enclosing them in parcels sent out) or done on the basis of mutual exchange (you display their material/send it out). For example, if your novel or memoir relates to the work of a particular charity, and they like what you have written, they may be happy to establish a formal link.

How to draw up a marketing plan

Whereas the previous paragraphs may have given you ideas about how to market your book, it is a good idea to consolidate your ideas before progressing further. Resist the temptation to keep firing off emails, try to be strategic about what you will do in what order.

A marketing plan is best thought of in stages, and for each one I will return to our previous example of a teenage read.

1 Where is the market for your book?

2 What benefits does it offer *them*?

3 How can you group them to tell them what you offer?

4 What means will you use to get your message to them?

5 What will you say?

6 What will the product cost; is there an associated offer?

7 How will they order?

8 How will you get it to them?

9 How will you work out if it was worth it?

10 How will you develop the relationship?

Where is the market for your book?

What kind of people buying in what kind of circumstance? Do some research into who is buying your kind of title, and make a list. So for our fiction for 8–12 year olds from a local author we could assume the children; their parents; their grandparents and other relations who buy presents (often called 'graunties'); teachers and librarians. Don't forget that end-users may not be buying themselves, but rather being bought for, and that intermediaries through which they are likely to purchase are also your market, and may include retailers (book as well as gift) as well as other retail outlets such as supermarkets and wholesalers.

What benefits does it offer them?

Entertainment and the chance to keep children quiet; the promotion of reading (which they may think is a good thing in general and may attract approval from the recipient's parents or carers); an attractive gift and one that they can be reasonably sure the likely recipient won't already have; the chance to appreciate the location where one of their parents grew up; the opportunity to support a local author; new material for lessons/libraries.

How can you group them to tell them what you offer?

This is often referred to as 'segmenting the market'; dividing the range of potential customers into groups that may be contacted with a similar message/offer. These may include:

Retail outlets: retail sales outlets need information on what you are doing to promote local/national interest; sales patterns of similar titles and proof of customer demand. See previous chapter.

Potential readers need to know the work exists, that others like it, and that it is something they would enjoy too.

Potential third-party purchasers (i.e. they are buying on behalf of someone else) need advice on appeal and availability, either received through their associated school, library, usual sales outlet or through the press and media (especially local).

Other intermediaries. Libraries and other information distribution points (e.g. tourist information centres; local museums; council offices and tourist locations) need to be informed and may display marketing material for you.

What means will you use to get your message to them? (marketing channels, marketing materials)

Retail outlets likely to stock will probably need individual presentations, with information also sent to the associated head office if buying is coordinated centrally.

Schools with the right age of children for your product may be willing to accept a talk or workshop from you on your book, and may help you organise a competition (tailored to the curriculum) with the children afterwards. They may hear of this through your individual approach, perhaps via a teacher you know, or via the press.

Once they know about it, schools and libraries may include information you send/they find within a school newsletter or emailing, or load it on their website if information is provided in time. Similarly there may be other local agencies which might incorporate your information (councils, institutions, related charities).

Local and national press need information to prompt them to commission a feature on you or include the information you offer. This is usually done via a press release (see next chapter).

It is important to cross-reference your various marketing materials so that those who find a leaflet or read information on a third party website can discover more, perhaps via another website, your own or someone else's.

What will you say?

The words you use will probably vary according to the formality of the vehicle chosen (in general the text used in emails will be more informal than print), but should be consistent in tone and branding; for example through typeface, colours and the type of words chosen. While it's tempting to arrive at one description, and use it constantly, it is helpful to have a few variations, each offering different supporting (but related) details. Journalists who pick up a press release will often try to access more information on a writer via the web, and get a bit frustrated if only one standard paragraph is available; similarly, general readers can be further enticed through the gradual dissemination of information. Details about the author and the process of writing can be just as useful as information on the book. For more on writing blurbs and other marketing materials see the next chapter on copywriting.

What will the product cost? Is there an associated offer?

The price you set is part of your marketing. You will find that your market has standard perceptions about what a book should cost, based on the prices charged for others, and if yours is to be out of line (either more expensive or cheaper) you need to explain why. Consider discounts, offers and how to get the money in quickly. See chapter 17.

How will they order?

Who will stock the title and what does this say about its value and brand? Selling on a street corner out of a suitcase may offer good availability but not affirm the associated distinction. See chapter 17.

How will you get it to them?

Mechanisms for managing distribution – to shops, to individual customers, to the media – need to be thought through and planned for.

How will you work out if it was worth it?

For the retail trade this means recording sales, special orders and anticipating future developments. The self-publishing author may note these but there may be other, more intangible benefits – seeing your work read by others; the response gained from workshops in schools which gives you ideas for development materials; the allocation of associated costs and experiences acquired in the process (research trips to interesting places).

How will you develop the relationship created by marketing?

Marketing is best thought of as an ongoing relationship, not a one-off sale. If you are supplying direct you are gaining the names and addresses of customers, and within the confines of data protection legislation you need to think about how to keep in touch with them, and what you might have to offer to them next.

Timing

Think too when information on your work would best be circulated. There are regular cycles within the book trade, and if you want to look professional it may be best to fit your title within these. So 'how to' books connected with new year's resolutions tend come out in January, and 'beach reads' in the early summer – although information for both will be needed by potential stockists much earlier. See the draft schedule in chapter 5.

A launch at publication time for a self-published book is often effective, helping you to attract the attention of local press, encourage others to buy – and promote general enthusiasm. You could consider organising one through a local bookshop (see chapter 17 on distribution) or having one in your home.

Spending on marketing

I am often asked how much a self-publishing author, or indeed a professional publisher, should spend on their marketing. A simplistic answer is to quote what other industries do, and say allocate 10% of the associated/anticipated profits, or a percentage of the retail price.

This is tricky because the book business works on lower margins than others and the low purchase price means that even a generous percentage of the eventual price is likely to yield little budget. There is an associated difficulty in that the retail price is seldom fixed, and retailers can chose to sell at below recommended retail price to secure a competitive advantage.

I would emphasise the expenditure of thought before the commitment of financial resources. It is possible to alienate through spending too much as well as too little, so think before you commit yourself. You need to think about what kind of atmosphere you want to create around your book, through the marketing materials you prepare; be conscious that whatever means you use to market yourself, from your website to how you dress for an evening talk, will be part of your overall marketing presentation. Marketing theoreticians call this positioning; the emotional relationship you create between your product (including yourself), and your market.

One marketing method may lead to the offer to spend on others – so the local paper which features your press release may return to offer you a paid-for advertisement in the same format, perhaps as a condition of featuring your work (this is sometimes called 'sponsored editorial'). Examine each suggestion for free and paid-for activity in this light: will it impress your customer appropriately, and does it reinforce your overall marketing thrust? And if so, is it worth the associated spend, whether that is financial or effort?

Producing marketing materials

If you want to promote your title for sale, you will need to have the following:

1 A basic book blurb

2 An author blurb

3 An AI

4 A press release and/or

5 A leaflet or handbill

6 A website and possibly a blog

7 Involvement in social media

All need to be recognisably promoting the same brand (book and author). For information on how to prepare and write copy for these various materials, see the next chapters.

Pursuing 'free publicity'

Books generally sell at low prices and in short runs. It follows that there is seldom the money available for high-profile advertising campaigns and mass market communication. The self-publishing author will need to dig deep; to think about their various connections and how to ensure information on the product they have for sale comes to the widest possible attention of those who might buy, recommend or endorse it.

'Free' advertising is available through seeking interviews in the media, public relations and general discussion around the subject of a new book in public forums such as literary festivals and society talks. Some may find this terrifying, but most of us improve with practice, over time. You will notice too that even famous authors still pursue publicity each time they have a new book coming out. It's getting harder and harder to be inscrutable. If you still find the whole process difficult, try this mantra:

> 'I am not pushing myself, I am simply making my work accessible. If people don't know of my writing, it cannot get read.'

How to set about securing free publicity

Try to distance yourself from your book and think about it as an object. How would you describe it to a third party; what kind of words would you use? This process may be best worked through with a friend, as writing puff for your own work is very difficult.

Then start listing the opportunities. These may include:

* A launch party, perhaps in your home or in a local venue or bookshop. Ask the local press along and you may get publicity off to a good start.

* Local organisations or groups, societies to which you belong/ know of, which might include a mention of your book in a newsletter or on their website or ask you to be a speaker (contact their programme secretary who is often looking for suggestions).

* Relevant media that might review it and in particular any names you know of journalists or others working there.

* Amazon reviews.

* Libraries. Could you give a free copy to your local library with a request that they display it on the 'just arrived' table which all libraries use to show recent purchases?

* Events. Could you offer a reading or to run a workshop for other local authors?

* A local museum or heritage centre to which your work relates? Might they stock or display it – or host an event?

* A local literature or arts festivals? Writers' groups?

* Reading circles. Can you find out if there are any run by local libraries, bookshops or independently? They may choose your book if you are willing to go along and take part in a discussion about how and why you wrote it.

In each case, you need to make a specific pitch, thinking about what they will get out of it rather than how much you want to do it. Remember they have a choice – and acknowledging the particular fit between what you offer and the kind of opportunities they service is often a good starting point. At all costs remain civil.

Anyone thinking of covering you in their medium, or booking you for an event, will need to be convinced that you can both engage interest and talk coherently. Prepare for this by being able to talk about your book briefly and seamlessly. Develop a short summary, often called an 'elevator pitch': what it is and how you would explain it simply to someone who was in a lift with you between floors. You will have time only for a summary of your title's overall interest, not a detailed exploration of the themes. You might have time to say – 'a fast-paced saga set in Victorian England following the rise of an illegitimate under-housemaid to mistress of the house'; it's unlikely you could read them the first chapter (unless the lift got stuck).

Most authors want to have their voice heard, but find talking about themselves difficult (there seems to be a common personality combination amongst authors of big ego, low self-esteem) so the ability to provide key information quickly is of fundamental importance. It's worth practising this so that your touch is light and your tone engaged – rather than over-rehearsed. Involving someone else may help you both identify merit and remain objective. Whatever your path to being able to describe your work, it does need doing – because you will be asked.

Case study: Nick Green, author of *The Cat Kin*
www.nickgreenbooks.webeden.co.uk

Deciding to self-publish *The Cat Kin* had a very positive outcome for Nick Green. He had been accepted by a literary agent for just over a year, but was not getting very far in finding a publisher (other than accumulating a pile of rejections). Feeling that he wanted to progress the project he decided to self-publish the book using Lulu. The typesetting and proofreading were done by him and a friend did the jacket – it was all very homespun. But the book did have an ISBN and it was listed on Amazon. It did not get many sales but did get a few reviews, one of particular importance.

He sent a copy to Amanda Craig at *The Times*, with a letter. He knew her column well as he read it each week – and thus felt he could offer material likely to be interesting to her in a way that might attract her attention.

By sheer good fortune (or appropriate reading of the prevailing Zeitgeist) Amanda Craig was planning a feature on books that centred on cats – she had already got the third in the *Lion Boy* trilogy by Zizou Corder and the second *Varjak Paw* book by S.F. Said, and so Green's title slotted neatly into the piece she was thinking of writing. A positive review in a national newspaper for a self-published book, alongside other well-established titles, could not have been more helpful. He was approached by Faber, who had had his submission for months but had so far not responded. They now snapped up the book.

The story does not have an immediately happy ending. Sales were good and review coverage positive, but Faber decided they did not want to take the sequel, and so he had to look for a new publisher. But having looked around he found Keith Charters' newly established Strident Publishing,[142] they agreed to publish the title and took the first book too. 'Keith is wonderfully proactive and handles the marketing, which is the bit I most hated doing – it's great to have someone to speak up for you.' He liked doing (and still does) events in schools and the energy of the children as they respond to his book, but hated trying to sell his titles in bookshops himself: 'Walking into a bookshop and offering your book for sale is awful: sometimes they look at you as if you are something that has been picked up off the street.'

His conclusion: 'Right now publishers are paralysed by the thought of what is – and what is not – commercial, and they have real blind-spots. They have a profile of what should be a successful book in mind, but as the slow progress of Harry Potter's path to publication indicated, there is no such template: it is simply about what is and what isn't a good story.'

He continues to work full-time as a business writer, working on his fiction mostly during his daily commute into London, and in the evenings and at weekends. He says, 'I wouldn't ever give up the day job. In fact, that would be my advice to any writer: Don't give up the day job. It's insanely risky.'

[142] www.stridentpublishing.co.uk

Case study: Bill Munro[143]

'There are, broadly, three routes you can take to self-publish, and whichever is right for you depends on what you are capable of, what you have time to do and what you are prepared (or not prepared) to learn to do. The first way is to do it all yourself. The second is to farm out a portion of the work that you don't have the time, the skills or inclination to do, for instance, layout and typesetting. The third is to use a self-publishing house, such as Matador or Completely Novel.com, who will provide the complete package. These people are not vanity publishers. Every book they produce will be your property, not theirs. You pay for the service and the product. As you are paying for the entire job (plus you will still have to do all the marketing on top of it) it is a bad business move not to have ownership of every copy printed.

Glutton for punishment that I am, I did it all myself: writing, taking many of the photographs, typesetting, arranging the printing, finding a specialist wholesaler and doing the marketing. I'd been editing and typesetting a car club magazine for the previous four years and had done similar jobs before that, so I was no stranger to publishing in one form or another.

Why did I do it? My first self-published book is about what must be the most recognisable motor vehicle in the world, the Austin FX4 London taxi. My day job for almost forty years has been to drive one and I had written three other books on the broad subject of London taxis. I'd lined up a specialist publisher for it, and although the format he offered was not the best I'd seen, I began negotiating with him. Sadly, after a protracted illness, he died and the publishing house was wound up. As it has always been in my nature 'to have a go', I took a look at publishing it myself, and the idea immediately appealed. I'd established a very good working relationship with the printers of the car club magazine, I already had DTP software on the iMac, I did some basic costings, saw that the sums added up, and dived in.

Marketing is an aspect of publishing to which the self-publisher must apply every available resource, or he will fall flat on his face. For

---

[143] www.elitelondontaxis.co.uk

my book, marketing began, not when the finished product arrived, but with the concept. A previous project of mine, *A Century of London Taxis*, (Crowood Press, 2005) a 200-page hardback, grew out of a small volume I'd planned, about another type of London taxi. This was to be a low cost, impulse-buy volume. I applied this 'impulse' concept to the new book, and this decided the format, A5, 80 pages, full-colour, paperback and the price, £7.99.

As retail outlets, I had motor museum gift shops in mind. There seems to be something of a gap in their prices, with books and other goods at a premium price at one end and tiny, pocket-money things like pencils and fridge magnets, but not so much in between. An £8 book on a topic of some interest that had not been dealt with before seemed to fill that gap. But none of the people running these gift shops had heard of me, or my new publishing company, Earlswood Press, so I sent a copy of the book to every motor museum book or gift shop manager I could identify, and also to London's two top transport book retailers and to some transport literature wholesalers, just to get my product under their noses and let them judge its quality for themselves. This is not something I'd recommend you doing if you've published a £40 academic book, but with the printing cost of each of mine being less than £1.80, the whole exercise cost me just over £50, which must be good value in anybody's book.

One of the wholesalers was delighted to take the title, as he only had two other books on taxis out of a range of over hundred titles. Crucially, he could provide account facilities for the museums and other retailers and also retailed it alongside his other titles on his show unit around the country. Within a year of publication, I had recouped over half my investment from sales of one third of the print run, and wholesale orders continue to come in on a regular basis.

I am now working on four new titles of my own, two of which are due for publication this year, and I have taken on a title from an outside author. This is a travel biography, in the same genre as Peter Mayle's *A Year in Provence* but set in a village by Lake Como in Italy.

The DIY route is not for everyone. If you enjoy writing more than you relish the idea publishing, then you're better off using a self-publishing house and concentrate on being a project manager for your book production, marketing and publicity. If, like me you have realised that you always wanted to be as much a publisher as an author, then it will work for you. But whatever your chosen way, make sure that it suits your time and your talents; be honest with yourself, and do it the way that's best for you.

Case study: Peter Mountain[144]

Always considered a good raconteur, professional musician Peter Mountain was encouraged by friends to write his stories down and worked with his son-in-law and author solutions company Authorhouse to produce the two volumes, published when he was 84 and 00 respectively.

'I held a belated book launch for my two autobiographical books, *Scraping a Living* and *Further Scrapings*. During the evening I reminisced about people, places and events and chose some of my favourite music to illustrate the stories. This was provided by the Melandra String Quartet (which included my daughter) and featured work from various composers including Vivaldi, Beethoven, Schubert and Sibelius. We served a wine punch in the interval and made books available to those who wanted a look at the end of the evening.

The books tell the story of my life in music, and are based on the premise that most people don't know what it is like to be a professional musician. My career has been varied, and lasted 80 years. I went to the Royal Academy of Music just as The Blitz started; was Leader of the Liverpool Philharmonic Orchestra; spent time with the BBC and was finally Head of Strings at the Royal Scottish Academy of Music in Glasgow. I have worked with many of the great figures of the 20th century including David Oistrakh and Arturo Toscanini, and my role in the development of professional music education in the UK was very important to me.'

[144] www.petermountainviolin.co.uk

Having ordered stock to give away to family and friends, orders are now made via his website, produced by print on demand and sent out through Amazon. 'I don't do much more to promote than that. The local paper featured the concert and led to a bit more publicity about the books.'

19

Copywriting: how to describe your work effectively

A whole chapter on how to describe your work – is this really necessary?

It is crucial. There is no clearer predictor of a self-published book likely to disappoint than poor associated copy. The words with which you describe your work have a massive impact on the customer's willingness to perceive value; whether they buy your work – and then hang on to it if they do.

Copywriting involves producing the text to describe your offering; it entices the recipient towards further involvement. In the case of a product or service this may mean purchase, either for themselves or on behalf of someone else; in the case of an idea, it might mean trying to secure agreement – or at least acknowledgement of an alternative point of view.

The process is a lot harder than it looks. You have to work out who is likely to be purchasing and/or using the product or service (not always the same person); establish the associated benefits that are most likely to appeal; consider how much argument to present (too much information can be as alienating as too little) but all the while support the consumer's perception that it is their decision over whether or not to buy – most people hate to be 'sold to'.

Meanwhile, the rest of the world is not inclined to see copywriting as an art. There is a general assumption that the briefer the copy you have to craft, the more speedily you will be able to produce it – and as we have all been to school, and learnt to write, how hard can that really be? But it is far more difficult to write short than long text, and effective copy needs extensive crafting, usually through a time-consuming process of getting your ideas down, allowing a meaningful theme to emerge, and then a long process of refining the message. As copy is often not only the main motivator for purchase, but also the basis for a continuing relationship with the customer,[145] its creation needs to be taken with appropriate seriousness.

Effective copywriting is often best spotted rather than explained; it creates a relationship between consumer and organisation, and hopefully promotes an organisational brand, making the customer both want to return – and recommend it to others. It also needs to be based on trust: an effective description will feel hollow if the product/service fails to live up to the promises made. In the case of a book that has been falsely sold, the reader may not only not trust the promise-maker again, but also allow their disappointment to spill over into their attitude to the type of book, or reading in general.

Later in this chapter I will explain the specifics of writing copy for various different formats, and offer particular tips for each type, but I will begin with an interview with an organisation whose copywriting I think is excellent: Lakeland, based in Windermere in the UK, an organisation that describes itself as the 'home of creative cookware'. Founded in 1964, offering a wide selection of kitchen essentials, they have now extended their range to include cleaning and storage products, garden-ware and presents. Quoting an example from outside the book world is deliberate. I think there is much to be learned from looking further than your immediate competition; people do not only buy books and are presented with a range of buying stimuli which may compete for the same budget. Many of Lakeland's products are similarly priced to books, and require a similar investment of time and imagination to appreciate their benefits. Significantly two of the Lakeland copywriting team used to work for the booksellers Ottakar's. Claire Forbes, a member of the Lakeland copywriting team comments:

Case study: Claire Forbes, Lakeland copywriting team

'This organisation has a really strong customer focus – the customer is represented at every stage of what we do, including at board level – and we are always thinking about how we would like to be treated and how the company can make a difference in

---

[145] Marketing experts refer to this as 'CRM' or customer relationship management

people's lives. So when it comes to writing copy to describe the company, our products, and the services we offer, we try to make what we say special.

The facts and figures about a product are of course important, and are offered by all retailers, but we would never make these the main focus of our explanation. Our copy always concentrates on the user benefit; the details that make a difference to our customers' lives and enhance their interests, pleasures or concerns. We try always to make what we say friendly and approachable; often we do this through describing a situation or telling them a story about a product that they relate to.

When it comes to starting to write, the marketing team is involved at an early stage. We are part of the process of product testing; buyers will regularly introduce product samples and ideas to us, either informally because they have found something they want to tell us about, or formally through our regular Product Awareness Meetings. At these meetings new products are described, discussed and often tried out – and then they go out on long term-trial with various members of staff. This often gives me a good starting point; listening to colleagues talk about why they like a product; hearing enthusiasm from those who try it out. For example, we recently discussed a box of Christmas crackers that included a series of whistles which played different notes and the instructions for playing a tune by numbers – so the description we wrote for the catalogue, about the fun we had trying them out during the meeting, was just a reflection of what had happened.

We discuss everything from what the manufacturers have said about a product to what it is called. To make things clearer, we rename quite a few products, as we want our customers to be able to identify, from a product's title, what use it is to them.

Members of the copywriting team draft copy for a wide variety of different purposes, from website and email text to catalogue copy. If I have a copywriting job coming up I like to come in early with that particular purpose in mind for that day and have a good run at it – rather than chop and change between different activities. To prepare myself, before I start writing I will read previous descriptions in our catalogue, and think about how the product might get used or felt about. I will browse on the internet to see how related products are promoted and note the key points that are stressed. I will look through customer feedback on our website to see what our customers have been saying (we get lots of feedback in this way). I am a keen reader and often make lists of phrases and words that I like, and those that I think get used too often (in any context, not just in marketing information). We have a clear idea of what Lakeland customers want and need, and this helps us maintain clarity in our copy – we are empathetic, encouraging and consistent. Most of the time they are buying for their own needs, or those of other people, and so our tone is straightforward, but when it comes to writing copy for the Christmas catalogue, a touch of humour may just creep in!

The sorts of questions I ask myself are:

- How is this different from what else is on the market?
- How will the customer benefit?
- How will it make a difference to their life?
- What will it do for them in their home?
- What would the product say about itself; what would be its voice?
- What associated stories might be useful to the customer to help them appreciate why we are offering them this product – perhaps about how it was created, sourced, and feels to the user?

I find copy that talks about how customers feel and think often has a strong impact with our market, and spend a lot of time thinking about these various questions. Everything that we sell has a value and usefulness, so presenting it to best advantage is not difficult; we just have to find the right words to make the benefits clear.

My first draft includes everything that I think is relevant, but then I do a check back against the manufacturer's documentation and the notes I compile about each product. I then think of a starting point; often a story of how it gets used, the problem it solves and how the user feels without it, or how those who are trying it out have told us it feels. I then put it aside for a couple of days, to come back to; it's important to be able to step back from the copy you wrote and return to it afresh – and think again about the customer and what they are likely to want to know.

Once I have edited it some more, the resulting text is shared between colleagues and we all comment – we try not to get precious about what we have written; ultimately the product has to shine through not the individual copywriter. When I look through our catalogue I can't remember which parts I wrote – it really is a team effort.

From then on it's a process of editing, reediting – and sometimes starting again if I suddenly have a better idea for how to present a product. These can strike at any time, sometimes when I am out walking in the fells (I am a keen walker), or maybe when I am at home relaxing. And provided the catalogue has not already been passed for press, there is always time to change the copy if we think of a better approach. We allocate responsibility for sections of the catalogue to three different individuals, but then do a final check on how the whole fits together; how the reader is likely to move through the publication; the pace of the text and the 'feel' of the spreads included. We want them to regard the brochure as a valuable resource that provides useful and friendly content, as well as a means of accessing information on our products.

The demographics of our customers vary, an acquaintance with/enthusiasm for the company gets passed on between generations or communicated to friends and neighbours, but in general I would say that our customers are home-orientated; like to "treat" their families; appreciate the value of home-made and "making to give" as being more special than buying ready-made and appreciate products that enable them to show care, love and nurturing to others.

I arrived in this job by accident. I left school at 16 and worked in the Lakeland café for a year, and then in the store for another five, before moving to catalogue production. So with this background I got used to the sort of questions customers ask about products, and why they ring up for clarification or with the occasional problem. And knowing the Lakeland brand and our customers is the best possible preparation for writing to them in future.

As to how I keep my enthusiasm for writing up, I read a lot – all sorts of books and magazines, I will even read cereal packets! We have a reading room at Lakeland headquarters, with a lovely view of the fells and a handy stock of books, and I generally go there at lunchtime to read. People often ask me why I want to read when my job involves so much writing, but I can't stop myself.

We have a regular monthly company meeting, drawing together one member from every department (staff are allocated on a rotational basis so everyone gets to go at some point) and then the ideas and outcomes are shared with other colleagues. I find this a really useful method of keeping up-to-date with what is going on, both within the company and in the wider world, and how the two relate. And of course the headquarters where I work is attached to our flagship store, so we meet our customers constantly – as well as getting email, telephone and written feedback from them. If we have a quote from a customer that we would like to use we always check that they are happy for this to appear – and I have always found that they are really excited to be featured.'

What shines through this interview is the pride and care taken in communication with customers. Have a look at www.lakeland. co.uk to see how this works in practice, and here are five key points to take away to make your copywriting more effective:

1 To work effectively as part of a long-term relationship, promoting confidence on both sides, copy has to be true. Can you, hand-on-heart insist that your reader will be satisfied with what you say you are making available? Does your work live up to the claims your copy currently makes? If you cannot pass the Lakeland test, of being able to sustain an appropriate enthusiasm based on a near certainty that the reader who invests their own time and effort will not be disappointed, proceed no further right now. Consider instead drafting copy that describes what it is you *want to create*, rather than telling the world that this is what you *already offer*?

2 Can you envisage your readers and the kind of benefits that will most appeal to them? How will your work make them feel, act and understand themselves? Step away from the copy and review it objectively. What wider situation, story, or human appeal

will really speak to your market? Are you describing what you think is important about your product ('a novel set in Regency England') or what they will find appealing ('How does it feel when the man you wanted to marry elopes with someone else?')?

3 Take a pride in the crafting copy that has a wholeness to it; a definite shape. Can you describe it in a linear form – maybe charting levels of excitement or emotion over time? Does it have a beginning, a middle and an end or are there still rough edges to it?

4 Is it too pushy? Remember most of us enjoy buying, and like to have our needs recognised and taken seriously – but we also want to feel that it is our choice to spend money rather than being over-directed towards purchase. Psychologists studying marketing talk of 'post purchase dissonance' – the uncomfortable feelings that occur when we have just spent money. Encouraging the customer to feel that they have made a rational choice may help them cope with this – and return/recommend in future.

5 Are you happy to be judged by your copy? Words can form the basis of a long-term relationship, and this can be negative as well as positive. Every word matters, and the sense of the whole is vital in promoting a positive feeling within the reader. Don't finalise what you circulate to promote your work until you are happy for that to represent you.

Preparing to write copy yourself

As a generalisation, all copy gets read in a hurry. The reader browsing in a bookshop, the web surfer looking for ideas on what to read, the potential customer reading a poster on a notice board – all need quick access to information. The job of the copywriter is to create a relationship with the would-be purchaser who has other things to do than be sold to, and is likely to be resistant to marketing messages – before they move on and do something else.

Marketing copy often works best when it is reassuring but slightly unexpected – we don't read what we think we already know; so look out for words that might entice without appearing odd. Continue your research for inspiration on the packaging of products and organisational websites that appeal to a demograph similar to that of your own work, looking in particular for the 'about us' section. See how some companies draw the potential customer in by discussing information that interests both parties, or provide value statements about what they represent, hoping that their customers will spot the common ground and feel understood. There are many books on marketing and a browse around a museum of brands and advertising[146] will also help. You will see that marketers have always sought to preserve the essential and recognisable nature of a product or service, but have surrounded this with attention-gaining gambits such as promotions, product placements and public relations activity. Borrow from this. Going back to a familiar slogan or promotion can be a very effective way of cultivating a sympathetic aura of nostalgia for your product, and an associated feeling of well-being.

Writing about yourself and your work can feel very awkward. It may be a good idea to involve someone else in the process, to help you draw out why your work is worth an investment of time. It also helps to write your information in the third person. Thus 'in her new novel Mary Jones explores...' rather than 'In my new novel I explore...' Along the same lines, using a testimonial often enables you to report merit more effectively than by having to describe it yourself.

A word on grammar. Given that copy competes for consumer attention in an environment that is full of choice, it is often upbeat and staccato in tone. It's common for marketing sentences to start and finish abruptly, and lack a verb completely. Imperatives (commands such as 'Look!' or 'See!') are regularly used; sentences can start with 'and' and finish with two forms of punctuation (?!) – and these are attention-seeking gambits rather than evidence of poor English. You can break grammatical rules provided you know what you are doing, the unpardonable sin is to use incorrect English without realising it (e.g. singular subjects, plural verbs; different tenses in the same sentence; spoken rather than written English – 'It was like she was...'). Not only will this irritate, it will make your market assume the content of the work described is of a similar standard.

---

[146] E.g. sections of the Smithsonian in Washington US www.si.edu, or in London the Museum of Brands and Advertising www.museumofbrands.com

After this general introduction to copywriting, I will provide a detailed look at each piece of marketing copy you will need to create.

Your writing name

You may be surprised to find your writing name listed under options for copywriting, but there may be a sound pragmatism for wider consideration before making a final decision. Names have a strong resonance and tend to create an immediate effect – think how cleverly Daphne du Maurier never reveals the name of the young protagonist in *Rebecca*, other than allowing her to comment that her father chose it – to Maxim's evident delight.[147] Publishers who are particularly concerned to present a new author to a specific market will often consider all options for premium positioning – including what the author's writing name should be. And their real name will be just one of the options available.

Start your research by...

Thinking about whether you like your real name? Perhaps refashioning what your writing self is called may release creativity, enabling you to put yourself in a different place. There may be associated benefits of privacy – particularly useful if you are writing in a genre or about experiences that others do not know about, and you want them to maintain boundaries between what they assume is your imagination and your first-hand experience. You may find morphing into the writer when donning the name becomes part of the process of preparing to write, in the same way that many writers have special clothes, mugs, biscuits and music to support their work.

Does your real name match the genre in which you wish to write? Crime and thriller writers often have short sharp names (Lee Childs, Dan Brown, Ian Rankin). Other authors use different names for different types of book (Jean Plaidy/Victoria Holt; Sophie Kinsella/Madeleine Wickham; Joanna Trollope/Caroline Harvey).

---

[147] A gambit incidentally repeated in *Pretty Woman*. When Richard Gere asks Julia Roberts what her name is, she replies 'What would you like it to be?' Fantasies are potentially fulfilled.

Would a name higher up the alphabet benefit you? Research into retail sales patterns for books has implied that the first letter of the author's surname is statistically significant. Anecdotally this may be due to casual browsers in bookshops, where fiction tends to be stored in alphabetical order, starting at 'A' and then getting distracted by the time they reach 'G' or 'H'. Other hotspots in the shelving include proximity to authors who are a brand in their own right, thus children's authors close to Jacqueline Wilson may benefit. If the browser cannot find a book that they want (or have not already read) they may move on to see what is next on the shelf.

I have heard no evidence, statistical or anecdotal, that alphabetical order has any effect on non-fiction buyers. These browsers tend to be looking for titles on a particular subject, and are thus more inclined to look in a specific place; and once they have found it to consider all the options presented.

You might also consider a genderless moniker. The Brontë sisters submitted their novels under male pseudonyms – Acton, Currer and Ellis Bell. You could consider using the initials of your first names; thus J.K. Rowling famously concealed hers from the first generation of Harry Potter readers. This could be important if you are creating work that you hope will appeal to both genders, and is likely to be particularly significant in the young adult market. Girls may be less influenced by the gender of the writer, but boys more resistant to reading work by female writers – and the same apparently goes for their adult selves.

For those who are embarking on self-publication because their recent sales with a professional publisher have been disappointing, changing your name can be a pragmatic move. The new name will have no associated sales record, and you can escape previous negative history.

The book title

Why does the book title matter so much – surely it is content that truly matters? If you have tried to get published via conventional routes you have probably wondered why agents and publishers so often want to hear what your budding work of genius is called.

It's worth standing back and thinking about the situation from the intended recipient's point of view. Retailers and readers are assailed by thousands of titles; what makes one stand out tends to be something that draws attention to its specific flavour rather than leaving it to languish as one of the crowd. An enticing title, drawing the reader in and conveying the kind of book, immediately sets it apart.

An effective title will speak to the market, use words that are familiar but not overused, have a particular resonance or perhaps a nostalgic feel. It will create intimacy; exude buyability. Lines from songs work well (although watch out for copyright issues), or from other books. Poetry can provide a rich resource, and of course Shakespeare has already provided a wealth of effective titles.

Start your research by...

Reviewing good examples already in existence. *Fever Pitch* is Nick Hornby's autobiography through football. His editor came up with the title by making a list of technical words about football ('goal', 'referee', 'pitch') and then a series of words about how the game makes you feel ('angry', 'enraged', 'passionate', 'feverish'). Then by putting the two lists together the useful link was made – and a ready-made cliché identified.

Some words work well in particular sales locations – references to 'weddings' in supermarkets, where misery memoirs with short titles offering a double-meaning also do well. Books destined to be read on beach holidays compete for attention in airport bookshops, and the titles need to be short, interesting and often spark a question. Some authors go for an interesting single word titles (Robert Harris has had *Fatherland*, *Enigma*, *Archangel*, *Lustrum*, *Ghost*).[148]

It is often suggested that humour does not work well in advertising, as the joke may be missed, offend or feel dated, but in a book title wit can be very effective. It can create empathy with the market as in Linda Kelsey's *Fifty Is Not a Four-letter Word* or highlight a title of interest to a sophisticated market as in Martin Amis' *The War Against Cliché*.

[148] All published by Arrow

If you want a particularly enigmatic title, a subtitle can be used to explain its meaning more precisely – this technique is much used in academic publishing.

The shout-line

A shout-line is a single line of copy (it does not have to be a complete sentence) that often appears on the front cover of a trade or mass-market paperback, summing up the content and drawing the reader's attention. Alternatively, some books display a quotation or endorsement from someone the market respects, or an announcement of the book's previous success or history (e.g. how many have been sold or 'new in paperback'). These are really hard to write.

Start your research by...
Looking at the posters promoting films. Film promoters have truly mastered the art of the effective shout-line. They do not tell us the plot; rather they sum up the feeling of the film as a whole, so:

> 'Just when you thought it was safe to go back in the water' (*Jaws 2*)

> 'In space no one can hear you scream' (*Alien*)

> 'Love means never having to say you're sorry' (*Love Story*)

The book blurb

This is the text that appears on the back of a paperback book, or the flaps of a hardcover dust-jacket, along with some information on the author. It is vitally important. A novel may contain 80–100,000 words, but it is the 200 on the back cover that matter most.[149] Along with the opening paragraph of the book they are the most visible parts of the title, and will have the most influence on potential readers. Regular surveys of book buyers have confirmed

---

[149] As an indication of how much time this can take, see Michael Frayn's delightful novel *The Tin Men*, of which the hero (if that's the right word) spends all his time writing the blurb of his putative bestseller, but never actually gets around to writing the book.

that although it is the book jacket that attracts the consumer's attention, it is the jacket copy that makes them decide to buy.

The function of the cover copy is to create an awareness of value or need rather than to describe; it should persuade the reader that what they are holding is relevant and valuable and worth further investment of their time, rather than giving them sufficient summary that they can talk about the title without the bother of actually owning or reading it – and it should do so without giving away too much of the plot/key benefits. It will thus probably concentrate on how the audience may feel or react through reading the text rather than what is in it; descriptions of character and plot will be less important than the take-home benefit to be acquired by involvement and or ownership, whether that is pleasure, amusement, self-improvement or one-upmanship (although as these may be more effectively conveyed as implicit rather than explicit benefits, a light touch is needed). A book blurb needs to tantalise, tempt and engross the potential reader, but to do so in a style that reflects the content of the book.

Most authors find this difficult. They see their work as unique, and hence that there is nothing else quite the same. The reader rather will see the book in the context of a wider genre – everything else they have read/would like to read – and the challenge will be whether they want to make time for this one too.

So whereas it may help you to get started by drafting a full paragraph on your book's wider significance, seek objective feedback from a third party (or just a cooled-down version of yourself) on whether or not the text feels right for the market. Maybe 'a complex examination of a family in crisis, which will have repercussions for anyone who reads it' might better be described as 'an engrossing family saga'.

Cover copy also often works best if it is:

- Short, because shorter paragraphs and sentences attract attention more than long ones (think how your eye is generally drawn to the shorter letters on the correspondence page of a printed newspaper).

- Spaced out. Separating one long paragraph into two of uneven length may considerably increase readability.

- Familiar. It will probably include some words that feel predictable – 'moving', 'compelling', 'heart-rending' – because these help the reader identify what kind of title is being offered and many of us buy and read and buy within our comfort zones.

- Infiltrated by the words of others. A blurb may contain more words from/about other people than concentrate on describing the work in question. A relevant endorsement is an excellent way flagging to potential readers that this is something for them (see chapter 8).

Start your research by...

Accepting that a book blurb is really hard to write and that you will take time to get it right. Don't set yourself unreasonable goals (e.g. by the end of today).

Becoming an active reader of other people's book blurbs; photocopying your favourites and building a file of inspiration.

Reading product pack information (because that is what a book blurb is) on other sorts of products; sandwich packs and drinks cartons; album covers from a collection and gadget boxes. See how they haul in consumer attention.

Taking a field trip to a local bookshop. Stand near the front, and with all the shopping that you may have with you from a Saturday morning expedition. Keep half an eye on your handbag or wallet (pickpockets haunt bookshops because the market is so engrossed) and then pick up a book from the table that is always near the entrance. Turn it over in your hand by revolving your wrist. Note the pressure on your wrist as you do so and how holding the book in this position is difficult. Appreciate the importance of short, impactful copy. Next pick up others from the table and try to decide which has the most appealing book blurb. See how you make decisions quickly, and find some text easier to read than others. And note how a particular sentence, or even word, can be the turning point in copy that either draws you in, or leads to you putting the title in question back down on the pile.

Start building a list of words that appeal to you and are relevant to your writing. Given that a book blurb is trying to strike an immediate relationship with a reader, it should never be compendium of little-used words, but the occasional unfamiliar term may intrigue the reader and draw them in. Examples might include: 'beguile'; 'crushing'; 'entranced'; 'high-flavour'; 'abrupt'.

Author information for the book cover

If a product interests them, the potential purchaser may read the section on who wrote it; perhaps subconsciously looking for something that sparks a relationship; an understanding that the author is to be trusted as offering a good use for their time. A quirky or light touch is particularly recommended, showing that you do not take yourself too seriously. For example, John Harding's author information mentions that while at university, he once sat next to Martin Amis during a lecture. Katie Fforde for many years listed her hobbies as ironing and housework, for which she regrettably had very little time – because the afternoon chat shows required her full attention.

Start your research by...

Dispensing with your CV. This is designed to impress a potential employer with your value in the workplace, not support your work as worthy of a reader's time and money. Similarly, your reader is not generally interested in your educational or professional attainments. A lack of formal qualifications may be interesting but does not sit well with the proffering of a title that is self-published. And a display of over-achievement may equally repel the potential reader, as it offers no bridge between your heights of significance and their own life experience. Failing to perceive a link they may decline to award you their attention.

Try instead to hunt for anecdotal information that demonstrates your qualifications for writing, supported by information that sparks a relationship with the reader. You can see how others have done this by looking at their home pages on Twitter or LinkedIn. Alternatively, read the personal column in a quality publication – these can be particularly effective in creating a strong impression in just a handful of words.

Writing an Advanced Information Sheet (often called an AI or Bookseller Information)

An advance information sheet is sent to all who need to know about a forthcoming title 6–9 months ahead of publication. It allows them to log the title in their systems, plan possible promotions and prepare for its arrival. It is possible to publish books more quickly than this, but if you want to get into the trade, and be treated as a responsible publisher, it's a good idea to manage the systems they expect.

An AI, which can be sent as a PDF or as a physical copy with the book, should include:

* Information on the author, their credentials and qualifications for writing this title. Their location as this can be useful for local coverage

* The book title, subtitle, series (if relevant), ISBN and details of the format

* Details of the publisher, and how to contact them

An example is shown on page 340.

Writing press releases

A press release is an announcement to the press of a particular event or issue that the sender hopes will find coverage in the media. More specifically, the sender is usually hoping for one of two things:

* That the press will use the release whole, absorbing the text into their format

* That it will prompt the press to get in touch and commission an original feature about the proposed issue/subject matter

Both outcomes are likely to result in press coverage, a resulting general or specific awareness – and whatever longer term outcome had been hoped for – sales/visitors/behaviour change. Journalists

Bookseller Information

SilverWood Books
30 Queen Charlotte Street
Bristol
BS1 4HJ
T: 0117 910 5829
E: info@silverwoodbooks.co.uk
www.silverwoodbooks.com

SilverWood

Between the Lines of Autism
Joshua Davies

A collection of poems exploring the effect of Asperger's on an intelligent young person.

ABOUT THE BOOK

Between the Lines of Autism is a collection of twenty poems by Joshua Davies. Each poem is a window through the eyes of a 19 year-old Autistic youth who suffers from Asperger's Syndrome. Joshua sees the world from a different perspective to others. Some of his poems demonstrate the grueling obstacles he faces in ordinary life whilst others demonstrate his interest in literature and general art. Each poem has been difficult to write, as some people with Asperger's find it challenging to explain not only their emotions but also the sights and visions stored within their minds.

Read on and look between the lines of these diverse poems, written so anyone of any experience can understand their meaning and deep symbolism. See the poetic views of a determined young adult who lives between the lines of normality and abnormality.

ABOUT THE AUTHOR

Joshua Davies suffers from Asperger Syndrome, a form of Autism. His symptoms are constant extreme anxiety and reluctance, difficulty communicating and expressing ones-self and emotions. He has a constant compulsion to appear as normal as possible so not to give away any of his quirks. Apart from all the negative aspects he experiences, Joshua has shown to his family and peers that he has a high level of intelligence and willpower, advantages for him coping with his condition. He has constantly tried to show his intellect and talent over the years; only recently has he found a passion for English – a subject he was never expected to excel in. Other than this collection he has drafted two novels.

Joshua also won the Prince's Trust GoodFund Educational Achiever of the Year for the North East in 2009.

Title	Between the Lines of Autism
Author	Joshua Davies
ISBN	978-1-906236-48-9
RRP	£3.99
	203mm x 127mm
	34 pages

Bookseller and library discounts available
Published in paperback by SilverWood Books

expect press releases – most get hundreds every day – and a standard answer to any hopeful author ringing a newspaper or radio station to seek coverage for their new book or event is a request for the associated press release. But while the theory of press release compilation sounds simple, in reality many press releases are not well put together, and the journalist has to either hunt for the message – or quickly decide to delete/bin what has been received.

Unless you make friends with a journalist, you are unlikely to have seen a press release before. Here are some tips for producing one that has an impact; the illustration overleaf shows the commonly used layout.

1 **Ensure you have news to impart.** If not, don't bother sending a press release. Journalists get a nose for those whose information is boring, and if they feel you do not value their time, may delete whatever you send in future. News means something they want to tell their audience, right away. Put a date at the top and say if they should not release the information before a certain date and time (this may not be observed).

2 **Make the information you send it specific to the media you are approaching.** You may not have time to write a separate release for every publication or programme (although those you are particularly keen on may repay special attention to detail) but do target appropriately. The producers of daytime television will have different priorities from those of broadsheet journalists; the respective editors of *Farming Today* and *The World at One* may both cover your proposal, but they will need different associated narratives.

3 **Start with an interesting headline.** Telling them that someone has written a book may not be the most fascinating opening – it matters to you more than them. Instead think about angles – the path to publication ('author finally publishes a book after 20 rejections'), the subject matter ('author distressed by rubbish in his neighbourhood') or controversy ('author in crisis over family memoir'). A book title is very seldom a headline (unless it is very strong or topical). The headline should also be relevant to the media being targeted, so if it is going to local press, the particular

Matador

PRESS RELEASE

WWW.TROUBADOR.CO.UK

WHO LIVES IN A HOUSE LIKE THAT!

Amazing new book lets us peek into the most amazing houses in England and Wales

A new book by Robin Whitcomb is the ultimate bible for everyone who has ever seen an amazing house and longed to own it. Historic homes, quirky homes, houses with beautiful surroundings, houses in ruins and boats, this book has it all. Each house is beautifully photographed with interior and exprerior pictures, and accompaning text which sets out the history and manner of the featured houses. Divided into regions, the book gives us glimpse of the way the British live today and features over 48 unique and amazing homes. 'It was the experience of visiting the remote and unique Cliff Cottage in Cornwall that set me thinking about the buildings we live in. I wanted to try to capture the amazing variety of places that we call home,' says Robin, whose research took him the length and breadth of the country

'Robin Whitcomb has struck upon a most imaginative idea with this book since people love to see where other people live – especially if their home is a bit quirky and different. I have thoroughly enjoyed Robin's book.'
The Duchess of Northumberland, Alnwick Castle

About the Author: Robin Whitcomb was born in Scarborough in 1945. After leaving school he spent two years working for his Grandfather's oil business in Tulsa, Oklahoma. In 1965 he joined up with Sonny and Cher and played drums on their hit *I Got you Babe*. Latterly, he has also worked as a journalist and played cricket for the MCC and rugby for Richmond RFC. He now coaches sport at St. Paul Junior School and has two sons, Patch and Beanie.

PUBLICATION DATE 1ST JANUARY 2011
ISBN: 9781848764798 PRICE: £15.99

PRESS PACK

FOR AUTHOR INTERVIEWS, REVIEW COPIES, ARTICLES, PHOTOS OR EXTRACTS
PLEASE CONTACT JANE ROWLAND
TEL: 0116 279 2299   EMAIL: MARKETING@TROUBADOR.CO.UK
TROUBADOR PUBLISHING LTD, 5 WEIR ROAD, KIBWORTH BEAUCHAMP, LEICESTER, LE8 OLQ

location should be flagged here ('Kingston author speaks to the world'). If you are sending your press release by email, your 'title line' needs similar consideration.

As you develop your arguments in the release, keep asking yourself: is this interesting? But think carefully about sensational supporting details. It will undoubtedly get you more coverage, but may haunt you forever. Do not mention that the book is self-published.

4 **One page is plenty, two at most.** All journalists are pressed for time, and they will also have received many others the same day. Ensure the opening paragraph has all the relevant information (who, what, where, why and when?). If the release gets used whole it will probably be cut from the bottom upwards – bad news if that is where your key points lie.

5 **Include some quotations.** Journalists always like to confirm any story they print with supporting quotations – from locals, from influential people, from experts, from readers. If you provide them, you offer them the opportunity to substantiate an argument without further research.

6 **Provide a source of further information:** at least two names of people who can be contacted to provide supporting detail. Give their mobile telephone numbers, not just those operating during office hours (journalists often work late). Provide supporting detail that sounds tempting: the opportunity to interview the author; to visit a key scene in the book; a local angle to the story. A list of top tips, a couple of interesting statistics or a quiz are all good ideas – these tend to be popular with journalists as they offer a break from solid text and may pull in readers (remember that the role of the journalist is to keep readers reading, not provide complete coverage of a particular topic). Ensure that the information you provide is available on your website if you have one (along with more supporting detail) before your press release goes out.

7 **Send it to the right person.** Take the trouble to find out the name of the particular correspondent with whom you want to be in touch. Don't assume that all books are best reviewed by the literary editor – it may be that a news editor might be more

interested. The names of the relevant correspondents can be found in a current almanac, e.g. *The Writers' and Artists' Yearbook* (Bloomsbury, UK) *The Essential Guide to Getting Your Book Published* (The Book Doctors, US).

8 **Read the paper/watch the television programme you are planning to approach before sending anything.** All journalists expect you to know their format and what they have just covered. This also enables you to sell a particular story in a way that might particularly appeal to them ('After that intriguing story on how ferrets are becoming an increasingly popular pet, this new novel shows that rats make better household companions than people.').

9 **Send it out as an email, with a picture of sufficiently high quality that it can be reproduced, to any news or feature medium you think may take it.** But if you are also sending out physical copies of the books, include a copy of the press release in the parcel too.

10 **Coordinate your timings.** The purpose of a press release is to promote sales, not just awareness, so don't send one out until the books are in stores ready to meet demand – and ensure your release mentions where the title can be obtained (stores and online through your website).

Writing author information for press releases

Journalists tend to have a short attention span, and you are more likely to prompt their attention if you include different information from that presented in your book blurb or on your website. Rack your brains for any good stories connected to you or your writing. For example:

* How did you come to choose this subject? Why did it appeal to you?

* What professional expertise qualifies you to write about this? For non-fiction titles this is particularly important. Even if you are a newcomer, a growing passion for a subject that you explore along with the reader can be explained.

- Where do you live and is this significant to the work or its development (this might make an interesting photograph)?

- What have others said about you? Positive and negative feedback can be used. The back cover copy for *Great Parliamentary Scandals* offers the following on one of the authors. 'Peter Mandelson once said: "Kevin Maguire only wants to cause trouble".'[150] Highly effective.

- Is the subject matter of your book topical and in the media already – in which case provide a link and offer a journalist a ready-made issue-based piece, with your book as supporting proof. For example: have you wondered how those who try to have a child through IVF but are *not* successful feel afterwards?[151]

Most author information, both on-book and destined for journalists, ends with a note of your personal circumstances, your marital status and whether you have any children. You don't have to provide this, and could produce a rather elegant alternative: 'Hamish Maxwell lives in the Scottish Highlands with a particularly talented cat'.

Printed flyers and leaflets to promote books

Printed information retains a strong role in generating future sales. A *printed* leaflet offering a taste of the *printed* book is neatly predictive. Writers tend to resist marketing vocabulary, but advertisers are aware when there is a desirable synergy to be achieved through 'using the medium to sell the medium'.

Leaflets also tend to be kept; we like to have a permanent record of things we plan to investigate in future (why else do so many emails get printed out?). A leaflet can also reinforce an impression gained – if you have heard an author speak, and liked what they had to say but do not want to buy the book right now, you can take their information away and think about it – or pass it on to someone else.

---

[150] M. Parris and K. Maguire, *Great Parliamentary Scandals: five centuries of calumny, smear and innuendo*, London: Robson Books (2004)
[151] Explored in *Cells* by Harriet Grace, see page 237

Start your research by...

Thinking about what to say about your writing as a whole. Sum it up, say what you have in print, and who else likes it.

Expanding your arguments and saying new things about yourself and your writing. A leaflet offers good value for money as both sides of the page can be printed.

A few tips for preparing information for leaflets and flyers

1 Make your leaflets as multipurpose as possible. Thus if you may end up handing them out in bookshops or other retail outlets, at the end of a talk, don't include a discount for buying directly from you (if you are diverting sales, you are less likely to get stocked).

2 Try to write a paragraph about how your work makes readers think/feel/see the world. This is a 'take-home benefit' and is likely to be more appealing than just describing the plot or content.

3 Can you include a photograph? This is not because writing is a beauty contest, but because would-be readers are interested in knowing more about the person in whom they are investing their time. Having a shot professionally taken is not as expensive as you might think, and you may be able to negotiate further if the photographer ends up with their image on the back of a book, with an appropriate credit.[152]

4 The same goes for locations that feature strongly in your work. Those who live there may be interested in reading more about where they live. All photographs need captions (studies have shown these get read first).

5 Provide a route to more information – the place where your new speaking engagements get advertised, your own website if you have one.

6 Give stock to friends and supporters to hand out. Most writers find handing out their information difficult, because promotion of their writing is such a personal thing, but your friends and relations may be less inhibited. Perhaps your mother would send it out with her Christmas cards?

[152] See chapter 11

To summarise, the work naturally has to be the writer's main point of effort; without a manuscript that is worth sharing, any associated enthusiastic description will ultimately feel hollow. The package of descriptive words with which you surround your work will however be vital in drawing an audience, creating awareness and encouraging potential customers to invest their time and resources. So don't compromise your chances of finding readers by giving the associated copywriting less time or attention than it truly needs.

20

Marketing online

'Believe it or not, this is the very best time to publish a book. Yes, there is a recession and it is more and more difficult to find a publisher or an agent – but this is the time of the consumer.

Let us begin with the hope that the book that you have written and published – be that with the traditional publisher or through the myriad of opportunities that exist for you to do it yourself – is well written and has a potential audience.

For the first time consumers – readers – are in control as to how they read it and where they buy it; no longer do they have to search bookshops from one end of the country to another in the hope that it is there, or they can order it and then return to pick it up.

Today your fingers do the walking. You find the book on the internet – whether it is Google or Amazon – and then you choose how you want to read it. That may be hardback (or in an even more luxurious, perhaps bespoke format – with gold edging and book mark ribbons), paperback, audiobook, ebook, or chapter by chapter. You can borrow it from a library or a virtual library. The important thing is that you choose how you want to read it; it's your money and your choice.

But there is one major problem. How do you, the consumer, know it exists? And how, as an author, do you tell the consumer that it exists?

That's where PR, marketing, advertising, and profile-building comes into the frame.

Authors and publishers have to create awareness and visibility for the book and you have to do whatever is necessary to make that happen before the window of opportunity disappears (unwanted books get pulped and become landfill). Remember that the media want something interesting, unusual, different, newsworthy, dramatic, revelatory, controversial – so it is up to you to deliver the goods for all sections of the media; to encourage them to mention you and your book. You need to target traditional newspapers and magazines, television and radio and all of the digital opportunities. You need a good website, or as a minimum a good homepage – because people need to find you and know where to get your book. You need to blog, tweet, participate in LinkedIn and Facebook – you need to make as much of the opportunity that the publication of your book has presented. If you can't do it yourself there are a number of PR agencies that specialise in this area. From our point of view, we see this as such a big opportunity that we are not only getting involved in promoting self-publishing, we are participating in helping authors widen awareness of their product. We think it's that significant.'

Tony Mulliken, Chairman, Midas PR

www.midaspr.co.uk

This chapter covers marketing through electronic media: using email; a website and social media to spread awareness of your writing. I will deal with the main vehicles in turn, but will start with a few general comments.

Online dissemination of both writing, and information about it, has changed the relationship between author and reader

When I began in publishing, publishing houses controlled access to not only the means of producing books, but also their marketing. The way to get a book talked about was to get it reviewed in a respected paper, and then to quote from the review on the back of the jacket; and book reviewers would not consider featuring anything self-published. Now, effective online communication can promote the wider dissemination of anything worth reading. Meanwhile the previous mediators changed; many literary editors lost their jobs (the pages they edit gained little advertising revenue) and chat show hosts who demonstrated sustained good judgement in recommending books that other people liked, found their future . observations got noticed. And as we saw in the opening chapter of this book, self-published books can now win prizes.

There is also much less deference within society.

'In this digital age, in which there will be no more facades, no more walls, no more privacy as we now understand it, no cordon sanitaire in which we can be something that we are not, this need, this demand for authenticity and the "real" will become more and more important.'[153]

The internet has fuelled our curiosity, enabling us to ask questions, and to do so without having to engage eye contact with those who interest us. This has impacted on the relationship between writers and readers. Time was when readers who wanted to communicate their enthusiasm for the work of a particular author would write a respectful letter to their publisher and request that it be passed on. Nor would they necessarily expect to hear back; anticipating that writers were unusual people, and that might include offering a 'my book says it all' reticence. Today readers are unafraid to ask questions and are empowered to do so. In some purchasing situations (e.g. the responsibility of choosing a title for their book group or for a significant present) they may need more information than is available in a bookshop. Today writers are more accessible: through literary festivals; in the media (much interviewed as they provide cheap copy) and now through the web. If readers like the sound of you, or your work, they may look first online.

An unmediated relationship

If you set up a website, email, tweet or blog, decisions on content are obviously yours; online communication is usually unmediated. There are no editors to get past, no sub-editors to rewrite your content, no publishers to decide you are not the voice of the moment (the publishing equivalent for the retailer's 'there's no demand' when you know there is). While this may give you freedom, and your readers a linear route from first hearing about your title to online purchasing, there are associated dangers. As critic and author Clive James has said:

[153] Bonnie Greer, writing in *The Daily Telegraph* about Michelle Obama, 24 May 2011

'My website has an inbuilt fault that all websites have; it is edited only by me. I have always been at my best as a writer when I was edited by someone else. Newspapers do that. Newspaper editors have this awkward habit of asking you what you mean, checking up to see whether you have got it right and they bring the whole force of the publication to bear on helping you to be better.'[154]

What is more, online media invite you to open up and share. Long term, this may not be in your best interests. Facebook places an emphasis on how you are feeling about things – 'What's on your mind?' is the question awaiting you as you log on. But there is no eye contact on Facebook, thus no opportunity to see how others are responding to what you have to say, other than their impersonal opportunity to 'comment' underneath what you have shared. Tweeting to your followers can breed a false sense of security – and a corresponding lack of judgement. Beware of getting the tone wrong. Over-ebullience may alienate; writers are notoriously jealous and hearing how well the publishing process is going may not endear you or your work to those who are finding it more of a struggle.

So if online communication is new to you, before you get further involved check out the territory; look at lots of websites and see how they feel to use; read other people's blogs and read the posts they get back; think about how you would feel if the responses made were directed at you.

What kind of information to share

When you start communicating online, the pace tends to be rapid. Writers who are regulars online often say that it is the sharing of *general* thoughts and information that leads to interest in their work; too direct a plug may produce the opposite effect. So consider: 'This is what I am currently pondering' (subtext 'Have you read my ponderings in book form so far?') rather than 'Get out and buy my book'. Provided your website offers material for those who decide you to Google and find out more, you may attract readers.

[154] BBC Radio 4, *Heresy*, 2009

Quirky (but not odd) and interesting is best. It is engaging to find out more about the preferences and habits of an author: what they like to eat; where they live; how many children they have – and it is likely to be even more engaging if you are specific rather than general. So don't say your hobby is reading, without qualifying to say what kind of books you like; or walking, without saying at what altitude and where for preference; state your favourite foods if they are interesting (haggis and watercress for some reason spring to mind).

But given that online information can be shared immediately, and far more widely than you perhaps originally intended, don't volunteer more information than you are happy for your readers to know. Once information is in the public domain, it cannot be recalled; material on your website can be copied onto other sites. So if you are suffering from writers' block or depression, but trying to battle through it and just keep going, your website is not the best place to announce this for the first time. If on the other hand you would like your readers to know why your fourth book is so horribly late, and not for them to assume that strong sales have made you disdainful of public reaction, then a website may be the ideal place to make an announcement. Sharing something personal may deepen their bond with you.

Using online channels for research or a warm-up for writing

Writing online can be an effective warm-up exercise; the prescribed word limit of Twitter can sharpen your brain. Some writers find it motivating to use social media to gather support; announcing their intention to get started and receiving encouraging tweets that help them keep going. Blogging, Twitter and email can all offer you a good break from your current involvement; the opportunity to avoid cabin fever and to take part in some banter which has a prescribed extent and does not require you to leave your writing place (it can take much less time than going out for coffee). They can all also be an excellent way of researching particular issues – throwing out a request for information ('does anyone else remember the swimsuits criss-crossed with shirring elastic, before the invention of lycra?').

The risks of being online

Loss of ideas
What you display can be used by others – who may not trace the origin of their material back to you.

Loss of time
Time goes quicker online. Involvement quickly becomes super-absorbing, draining time and energy from your writing. Online communication can so easily move from being a necessary activity in support of your writing to the point of main effort, and writers need to maintain sufficient self-discipline to have time to craft their work – disengaging from social media may be part of this.

Loss of energy
Although online communication often appears informal, effective management of the media requires a very precise attention, and this can drain your writing brain. There is also a danger that the heightened reality of life online will come to replace a writer's ability to remain in touch with the real world (although obviously this can be cannily avoided if you set your work in a world where the characters are also constantly online).

Life online can also feel crowding. The frequency of communication of some Tweeters is amazing, as is the surprisingly large number of people following them. The first time you sign up for Facebook, up pops a whole list of people you already know through email, and the impression of so many smiling faces can be daunting. And as fast as you click, more appear. If you are a writer who thrives on privacy; the cherishing of fleeting thoughts as they grow into ideas and gain a tangible form through words – that have still not been voiced to those to whom you are closest – this may feel inappropriately brash and hurried. Prolonged exposure can de-motivate, particularly if you are feeling blocked and keep reading about how other writers have written thousands of words that morning (whether or not this is true).

Talking about a project in too public a forum can drain it of energy, whereas inside you it still had a real burn. The same goes for talking about yourself and your writing method. Others blogging back may regard your honesty as either self-pleased or pretentious (or perhaps both) and if they tell you it can feel invasive; you may end up wishing you had never shared your thoughts in the first place. It's hard to be prescriptive about this, but go with your instinct and don't share stuff you (or those you value) may come to regret later. And of course the internet is not a legal-free zone – all the same restrictions to what you say on the printed page apply to what you say on screen.

Loss of impact

Every tweet you send is displayed on the screens of your followers; every minor change to your Facebook profile results in the announcement of your changed details to your entire network. This may draw more attention than you want.

Which online medium to use?

Using your email contacts

If you have not communicated online about your work before, then an email account is an essential starting point, and there are many basic things you can do before embarking on more complicated communication methods. For example, do you have a line under the signature on your out-going mail, giving the name of your latest book or talk/lecture/book signing? And if so do you change it regularly (content and colour)? Have you communicated with those in your email inbox recently?

Along similar lines, are there friends who blog or tweet who might do so on behalf of your work? Although directing them to a physical bookstore will mean the momentum from first information to purchase will necessarily be interrupted.

How many social media should you use?

Writers involved in social media seem to concentrate their efforts on one form, although it is possible to use 'feeds' that integrate your various online communications. There are also generational biases and trends that affect the use of social media; in general the young are more likely to use Facebook than Twitter; LinkedIn functions as a Facebook for people in business and the Facebook has become much more popular than MySpace.

Having a website

At its most basic, a website is a place online where those who want to know more about you can look you up.

Start your research by...

Thinking about what you want a website to do for you – because this may help you think about what to say. Examples of what a website can do for you:

1 Provide information about you so that those who are interested can find out more. This is particularly useful for journalists who often look on the author's website for information to humanise what they have discovered so far.

2 Sell your books. Even if the supporting structure behind your website is just you putting books in envelopes and taking them along to the mail, having a formal portal depersonalises the selling experience – useful if, as many writers do, they find accepting money for their book a curious mixture of demeaning and validating.

3 Answer routine questions that you don't have the time or inclination to deal with, or as a very famous academic gave as his rationale time allocation: 'to explain what my theories are, not use up my time explaining what they are not'; presumably to those who have taken insufficient time to investigate themselves.[155]

4 Allow you to get on with your work without interruption.

5 Provide a sneak preview on forthcoming work.

6 Pad out the back story of your work, perhaps by giving more detailed background information on characters, key locations and your own inspiration for writing.

[155] Peter Checkland, Emeritus Professor of Systems, Lancaster University and creator of Soft Systems Methodology (SSM)

7 Trawl for ideas – perhaps by discussing a dilemma in your writing or seeking feedback on previous novels. Which character from a past book they would your readers most like to meet again in future?

8 Announce forthcoming appearances or the launch of new titles.

9 Deepen the relationship with your readers. To make them feel they share something with you.

Ironically, rather than being an intrusion into your privacy, a website actually helps you keep some distance. You provide the information you are happy to share. If you want to see how this is managed at a more tactical level, wait until a specific organisation is in crisis and then start monitoring their website (e.g. BP's reaction to the oil spill in the Gulf of Mexico). The organisation under pressure tends to use their website to provide the information it wants the world to absorb, and in the particular case quoted, the opinions of individual staff members were offered; presumably to offset the immense size of the corporation. Individuals have been known to use the same technique; to make announcements they would find difficult in person – and when they don't want to be cross-examined.

I am going to steer clear of the formatting questions – what typeface works best, how much to write, how often to update – as these are beyond the scope of this book (and lots more advice is available). Rather, I would encourage you to read other people's sites, analyse your personal response, and then consider the few rules I offer below. To get you started, I really like www.innocentdrinks.com (see in particular 'us' and then 'our story') and www.writersandartists.co.uk.

Three top tips
- If you are going to offer a website, it needs to be updated. Not as often as a blog, but often enough that it feels fresh and cared about; to ensure that the date on which 'site last updated' is within recent memory and the material feels recent (you also need to read it every now and again). If readers are to build a relationship with you through your site you need to think about what might draw them back. Maybe you could feature information on things you have discovered that you like (see

Gwyneth Paltrow's site www.goop.com or a statement of what you plan to do with your day ('Today I am in... and I am.... See www.chriscleave.com).

* Don't promise more than you can deliver. If you install a 'contact me' button offering to respond to readers' questions they will expect you to be as good as your word. If you suspect that you won't want to bother responding, then don't offer. That way no one will be offended. There is a clear message embedded in the websites of authors who do not have a facility for getting in touch – and it is not necessarily resented.

* If someone else is building your website for you, ensure it is set up so you can update it yourself, and ask for a package of information on how to do so. Once you get used to using it, and start incorporating it into your thinking about your writing and spotting things to share, you will find having to update it through someone else is not fast enough.

Blogging

A blog is a type of website; a different way of managing website content. It usually functions as an internet journal (blog is short for weblog) and in its simplest form it's like an online diary that can be updated frequently and enhanced with video, photos, links to other sites and even advertising. No real technical expertise is needed to set one up, and if you have a computer and access to the internet you can be up and blogging within a couple of hours.

Another option is to contribute to someone else's blog, either by submitting a response to what someone else has said or by starting a discussion yourself as one of the official contributors. This allows you to post every now and again, without responsibility for site maintenance (e.g. www.writersandartists.co.uk). If you have your own blog you have the option of whether or not to accept feedback – and so monitor what is sent in. If you blog on a site managed by someone else, feedback will be actively sought (because it drives traffic to a site so the more comments the better) and so you will have to be prepared to contribute sparkly articles, interesting if not controversial, and that those blogging back may disagree so profoundly that they decide to publicly rubbish what you say.

There are easy options for starting a blog (see Blogger.com) – this is ideal for first time bloggers as it is simple to use. Once you know what you are doing you may want a more professional site, and may consider other options (see Wordpress.com)

Reasons for blogging

Blogging feels fresh and immediate – because (if it's your site) you can say what you want to say and it can be up within seconds, allowing you to take comment on, and contribute to, contemporary conversation. You can be articulate, making your point with wit, charm and brilliance, and talk without being interrupted.

Blogging also offers a discipline for reflection; a space to put stuff – perhaps things that you want to hang on to, or reflect upon, but which are not part of the 'work in progress'. Many writers use it as a diary to themselves, helping to clarify their experiences and in the process funding some understanding amongst the readership of the difficulties of the creative process. Some writers use their blog when giving talks to interested groups – so children's writer Shoo Rayner discusses what's going on in the pond outside his writing space[156] and others will show images of where they have just been.[157]

For several authors blogging has also provided a way to get published (see www.wifeinthenorth.com which began as a blog before Penguin turned it into a book), although recent research by Dr Sarah Pedersen of Robert Gordon University in Aberdeen found that those moving from blogs to books were usually journalists or writers already; the blog was thus a means of drawing their work to the attention of potential investors via a new format.

Twitter

Twitter is a service for people to communicate and stay connected through the exchange of short (140 characters or fewer) and usually frequent messages. Those involved write quick messages, often called 'tweets', post them to their profile or blog and they

[156] www.shoorayner.com
[157] www.yemisiblake.co.uk

automatically appear in your followers' Twitter feeds; they can also be searched for on the Twitter website www.twitter.com.

To use Twitter all you need are an internet connection or a mobile phone – and the best way to find out how it works is to try it out. Enrol on the Twitter website and then see what topics are being discussed. To create an account you will have to provide your full name, set up a user name (this could be a nickname or the name of something you do or admire), enter a password, and then give your email address. Before getting started you will have to copy some symbols to prove that you are human and not a machine.[158]

From then on it's a question of trying it out. You can search for your friends or the famous and decide to follow them, which means their tweets will be available to you (unless they decide to block you). Clicking the 'follow' button next to a user's name will 'add' them to the list of those you hear from – and they will get a message to say you have chosen to follow them. If you subsequently decide to stop following them, you can, but this time they do not get a message telling them so. When you decide to follow someone you can see how many followers they have, and how many you have in common. You can also decide to follow people on the basis of your interests – a new list of possibilities is suggested every time you click an interest. Twitter keeps running totals for every user of how many people you are following, how many are following you, how many lists your tweets appear on (usually based on groups you belong to or your place of employment) and how many you have sent. You can use Twitter to scan your email address books to find contacts and friends who are also users, and then contact them too – either en masse or one by one.

What kind of messages to send

People use Twitter for all sorts of purposes, but probably the most common is individual comments on what is going on: what annoys, inspires or excites you; what you are about to do/have just done. You can make a public reply to someone else's tweet and retweet messages that you think deserve a wider public. You can also send a direct message to a Twitter contact (if they follow you), by using the buttons on the right hand side of your screen.

[158] A 'captcha'

What's the point of Twitter?

1 **Instant communication and connection with a huge variety of different people.** It can be an interesting experience to watch a public event and read the tweets of others doing the same. For example, when watching a football match on television you can listen to the commentator and then take part in a discussion of both their comments and the match in general, with a wide variety of people, many of whom you do not know.

2 **Information.** The explosion of communication media means that no one can keep up-to-date with all channels for delivery. Twitter can help you to hear about serendipitous events and people of interest to you; that would otherwise pass your notice. You can cross refer people to websites, and shorten the links to avoid using up too many characters.[159]

3 **Rapid dissemination of information.** I first heard of the death of Osama bin Laden on Twitter.

4 **A source of articulate communication.** Given that each tweet is only 140 characters (that's including punctuation) many tweeters tend to sharpen their comments before pressing send. Tweets are often (but not always) pithy, witty and well written – taking part can encourage you to be concise and precise.

5 **Fascination.** Tweeters share their thoughts and experiences, and in the process you gain an insight into the lives of others – a snapshot of what is else is going on. And this might trigger a story, as sub-plot, a character, or provide you with useful reference material.

'The beauty of Twitter is how all-inclusive it is, reading Hugo Chavez's visions of the future of Venezuela, followed by an old mate from university informing me she has woken up from a five-minute nap is a scenario you won't find anywhere else, unless you go on holiday to South America with a sleepy friend.'   Alasdair Baverstock

---

[159] See http://bit.ly/ You can shorten websites on a one-off basis, but signing up permits you to give websites names of your choice and to see how those reading your Tweets use the information you provide – and how this compares with other users

6 **Widened participation.** Twitter makes people accessible. You can send tweets to people whom in everyday life you would never meet, and they may reply. Similarly direct messaging through Twitter may produce a more instant response from someone you wish to contact than sending an email to their overcrowded inbox.

7 **Showing off.** Twitter offers a medium for the wider sharing of good thoughts; a place to put your ideas rather than feeling them fade away. If you have ever polished a thought about what you should have said in a particular situation, feeling frustrated that this was less than what you managed in practice, Twitter may be for you.

8 **Attract readers for your work.** Writers who tweet have seen a direct relationship between the constituencies of those who follow them and those who buy and recommend their work.

Facebook

A facebook is the informal name given by US university administrators to a book of headshots of their new classmates, given out to new students to help them settle in. Facebook as an online network was set up by Mark Zuckerberg and classmates from Harvard in 2004 – if you want to know more, see the film *The Social Network*.

The vocabulary of Facebook has entered everyday speech, and now dictionaries. You will hear young people shout 'I'll add you' as a way of ending a conversation (meaning 'I will add you as a friend on Facebook') and 'to unfriend' (meaning to remove someone as a friend) was the *New Oxford American Dictionary*'s word of the year in 2009. At first restricted to Harvard, Facebook quickly became a standard means of communication and now anyone who declares themselves to be at least 13 years old, and has a valid email address (before your membership goes live you will receive an email that requires you to confirm details, and accept conditions of membership) can become a registered user of the website and attach a 'profile'. All usage statistics are out-of-date as soon as they are published, but it was recently estimated that users of Facebook spend 700 billion minutes a month on the site. They are to be found worldwide, although (according to the *Financial Times*) the US, UK and Indonesia are the countries with most members. Certain national governments (e.g. China, Pakistan, Syria, Vietnam and Iran) have at times blocked access, and it is often banned within the workplace to prevent the misuse of employees' time.

How it works

Potential users log on to www.facebook.com follow the prompts, create a personal profile on their home page (sometimes called the home feed), which they can augment with photos, lists of personal and other information, add other users as friends, and from then on exchange messages. The screen where comments arrive on your profile is called your wall. You can also join common interest user groups organised by your place of work or education, or other specific interest pages.

To allay concerns about privacy, Facebook enables users to choose their own privacy settings and hence who has access to specific parts of their profile. The website is free to users, and generates revenue from advertising, such as banner ads or 'like' pages on which the interested click and enter the advertiser's message or website. Each individual's profile page includes a wall, a space that allows friends to post messages for the user to see; 'pokes' (virtual prods to attract someone's attention) and a section where photographs can be loaded for friends or all to see.

Facebook for writers

It is a straightforward process to sign up and a natural place to post information on your work/recent successes; announcing to friends and others interested in finding out more about you. You can form special groups, a handy way of talking with like minds – and getting information out of people quickly. And in the process you may garner motivation and comradeship. Creation of a 'thread' (an email conversation between two or more people) can enable the maintenance of friendships you do not have much time for at the moment, but are reluctant to lose. You can also create a business page for your Facebook account, which allows you to display information on your work (tick the box that categorises you as 'artist, band or public figure').

Case study: Catherine Ryan Howard[160]

'I think in order to succeed at marketing and promoting your book online, you need to do ALL of the following: blog, tweet and maintain a Facebook page.

Your blog is the main hub of your online activities and really you should have a 'blogsite' or a blog with pages/sections that also serves as a professional-looking website, i.e. it has an "About" page, a "News" page, a "Contact" page, and so on. I don't believe there is any "right" way to blog, but I've found that filling a gap, doing something a bit different (or doing something that's already been done but in a new, different way!) and giving your readers something of use (e.g. self-publishing information, entertainment, etc.) is a recipe for success.

Twitter is for networking/making contacts and driving traffic to your blog. I think being on Twitter is the single most important thing I ever did for my writing career and all the things that have happened to me (selling books, getting speaking engagements, being in *The Sunday Times*, on the radio, etc.) can all be traced back to me being on there. But yet most of my tweets are not about my books; I use Twitter for fun, more than anything.

Facebook, I believe, is nowhere near as important to actually selling copies of your book as the other two but since it's the world's most popular social media platform, you should have a presence on there. Also, if your book is about a specific subject (like mine is about Disney) the chances are that Disney fans, or people interested in the subject, have already organised themselves into Facebook groups, and they are like readers/customers ready and waiting to purchase your book – they just need to find out about it first!

The two pieces of advice I try to give all writers trying to market their work online are:

1 Get people interested in YOU and YOUR WRITING, as opposed to your book. Not only is this easier but it's better for you in the long run (otherwise you'd be starting from scratch with every book).

[160] www.catherineyanhoward.com

2 Wait at least a year. I think that's how long it takes for things to take off, if they're going to.'

To the previously uninvolved, marketing online and in particular through social networking can feel an overwhelming challenge. But the opportunities are enormous. Viral marketing gets shared – and things can ignite very quickly (as movie stars who attract gossip, and hence millions of new followers on Twitter find out). The best advice is to explore before you commit, to think about what you want to say and how to communicate – but above all to get started. Just as putting off writing can leave you with nothing to improve, putting off getting involved in online marketing is neglecting the fastest growing means of disseminating ideas and information. It's that important.

ALL YOUR OWN WORK

THE WRITER'S TOOLS

DGill

Conclusion

Self-publishing has had a bad reputation. It has tended to attract those with anger in their hearts, and spleen in their vocabulary. Anger from rejection by the traditional industry, but spleen fuelling their inability to listen – both to the feedback they were getting/not getting (even more annoying) on their work, and the implications of being repeatedly rejected by potential external investors. Disinclined to consider a serious reappraisal of their writing, or their own self-cast role as misunderstood genius, they wandered off in the direction of a bunch of charlatans, who were offering them a shoddy range of services at a very high price:

> 'Come and read the manuscripts that turn up at Manutius. But if you want a more down-to-earth explanation, it's like the story of the man with a bad stammer who complains that the radio station wouldn't hire him as an announcer because he didn't carry a party card. We always have to blame our failures on somebody else, and dictatorships always need an external enemy to bind their followers together. As the man said, for every complex problem there's a simple solution, and it's wrong.'[161]

The world has changed. Today new products and services await, as well as a whole range of new buying situations: the single, commemorative book for a special occasion; a working copy of a manuscript in progress, that will both promote your objectivity and enable you to record your feedback in a format that resembles the anticipated final product; a permanent repository for information that you wish to hold on to; a slim volume of your poems for those who have kindly asked. And of this I have had personal experience.

[161] Umberto Eco. *Foucault's Pendulum*, Vintage (2001)

While writing this book both my parents-in-law celebrated their 80th birthday, and in each case my brother-in-law produced a book with a print run of one, including memories and photographs of their lives – and I can't think of a more precious potential gift.

One other unexpected consequence of this book needs mentioning. Over the years I have attended many gatherings of authors, at society meetings, literary festivals and special events. The prevailing tone has always been claustrophobic: discontent with almost every aspect of the process, fuelled by barely concealed envy. Any contract to publish carries within it satisfaction, but perhaps a range of opportunities for disappointment: the loss of friends who are less favoured; the threat of non-renewal by the investor; lower than anticipated sales; poor reviews – all underpinned by the terrifying question every newly published author must ask themselves, 'Can I ever do it again?' As part of the research for this book I have interviewed many self-published authors and the unifying factor between them has been their generally high level of contentment. I met a group who were energised by the opportunities available; enchanted to see their work in a finished format; who felt peace at having finally achieved what had long been desired, and who were proud to share the fruits of their labours, with friends, family – and the wider community. And those they dealt with on their journey found them pleasant to deal with; prompt payers and likely to comment on a job well done.

Self-publishing today feels a very fitting phenomenon for a society that is getting weary of the massification; wants slower cooking, more gardening, better relationships, fewer supermarkets, and a greater emphasis on concentrated pleasures. And my conclusion gradually became that self-publishing really can be a path to fulfilment.

Even the difficulties seemed to be positively managed. This book has allowed me to explore the processes involved, and hopefully offer a sense of the complexities involved. And while it is true that most of those I interviewed began by wanting others to take responsibility for getting their work more widely read, perhaps it was the requirement to take responsibility for themselves that augmented their subsequent satisfaction. Society has become very risk-averse; making the decision to allocate resources and time to a project you have long desired, and wresting judgement on your work from those you felt were insufficiently engaged, often resulted in a profound pleasure. As author Erica Jong said:

'Take life in your own hands and what happens? A terrible thing: no one to blame'

But take on the risk and you gain the opportunity to measure your achievement – and take the credit too.

Whatever combination of routes you decide upon, to do it all yourself and learn in the process, or instruct one/a series of suppliers to mange it for you, I wish you luck. And a speedy route to the same delight I saw on my mother-in-law's face, when she saw images from her childhood presented on the page in front of her. It was priceless.

Grace Baverstock at the party to celebrate her 80th birthday – even the prospect of pudding did not get in the way of her desire to read her book Photograph by Sue Baverstock

Acknowledgments

This book began its life at a two-day conference at Kingston University, with a live link-up with Mark Coker (and his cat) at two in the morning from San Francisco. I am particularly grateful to Margaret Aherne, Katharine Allenby, Darin Brockman, Lindsay Brodin, Mark Coker, David Gifford, Nicholas Jones, Kay Sayce and Judith Watts and for their contributions and encouragement; to my publishers, family, and Jenny Brown my agent.

I would also like to thank:

Barbara Abbs; Annemarie Allan; Penny Anstice Brown; Giles Armstrong; Julian Baggini; Elaine Banham; Adam Baron; Alasdair Baverstock; Clare Baverstock; Mike Baverstock; Sue Baverstock; Rachel Billington; Kevin Billington; Jane Birdsell; Yemisi Blake; Susannah Bowen; Beth Brewster; N.M. Browne; Akiko Bush; Helena Caletta; Siobhan Campbell; Steve Carey; Peter Checkland; Jane Cholmeley; Norma Clarke; Ed Collacott; Andrew Collins; Ray Compton; Andrew Crofts; Valerie Crofts; Matt Cunningham; Siobhan Curham; June Davies; Isobel Dixon; Lari Don; Cathy Douglas; Robert East; Mark Edwards; Justine Embury; Anna Faherty; Claire Forbes; Allan Fuller; Liz Gifford; Harriet Grace; Nick Green; Bonnie Greer; Hattie Gordon; Lisa Hall; Stephen Hancocks; Andrew Hansen; Helen Hart; Billy Hopkins; Barbara Horn; Catherine Ryan Howard; Jon Howells; Paul Hurst; Margaret Hyslop; Clive James; Liz James; Beth Steiner Jones; Alan Kenchington; Diana Kenchington; Mandy Knight; Brian Landers; Mary Lawson; Gwyneth Lewis; Helen Maroudias; George Masikunas; Robert Mayfield; Alastair McIver; David McLean; Roger Millington; Matt Moore; Kelly Morgan; Peter Mountain; Tony Mulliken; Bill Munro; Sarah Nock; Ama Page; Jessica Palmer; Jill Paton Walsh; John Peacock; Wendy Perriam; Jenny Plaxton; Jill Plaxton; John Plaxton; Sarah Pedersen; Lisa Piselli;

Kate Pool; Libby Purves; Lynne Quirk; Lucy Raby; Sarah Rayner; Shoo Rayner; Meg Rosoff; Caroline Rees; David Rees; Kathryn Richardson; Jenny Ridout; Jane Rowland; Patricia Saunders; Edna Scott; Don Seed; Elif Shafak; Lionel Shriver; R.D. Simek; Harriet Smart; Julian Smart; Nicola Solomon and The Society of Authors; Jackie Steinitz; Rebecca Swift; David Taylor; Jeremy Thompson; Stephanie Thornton; Inderjeet Tillier; Judy Tither; Dan Townend; John Rowe Townsend; Rachel Vevers; Louise Voss; Gale Winskill.

Further reading

On writing and getting published

Baverstock, A. *Is There a Book in You?* London: A&C Black (2006)

Blake, C. *From Pitch to Publication.* London: Macmillan (1999)

Brande, D. (with a foreword by Malcolm Bradbury) *Becoming a Writer.* London: Macmillan (1996)

Cameron, J. *The Artist's Way.* New York: Tarcher/Putnam (2002)

King, S. *On Writing.* New York: Charles Scribner's Sons (2000)

On marketing and publishing

Baverstock, A. *Marketing Your Book: an author's guide.* London: A&C Black (2007, second edition)

Clark, G. and Phillips, A *Inside Book Publishing.* London: Routledge (2008, second edition)

Hamilton-Emery, C. *101 Ways to Make Poems Sell: the salt guide to getting and staying published.* Cambridge: Salt Publishing (2006)

Horn, B. *Editorial Project Management, with exercises and model answers.* London: Horn Editorial Books (2006)

Horn, B. *Copy-editing, with exercises and model answers.* London: Horn Editorial Books and The Publishing Training Centre (2008)

OUP *The Oxford Dictionary for Writers and Editors,* Oxford: OUP (2005)

On self-publishing

Poynter, D. *Self-publishing Manual: how to write, print and sell your own book* www.parapublishing.com

Ryan Howard, C. *The Sane Person's Guide to Self-publishing.* Dublin: www.selfprintedbooks.com (2011)

On online marketing/building a social media platform

Reed, J.) *Get Up To Speed With Online Marketing*. London: Financial Times/Prentice Hall (2010

Faherty, A. *Social Media for Professionals* (online course, takes 4 hours). London: Nelson Croom see: http://bit.ly/YrCPDSMPro (2011)

On design and printing

Birdsall, D. *Notes on Book Design*. New Haven and London: Yale University Press (2004)

Bringhurst, R. *The Elements of Typographic Style*. Vancouver: Hartley & Marks (2nd edition, 1999)

Garfield, S. *Just My Type*. London: Profile Books (2010)

Haslam, A. *Book Design*. London: Portfolio (2006)

Hendel, R. *On Book Design*. New Haven & London: Yale University Press (1998)

Simon, O. *Introduction to Typography*. London: Faber & Faber (2nd edition, 1963)

Wilson, A. *The Design of Books*. San Francisco: Chronicle Books (2nd edition, 1993)

Index